"For all those convinced 'all is lost' fo  book!' Stonestreet and Smith aim to res and gloom narrative by pointing us to th still at work today, through people who and taking the opportunities right in fro .. .nspiring!"

—Eric Metaxas, *New York Times* bestselling author
of *Miracles: What They Are, Why They Happen,
and How They Can Change Your Life*

"*Restoring All Things* is an important and timely book. Smith and Stonestreet provide an insightful analysis of contemporary culture as well as practical steps each one of us can take to make a difference right where we are. I pray this book makes the wide and lasting impact it deserves."

—Sean McDowell, professor, Biola University; speaker;
coauthor of *Same-Sex Marriage*

"In a world that seems to be going to hell in a hand basket, Warren Cole Smith and John Stonestreet provide not just encouragement but a good swift kick in the pants. If we really believe that God came in Christ not just to save our souls but to restore all things in Him, then we cannot despair. No matter how hostile the world may seem to the gospel, it is still God's world, and the Good News applies to all of it. There is no pocket of society or human existence that lies outside of God's loving dominion. Smith and Stonestreet show how God's people are already advancing God's kingdom in the here and now as well as give concrete advice on how to take part. You should read this book."

—Jay W. Richards, PhD, bestselling author;
professor, Catholic University of America;
senior fellow, the Discovery Institute

"As a detective, I find my heart resonating with the work of Warren Cole Smith and John Stonestreet. Like me, they want to make a difference in a world often filled with despair and injustice. In *Restoring All Things*, Smith and Stonestreet make a case for how God can use each of us to impact our world. Like good detectives, they've interviewed and investigated the lives of many key witnesses used by God to transform their friends, families, and communities. Their examples will inspire and motivate you. If you want to make a difference, let this book be your call to action."

—J. Warner Wallace, cold case homicide detective;
author of *Cold-Case Christianity* and *God's Crime Scene*

RESTORING

ALL

THINGS

GOD'S AUDACIOUS PLAN
TO SAVE THE WORLD
THROUGH EVERYDAY PEOPLE

**WARREN COLE SMITH
AND JOHN STONESTREET**

BakerBooks
a division of Baker Publishing Group
www.BakerBooks.com

© 2015 by John Stonestreet and WORLD News Group

Published by Baker Books
a division of Baker Publishing Group
P.O. Box 6287, Grand Rapids, MI 49516-6287
www.bakerbooks.com

Printed in the United States of America

All rights reserved. No part of this publication may be reproduced, stored in a retrieval system, or transmitted in any form or by any means—for example, electronic, photocopy, recording—without the prior written permission of the publisher. The only exception is brief quotations in printed reviews.

Library of Congress Cataloging-in-Publication Data is on file at the Library of Congress, Washington, DC.

ISBN 978-0-8010-0030-0

Unless otherwise indicated, Scripture quotations are from The Holy Bible, English Standard Version ®, copyright © 2001 by Crossway, a publishing ministry of Good News Publishers. Used by permission. All rights reserved. ESV Text Edition: 2011

Scripture quotations labeled NRSV are from the New Revised Standard Version of the Bible, copyright 1989, by the Division of Christian Education of the National Council of the Churches of Christ in the United States of America. Used by permission. All rights reserved.

Scripture quotations labeled NKJV are from the New King James Version. Copyright © 1982 by Thomas Nelson, Inc. Used by permission. All rights reserved.

Scripture quotations labeled NLT are from the *Holy Bible*, New Living Translation, copyright © 1996, 2004, 2007 by Tyndale House Foundation. Used by permission of Tyndale House Publishers, Inc., Carol Stream, Illinois 60188. All rights reserved.

Scripture quotations labeled NIV are from the Holy Bible, New International Version®. NIV®. Copyright © 1973, 1978, 1984, 2011 by Biblica, Inc.™ Used by permission of Zondervan. All rights reserved worldwide. www.zondervan.com

Lyrics to "Don't You Want to Thank Someone" are written by Andrew Peterson © 2012. Used by permission.

15   16   17   18   19   20   21   7   6   5   4   3   2   1

In keeping with biblical principles of creation stewardship, Baker Publishing Group advocates the responsible use of our natural resources. As a member of the Green Press Initiative, our company uses recycled paper when possible. The text paper of this book is composed in part of post-consumer waste.

When the world is new again
And the children of the King
Are ancient in their youth again
Maybe it's a better thing
A better thing . . .

To be more than merely innocent
But to be broken then redeemed by love
Maybe this old world is bent
But it's waking up
And I'm waking up.

—Andrew Peterson
"Don't You Want to Thank Someone"

Contents

Foreword

In that day, Israel will be one of three with Egypt and
Assyria—a blessing in the midst of the land.

Isaiah 19:24 NKJV

Unless you've been living in a cave somewhere, you're probably aware
that followers of Jesus are up against a stiff challenge. Along with the
rest of our contemporaries, we're caught up in a cultural milieu where
conflict and controversy have become the order of the day. Everywhere
you look, society seems to have been reduced to a bewildering array
of warring camps. Pride, power plays, money, sex, and prestige seem
to drive the passions of people on all sides of every issue. If you're
like me, you wish you could do something about it. You're thinking to
yourself, "There must be a better way. There *has* to be a better way."

I've got good news for you. There *is*.

In Isaiah's time, Egypt and Assyria were the two heavy hitters on
the international scene. Like the United States and the Soviet Union
during the Cold War era, they defined the great power struggle of the
day. Everybody assumed that the contest would eventually be decided
in favor of one or the other of these two superpowers. But Isaiah's
eyes were opened to a third possibility: the possibility of God's true
servants becoming a *blessing*, and not only to the key belligerents but
to the rest of the world as well.

11

Warren Smith and John Stonestreet have caught the same vision. In the pages of *Restoring All Things*, they've mapped out a strategy for translating that vision into practical, everyday reality. Central to their thinking is something they call "the importance of the 'middle'"—the value of that vibrant "in-between place" where real people get involved in providing real services at the level of the local community:

> When a twelve-year-old Boy Scout is elected patrol leader in his Scout troop, he learns about elected office and leadership. When a homeschool mother organizes a local co-op, she empowers herself, her children, and her neighbors without having to depend on the government for services the co-op will now provide. Little League baseball. Kiwanis. Rotary. Lions. Fraternities and sororities. Professional associations. Faith-based ministries. Trade associations. All of these organizations teach participation, leadership, cooperation, and self-determination.

It's *here*, the authors argue—in the "middle"—where Christians have their best chance to make a lasting mark for Christ in contemporary culture.

I think they're right.

The clash of values in the public square has at times inadvertently alienated citizen from citizen and believer from believer. Even in our efforts to alleviate suffering and help those in need, we constantly run the risk of being viewed with suspicion and even contempt. Some of this is unavoidable. When it comes to supporting biblical principles, we have no room to negotiate. However, one of the best ways to counteract false impressions concerning people of the Christian faith is to get engaged in the lives of people right in your own neighborhood—people who might not share your views but who would be glad to have your assistance and encouragement with some practical project. There's no telling where those friendships might lead!

This is what Smith and Stonestreet are envisioning as "God's audacious plan to change the world through everyday people." And they've filled their book with uplifting stories of believers who are putting that plan into action in a number of exciting ways.

Sound intriguing? Then read on. I have a feeling you'll be inspired to jump in with both feet yourself!

Jim Daly
President, Focus on the Family

Acknowledgments

John and Warren

We would like to thank the writers, editors, and staff at both WORLD News Group and *BreakPoint* for allowing us to pick and choose from the thousands of great stories these two organizations have published and broadcast over the years. Among the stories we included in this book are those originally written for WORLD or *BreakPoint* by Mindy Belz, David Carlson, Jamie Dean, Daniel James Devine, Thomas Kidd, Jill Lacy, Sophia Lee, Eric Metaxas, Anne Morse, Daniel Olasky, Marvin Olasky, Dick Peterson, Heather Rice-Minus, Roberto Rivera, and Gary Spooner. Kim Moreland also helped us find many stories that were buried deep in archives.

Some of the stories from WORLD appear in only slightly altered form. Thanks to Kevin Martin, CEO of WORLD News Group, for permission to use this material.

Several people read drafts of this book or particular chapters. We are grateful for meaningful feedback on the manuscript from Jackie Arthur, Marvin Olasky, Joseph Slife, Cole Smith, Missy Smith, and Sarah Stonestreet.

A special thanks to Focus on the Family. This project took form as a companion book for the Restoring All Things events. Those events would never have come to pass had not Joel Vaughan, Paul Batura, and Jim Daly of Focus on the Family lent their support and active participation. Thanks, too, to Rajeev Shaw for his essential work in making the events happen.

Summit Ministries in Manitou Springs, Colorado, was, in many ways, a greenhouse for this book. John's association with Summit goes back more than a decade, as speaker, leader, and curriculum developer for this remarkable worldview ministry. Warren has been speaking at Summit for the past five years, and for the past two he has served as scholar-in-residence during Summit's summer program. The days and weeks spent together in Colorado, hearing each other's speeches, and then many hours more discussing the ideas in these speeches, allowed us to realize how closely aligned we are in our thinking. Out of that alignment came this book.

And, of course, we foremost thank God our Father who, in and through Jesus Christ, makes all things—and continues to make each of us—new.

John

I must begin by thanking my wife, Sarah, and three daughters, Abigail, Anna, and Ali, but not because it is obligatory. They have been more than gracious with me as I jumped out of one book project into another, and they continually offer in my life glimpses of thoughts and ideas that have taken form in this book.

To thank those whose thoughts have shaped my own on the scope of redemption would take more space than we have here, but I especially would like to note the influence of two friends from "down under," Rod Thompson and Paul Henderson. Also, though I began working with Chuck Colson just a few years before he died, his fingerprints are seen in the Kuyperian vision of this book, as well as in his consistent celebration on *BreakPoint* of Christians from all walks of life who are living out their Christian worldview.

And to say that Warren Smith did the heavy lifting on this book is an understatement. I'm grateful to be part of this project with him, but even more so for his friendship.

Warren

I would like to thank my wife, Missy, and our four children, Brittany, Cole, Walker, and Morgan.

I started thinking about this book soon after finishing my 2009 book *A Lover's Quarrel with the Evangelical Church*, a book that was highly critical of many Christian organizations. My publisher then, Volney James, suggested I write a book about what is *right* about the Christian church as a kind of sequel. I liked the idea but could never figure out how to implement that suggestion in a way that seemed authentic.

Then I heard John Stonestreet give his speech "God Loveth 'Re' Words" at Summit (a version of which makes up the first chapter of this book). A key idea of that speech is that the Great Redemptive Story of the Bible has as its last chapter the restoration of all things to God. Further, one of the truest measures of God's love for us is that He allows us to participate in that restoration. Our individual stories are like pixels in a massive picture of God's own making. So I would like to thank John, who helped me see these truths and provided the philosophical underpinnings for the stories in this book. I should also add that it was a real pleasure to work with him.

Introduction

God Loveth "Re" Words

There is not a square inch in the whole domain of our human existence over which Christ, who is Sovereign over all, does not cry: "Mine!"

—Abraham Kuyper[1]

There are a lot of "re" words in the Bible. Have you noticed? Words like *re*demption, *re*new, *re*pent, *re*store, *re*surrection, *re*conciliation, and *re*generation show up over and over throughout the Bible, especially in the New Testament.

The reputation of Christians today, however, often reflects a different set of "re" words: *re*sisting, *re*acting, and *re*jecting. These are biblical words too. The Bible commands us to "resist the devil," for example (James 4:7), and a wicked man is one who does not "reject evil" (Ps. 36:4), implying that Christians should be ones who do.

But *re*sisting, *re*acting, and *re*jecting are not the most important "re" words in the Bible. Not by a long shot. And if our Christian witness is to be taken seriously in our post-Christian world, we should spend more time reflecting on those other "re" words and how they can better shape our words and deeds.

That's what this book is about. We hope to articulate better language as we challenge one another to faithfulness and good works. We hope to clarify a more biblical posture toward the evil and brokenness we see all around us. We hope that Christians can become better known for what we are for, not just what we are against.

Think about it. "Re" words have to do with returning something (a person, a relationship, a project, a universe) to its original, intended state. For example, Scripture uses a word like *re*concile to describe how the relationship between God and people is made right again. But it also uses that word to describe what we are to be doing in our daily lives. We are reconciled to become reconcilers (see 2 Cor. 5:14–21). And a word like *re*demption describes how Christ paid for the sins of the world. But it also describes the "already not yet" state of all things, which are secured by Christ's resurrection and will be fully realized when His kingdom comes in fullness to earth.

In other words, the most common "re" words in Scripture are more than just repetitive words used to assure us we are headed to heaven if we trust Christ. They are also summary words that describe the role the church and individual Christians are to play in the overall story of the world. "Re" words flesh out for us the personal and cosmic impact of the work of Christ. Through them, we learn more about who we are in Christ, as well as about the future of the cosmos.

The True Story of the World

If our faith never goes deeper than personal moral and therapeutic reflections,[2] then we'll spend our time asking questions like, "How can I apply that verse to my life?" or "What can I get out of this passage of Scripture?" These are important questions, but the implications of Christianity far exceed ways to add spiritual decorations to "The Story of Us."

The Bible is both the story of God and the true story of the world. It is not the complete story of the world, but it is the story which God, in His sovereignty and love, has chosen to reveal to us. The "re" words we find throughout Scripture unlock, in all kinds of ways, the central plot of the grand story of God's cosmos, from its beginning in Genesis to its new beginning in Revelation. It is the story of God's creation of the world, of man's rebellion against God, of God's love and grace being so great that He sent His Son to redeem us, and—in the final chapter—of how He is in the process of restoring all things to Himself.

So the Bible is not, or not merely, a book about how to have a better life or how to handle life's problems. It is a book that explains the universe and how God is in the process of redeeming and restoring it to its original good, true, and beautiful state.

This idea that the Bible's primary purpose is to communicate to us this great redemption story is not original with us. It was the primary way of understanding the Bible for most of the Christian era. That may be why missionary Lesslie Newbigin repeated words that were said to him during an encounter in India, an encounter that helped him see his own Bible with fresh eyes:

> I can't understand why you missionaries present the Bible to us in India as a book of religion. It is not a book of religion—and anyway we have plenty of books of religion in India. We don't need any more! I find in your Bible a unique interpretation of universal history, the history of the whole of creation and the history of the human race. And therefore a unique interpretation of the human person as a responsible actor in history. That is unique. There is nothing else in the whole religious literature of the world to put alongside it.[3]

Those words, from the mouth of a Hindu scholar, sum up one of the most crippling problems in the church today: failing to grasp the biblical narrative as *the true story of the world*. As a result, Christians feel lost in this world, seeing both it and Scripture in "bits and pieces."[4] This fragmented understanding forces us either to disconnect our faith from any issues outside of personal holiness or emotion, or, as more things seem to go against biblical truth and morality, to sink into despair and hopelessness about "where this country is heading."

In the process, Christian witness suffers. Attempts to "save America" on one hand or to "stay relevant for the sake of the gospel at all costs" on the other hand, just lead the church to compromise and futility. And books like Joel Osteen's *Your Best Life Now* fail to take seriously the full scale of our own wickedness and the emerging glory of how God is at work in the process of restoring all things. These opposite but equally misguided attempts to confront the problems of the world may appear to be very different—one is political and the other therapeutic—but they share a common misunderstanding about the world. Namely, they fail to grasp the full scope of the biblical story, especially when it comes to understanding the true natures of God, man, and the world.

Here's another way to think about it. Is the world we live in a creation, an accident, or an illusion? Do we live in God's world, or is God an invention we brought into our world? Is the world we live in the one described by Jesus, Richard Dawkins, or Oprah? Are we nothing more than the biological by-products of time plus chance plus matter? Is the world nothing more than a fabrication of our minds?

Different religions and philosophical schemes offer different visions of reality, and it matters greatly which, if any, is right. What we think is real will determine how we live.[5] We need to know which world this is before we can know the answers to other important questions, such as: Is the world fine the way it is? Is something wrong with the world? Is it society? Is it us? Is it "them"? Can it be improved? Can it be fixed? If so, how?

"But I am no atheist!" you say. "I know God created the world and Jesus rose from the dead!" It's possible to get those very important facts right and miss others essential to a truly Christian worldview. Those "re" words in the Bible are gifts from God, designed to point us to these details, reminding us of the true state of the world in which we live (fallen but redeemed) and *why* we are here (to be agents of restoration).

For example, if we overlook what these "re" words tell us about how fallen or broken the world is, we'll be tempted to live for the promises *of* this world, seeing health and wealth as indications of Jesus's blessing. On the other hand, if we overlook how these "re" words point us back to God's original, very good design for the world, seeing instead only its evil and harmful potential, we'll make safety *from* this world our goal. Separation and distance become false indicators of Christian faithfulness.

But Christ followers are to see the world differently and have a different posture toward it. Rather than safety *from* or capitulation *to* the world, the grand narrative of Scripture describes instead a world we are called to live *for*. This world, Scripture proclaims, belongs to God, who then entrusted it to His image bearers. He created it good and loves it still, despite its brokenness and frustration. He has plans for it yet and invites the redeemed to live redemptively, for its good and our flourishing, even as we live for Him.

The Story of the "Re" Words

"The earth is the LORD's and the fullness thereof," proclaimed King David (Ps. 24:1), but this is more than the psalmist's adoring reflection. This is, in fact, the foundational fact of the Bible: God does not inhabit our world. We inhabit His world. From the very beginning of the story of redemption, this fact is assumed. First, God brings the world into existence by His command, and then He brings humans into that world by His creative hand.

In his book *Miracles*, C. S. Lewis wrote, "No philosophical theory which I have yet come across is a radical improvement on the words in Genesis, that 'In the beginning God made Heaven and Earth.'"[6] Lewis is right to identify the Genesis account of creation as a "philosophical theory." It's more than that, of course, but it is not less. Though even Christians might reduce Scripture to a collection of moral teachings and esoteric advice about the inner life, it actually offers a description of the nature of reality, the purpose of humanity, and the meaning of existence.

When the world begins, as Scripture tells the story, Someone is already there. Everything else has a beginning, but God does not. He simply is, not reliant on anyone or anything for His existence. His existence is, in the biblical picture of reality, the explanation for the existence of everything else.

"The earth was without form and void, and darkness was over the face of the deep" (Gen. 1:2). The second verse of the Bible, while often overlooked, shouldn't be. The rest of the chapter, in fact, describes how God addresses the formlessness and emptiness described in the verse. Simply put, He forms and fills.

"Let there be light," God says (1:3), and the empty darkness is filled with light. And when God "separated the light from the darkness" (1:4), the light is given shape. He fills, and He forms. He fills the world with new things: stars, land, the atmosphere, animals. Then He shapes these things: He separates day from night, He tells the water how far it can go, He divides the waters in the expanse above from the waters below, and He places the plants, trees, fish, and beasts into distinct "kinds."

God does His filling and forming work by speaking. He says it, and it happens. Everything becomes what He tells it to become. Even "nothing" obeys Him when He tells it to become "something." God is so thoroughly and completely in charge, nothing exists without His command.

God's language in Genesis 1 has a repeated rhythm: God says, "Let there be," and it is so. God looks over what He has made and pronounces it "good."

"Let there be . . . and it was so . . . it was good . . ." over and over and over, day after day. But midway through the sixth day, just as this rhythm is getting stuck in our heads, it changes. Human beings are not created by fiat command as everything else has been. Instead of a "Let there be," God utters a "Let us make" (1:26). This is new, and the next chapter provides further detail: "Then the LORD God formed the man of dust from the ground" (1:27). God not only employed a different language, He employed a different process when He created humanity.

Humans are above and beyond anything God has created thus far. "Let us make man in our image, after our likeness," He says. "And let them have dominion over the fish of the sea and over the birds of the heavens and over the livestock and over all the earth and over every creeping thing that creeps on the earth" (1:26).

Don't miss this very important point: The absolute Ruler of everything decides to make other rulers to take care of His world. The great Sovereign, who up to this point in the story has showed Himself completely in charge and without rival, creates human beings to bear His image and to "rule" for Him in the world. They are not puppets, nor have they been granted tourist visas to enjoy paradise. They have work to do.

And their work is the sort of work God has already been doing. Note the instructions: "Be fruitful and multiply and fill the earth and subdue it" (1:28). Just as God did, they are to fill the earth. Just as God did, they are to bring order to disorder. Just as God did, they are to bring life and fullness. In other words, they, too, like the One whose image they bear, are to fill and form. They are to begin this work in the Garden and continue it throughout the earth until it is filled and subdued for the glory of God. In other words, humans are to bring glory to God by living for the good of the world.

Why did we take you on that walk in the Garden? Because the story described in Genesis is *our* story. Here, we see clearly God's intent for us and His world.

Keep in mind also that the first ones to hear this Genesis narrative in this form were members of a just-freed nation of Hebrew slaves.

Having just witnessed the defeat of the gods they worshiped in Egypt, they now learn that there is only one God and that they are not His pawns but rather share in His image. These former slaves are being told that they were, in fact, made to be rulers. This is more than a theology lesson; it's a worldview lesson. They are learning they live in a wholly different world than the world they had been acculturated to believe.

We know where the story goes next. The first people fail at their task, futilely attempting to be their own masters and fatally attempting to remake reality. It doesn't work, and the results are catastrophic, for them and for the world they were supposed to steward.

As a result, they are separated from God and from one another. Their responsibility for the creation isn't removed, but it is frustrated by pain and toil. They are in need of rescue. They need to be reconciled to God and each other. And God does not abandon them. In Christ, He fully and finally enters the humans' story to make things right again.

That's where the "re" words come in. Christ *re*deems humanity from sin, *re*conciles us to God and one other, *re*stores us to our full humanity, *re*surrects us from the death that our rebellion brings, and promises to ultimately *re*store all things. The end of the story, as told in Revelation, is not really the end at all, is it? It is, as C. S. Lewis skillfully describes in *The Last Battle* of his Narnia series, a new beginning.

Even as we resist evil and reject the lies so compellingly told by the Enemy of our souls and firmly embedded among rebellious humanity, all those who are in Christ belong to a story of hope, not of despair. This grand, sweeping story of redemption is our story. Christ has risen. Indeed.

Imagine you were to ask someone whether they had read the Lord of the Rings trilogy by J. R. R. Tolkien (or at least watched the movies), and they replied, "Well, I started the first book, but I couldn't believe he killed off Gandalf! Why on earth would Tolkien do *that*? I was so mad, I threw the book away and didn't want to read any more!"

"Wait!" you would say. "He comes back! And not only that, he's way cooler as Gandalf the White. And he helps save Middle Earth."

Christian, we must not stop at the middle of the biblical story! The story we are part of, God's story, ends with Christ proclaiming, "Behold, I am making all things new" (Rev. 21:5). And He brings us into this story, not merely as observers or personal beneficiaries. We are participants, and even champions, in this story.

The apostle Paul summarizes what this story means for all who are in Christ:

> For the love of Christ controls us, because we have concluded this: that one has died for all, therefore all have died; and he died for all, that those who live might no longer live for themselves but for him who for their sake died and was raised. From now on, therefore, we regard no one according to the flesh. Even though we once regarded Christ according to the flesh, we regard him thus no longer. Therefore, if anyone is in Christ, he is a new creation. The old has passed away; behold, the new has come. All this is from God, who through Christ reconciled us to himself and gave us the ministry of reconciliation; that is, in Christ God was reconciling the world to himself, not counting their trespasses against them, and entrusting to us the message of reconciliation. Therefore, we are ambassadors for Christ, God making his appeal through us. We implore you on behalf of Christ, be reconciled to God. For our sake he made him to be sin who knew no sin, so that in him we might become the righteousness of God. (2 Cor. 5:14–21)

Three times Paul identifies those who are in Christ as those who have been entrusted with reconciliation. We are now "ambassadors" of the redemptive work of Jesus Christ, given both the "ministry of reconciliation" (vv. 11, 18) and the "message of reconciliation" (v. 19). Let's be clear on what that means.

First, we are ambassadors of the *full* redemptive work of Jesus Christ. This includes, but is also more than, the rescue of individual souls. The story, as told in Scripture, is the restoration of all things that culminates in the New Heavens and New Earth, when all wrongs will be made right again.

Second, we are not only saved *from* sin and death but also saved *to* the life God intended for His image bearers from the beginning. Humans were placed in the world to care for it, and though the fall frustrates our efforts, Christ restores that identity and calling. "Re" words are "again" words. They only truly make sense in light of God's original intent. As Thomas Howard says:

> The Incarnation takes all that properly belongs to our humanity and delivers it back to us, redeemed. All of our inclinations and appetites and capacities and yearnings and proclivities are purified and gathered up and glorified by Christ. He did not come to thin out human life; He came to set it free. All the dancing and feasting and processing and

singing and building and sculpting and baking and merrymaking that belong to us, and that were stolen away into the service of false gods, are returned to us in the Gospel.[7]

Third, nothing that happens in any time or any place in the history of the world—*absolutely nothing*—can frustrate the accomplished work of God in Christ. It's tempting to despair at times. But as Richard John Neuhaus said, "We have not the right to despair, for despair is a sin. And finally we have not the reason to despair, quite simply because Christ has risen."[8] His resurrection has secured for us, Peter wrote, "a living hope" that is "imperishable, undefiled, and unfading, kept in heaven for you" (1 Pet. 1:3–4).

Living Our Story

So what does this look like in real life? That's what this book is about. In the next chapter, we suggest both a specific *angle* and a specific *strategy* that Christians can employ to be effective as ambassadors of reconciliation. And in the pages that follow, we highlight everyday Christians who, across the scope and spectrum of culture, are living lives of redemption and restoration in powerful ways.

As you read their stories, we encourage you to think through what God might be calling you to do to join His redemptive work in the world. We offer some suggestions at the end of each chapter. But before we proceed, we'd like to offer a guiding framework for "re" word living, in the form of four questions that connect our actions with what we know to be true about the world from the biblical story:[9]

1. *What is good in our culture that we can promote, protect, and celebrate?* Christians believe that how God created the world was, in His own words, "good." Even after the fall, much of this goodness, such as beauty and truth and human dignity, remains.

2. *What is missing in our culture that we can creatively contribute?* Christians believe that humans were created to be creative. When something good is missing in a particular time and place, we should find ways to offer it to the world. God is glorified and the world is helped by properly ordered human creativity.

25

3. *What is evil in our culture that we can stop?* God hates evil, and so ought we. Throughout history, courageous Christians have worked to stop that which destroys and deceives. We must do no less. It's a basic requirement of loving our neighbors.

4. *What is broken in our culture that we can restore?* Ultimately, we reflect the gospel most clearly when what has been damaged by sin is restored to God's intended purposes.

1

Great News!

The only two things that can satisfy the soul are a person
and a story, and even a story must be about a person.
Men . . . are much oftener led by their hearts than by
their understandings.

—G. K. Chesterton

The most pressing spiritual question of our time is this:
Who gets to narrate the world?

—Robert Webber

There's a lot of bad news in the world.

As we write this book in the fall of 2014, daily papers and news
broadcasts are full of stories about the Ebola epidemic; racial tensions and riots in Ferguson, Missouri, and elsewhere; the beheadings
of journalists and ordinary citizens by radical jihadists; and ongoing
wars in Iraq, Afghanistan, Syria, and Ukraine.

As you read this book, that list is almost certainly outdated, replaced by a newer list of troubling stories that try our hope afresh. This
much we are all guaranteed: If we wake up tomorrow, new troubles

await us. It is tempting to despair and proclaim with the Teacher in Ecclesiastes, "Meaningless! Meaningless! Everything is meaningless!" And yet . . .

If you look closely, there's more to the story of our world than just bad news:

- At the beginning of the twentieth century, the average American lived only about forty-five years. Today that number is seventy-seven years.
- We used to argue about *whether* we ought to help the poor. Today we argue about *how* best to help the poor, with a track record of measurable success. For example, India was on the brink of mass starvation in 1960. Then came the innovations of American scientist Norman Borlaug, who set off a Green Revolution now credited with saving more than a billion lives. In fact, starvation-level poverty has been reduced by more than half in the past twenty years alone, with some predicting its eradication within the next few decades.[1]
- Totalitarianism wrote the most tragic chapters of the last century, but most of those terrible regimes had collapsed by the century's end. The religious liberty watchdog group Freedom House reports that more people now live in countries governed by democratically elected leaders than at any other time in human history.
- And think about advances in science that have all but eradicated polio, tuberculosis, malaria, and dozens of other diseases.

Make no mistake; ours is a fallen world. There is much evil and brokenness to lament. But to paraphrase Mark Twain, the rumors of the world's demise are premature.

As we said in the introduction, Christians are called to live for the good of the world. This requires understanding and action. We must think clearly about the world and engage deeply when and where we can.

How do we gain a balanced perspective on the good and the bad that exist in our world? Is it possible to see all that's happening and avoid both despair and naïveté? Can we take the brokenness of the world seriously and still be hopeful? Even more than *feeling* hopeful, can we actually live in such a way as to champion hope and make a meaningful difference in the world?

We think so, but only if we learn two things. First, we must learn to see culture differently. Second, we must learn the power of story.

The Importance of the "Middle"

In the 1830s, the young French aristocrat Alexis de Tocqueville visited the rowdy, adolescent United States of America and wrote down what he saw in a masterful book, *Democracy in America*. Even today, almost two hundred years later, his insights remain among the most profound analyses of the American experiment ever written.[2]

Tocqueville, even then, could see that something remarkable was happening in America. Historian and Baylor University professor Thomas Kidd offers this helpful summary of Tocqueville's findings: "America's strength came from its religious heritage, its tradition of local participatory politics, and its many mediating institutions and civic associations, all standing between the individual and the government."[3] In other words, America was strongest in the middle, with a robust civil society limiting the power of the state while allowing citizens to flourish and self-govern.

Benjamin Franklin often gets credit for forming the first cooperative association in America in 1736 when he helped organize Philadelphia's first volunteer fire brigade. Today more than 1.5 million nonprofit organizations operate in this country, with the overwhelming majority of them consisting of local people meeting local needs and solving local problems. The aggregate impact of the money and labor contributed by these "mediating institutions" runs into the hundreds of billions of dollars each year.[4]

It's easy to miss just how unusual it is in world history for a country to have such a robust civil society. Particularly today, in the divisive political climate of the United States, we often hear of only two options for fixing what's broken in our society: federally controlled social programs or individual responsibility. One side wants more federal intervention and wider government-provided safety nets. The other wants unrestricted freedom and personal autonomy. Each of these so-called solutions sees the top of culture as most important, either the remedy for all that ails us or the source of all our problems. The true strength of a society, however, comes from its "middle," in those activities and institutions that exist between the individual and the government.

Tocqueville observed that America was—and today it remains—unique in the number, scale, and scope of these mediating institutions. We also note that these organizations are valuable not just because of what they do directly but because of how they foster a strong citizenry and a sense of personal responsibility. When a twelve-year-old Boy Scout is elected patrol leader in his Scout troop, he learns about elected office and leadership. When a homeschool mother organizes a local co-op, she empowers herself, her children, and her neighbors without having to depend on the government for services the co-op will now provide. Little League baseball. Kiwanis. Rotary. Lions. Fraternities and sororities. Professional associations. Faith-based ministries. Trade associations. All of these organizations teach participation, leadership, cooperation, and self-determination.

In our own time, management guru Peter Drucker described our impulse for collective action as "that peculiarly American form of behavior. Nothing sets this country as much apart from the rest of the Western World as its almost instinctive reliance on voluntary, and often spontaneous, group action for the most important social purposes."[5] Charles Murray warned us in his book *Coming Apart* that one of the most significant (and negative) developments of the past several decades has been the emptying of the middle, the shriveling of local control and local action in government and in civil society.[6] It's important to note, though, that while this emptying of the middle has weakened our society, it also offers a huge opportunity for Christians to make a difference. Most of us will never run for governor or president, but while we may not provide leadership to change culture from the top down, we all have opportunities to do so from the middle.

A robust civil society, with strong local institutions and citizen involvement, is simultaneously the most effective means of limiting federal intrusion as well as catechizing new generations of citizens in the essential skills of self-government. That's why the Founding Fathers of our country carefully planned a culture and legal infrastructure that encouraged the formation and sustenance of mediating institutions. It also explains why the "freedom to assemble" is one of the essential freedoms outlined in the First Amendment to the Constitution.

Also in the First Amendment is the guarantee of the freedom of religion. Our Founding Fathers knew these freedoms were inextricably connected. The freedom to assemble allows cooperative action, and without it, the freedom of religion loses much of its meaning. It should come as no surprise, then, that the vast majority of the "mediating institutions" in this country—the vast majority of the associations and nonprofits—are faith-based.

Case in Point: Strategies to Elevate People

Take, for example, STEP (Strategies to Elevate People) Richmond, a ministry to the inner-city neighborhoods of Virginia's capital city. With a small paid staff, volunteers of STEP Richmond are the real "secret sauce." They lead the Bible studies, summer book clubs, camps, and field trips of the ministry, all with the active participation of Richmond churches, both large and small.

The success pioneered in Richmond spawned STEP programs around the country. A 2010 WORLD article featured STEPdc, a STEP program operating in the rough Columbia Heights neighborhood of Washington, DC. The breakdown of the family there is epidemic. For example, of the 175 households in a nearby government housing project described in the article, only eleven were led by men. STEPdc labored heroically in this neighborhood for twenty years, with many successes. The Reverend Jim Till, who led STEPdc, told WORLD, "We've had kids go through our tutoring program who came back to tutor others when they were older."

This sort of work is *hard*, of course, and success is mixed. As Till also admitted, "We've also had guys end up in jail." Indeed, a couple of years after the WORLD article appeared, STEPdc closed its doors.[7]

And yet even the stories that do not have happy endings can instruct. Similar work to confront the challenges of inner-city life continues all across America and around the world. The STEP movement is just one of *thousands* of grassroots organizations around the country confronting the local needs of the inner city with local solutions. The conclusion is clear: Localized work to rebuild civil society can make a significant difference.

How Stories Matter

Stories such as the one above teach in ways that bulleted lists and academic lectures simply cannot.

Consider the impact of one television program on the cultural imagination: *Will & Grace*. If you doubt the impact, consider this timeline. In 1996, the U.S. Congress passed the Defense of Marriage Act (DOMA). Democratic President Bill Clinton signed the bill into law. In 1998, *Will & Grace* premiered. It aired for eight seasons, and for four of those seasons it was the number one situation comedy on television. By 2013, significant parts of DOMA were overturned. By 2014, same-sex "marriage" was legal in more than thirty states. The program continues to be popular in syndication and continues to receive credit for changing attitudes toward homosexuality. In 2012, Vice President Joe Biden said the show "probably did more to educate the American public on LGBT issues than almost anything anybody has ever done so far."[8] The Smithsonian Institution added items from the program to its LGBT (lesbian, gay, bisexual, transgender) history collection.[9]

It's often said that politics is downstream from culture. This is mostly true. It's also said that ideas have consequences. This is true for both individuals and cultures. But there's another, even deeper truth that many miss: The ideas that shape politics and a culture are rarely advanced by argument. Rather, they are advanced by the stories that shape our imaginations. If you can control the stories a people see, hear, and tell each other, you can ultimately control what they think and even how they think.

Jesus, it seems, understood this, for the Bible plainly tells us of times when Jesus spoke to large crowds and "did not speak to them without a parable" (Mark 4:34).

To understand the importance of stories, consider the mathematical symbol *pi*. If you've had high school math, you know *pi* is 3.14. Some of you who had a bit of higher math know that *pi* is actually an irrational number: an infinite series of non-repeating numbers.

Now, if we asked you to recite *pi* to 10 places, few could do it. And 100 digits? Forget about it. However, most of us have hundreds if not thousands of numbers in our heads ready for easy recall: your 10-digit home phone number, your 10-digit cell number, your wife's or your husband's number, your nine-digit Social Security number, the year you graduated from high school or college, and many more.

We remember these numbers because of the stories behind them. Those stories give them meaning and context—and make them memorable.

But modern evangelical Christians often miss the power of story. We tend to proclaim the truth of Christianity as if we were reciting *pi* to 10 decimal places, forgetting that we live in a post-Christian and postmodern culture that has forgotten the great biblical story of creation, fall, redemption, and restoration. This story, sometimes called the biblical meta-narrative, is as foreign now to Western culture as Chinese history is. Yet this story is the context that makes sense of the truth we wish to proclaim.

Those of us who understand and believe the biblical meta-narrative know that we have facts, logic, reason, and history on our side. But we, too, often think that what is obvious to us must be obvious to all. It is not. Stories make the world come alive and facts memorable. We need to stop asking people to memorize *pi* to the 10th decimal point and start telling them stories that—in the end—will allow them to see the world more like it really is. We need to get better at telling stories if we want our message to be heard.

The strategy of this book is to tell stories. As we learn of the great work God is doing through His people in the world, not only will we be inspired to embrace the redemptive responsibility the church has in the world, but we will be inspired to join in. And as we tell these stories to others, we may find a lost world regaining familiarity with the truths of Christianity and, more importantly, being drawn to Christ, the Storyteller they need to know.

Stories to Get Us Started

It only makes sense, then, that we would begin by telling a couple of stories.

As we write this in the fall of 2014, Ebola is generating a great deal of fear around the world. Doctors are fighting outbreaks in other countries, both to cure patients and to prevent the spread of the virus. Among all the different angles of this story, one is that many of the doctors waging war against Ebola, and in some cases becoming sick and dying in the fight, are Christians.

We find it interesting but not surprising. Throughout history, Christians have often run toward, not away from, the misery of others. The sociologist and historian Rodney Stark recounts many such stories in his book *The Rise of Christianity*.[10] For example, between AD 250 and AD 270, a terrible plague called the Plague of Cyprian, after the man who wrote about it, devastated the Roman Empire. Up to five thousand people succumbed to the plague in Rome alone at the height of its devastation.[11]

The plague coincided with the first empire-wide persecution of Christians under the emperor Decius. Decius and other enemies of the church blamed Christians for the plague. That claim was, however, undermined by two inconvenient facts. First, Christians died from the plague just like everyone else. Second, Christians cared for the victims of the plague, including their pagan neighbors, unlike everyone else.[12]

We were reminded of this historical episode by a recent story told on National Public Radio's *All Things Considered*. Host Robert Siegel interviewed Stephen Rowden, who volunteers for Doctors Without Borders in Monrovia, Liberia, and has the grim task of managing the team that collects the bodies of Ebola victims.[13] Rowden and his team retrieve between ten and twenty-five bodies a day. Since close contact with the victims is the chief means by which the usually deadly virus is spread, Rowden and his team members live with the risk of becoming victims themselves.

What's more, living in the midst of this death and suffering takes an emotional toll. On the program, Rowden recalled entering a house and finding the body of a four-year-old victim who had been abandoned by her family. His typically British understatement failed to mask how the discovery had impacted him. "I found that a very sad case," he told Siegel.

Siegel then asked Rowden if he was a religious man. "I am. Yes, I'm a practicing Christian," he replied. When Siegel asked whether what he had seen tested his faith, Rowden replied, "No, I get great strength from my faith and the support of my family."

As our friend Eric Metaxas said in his *BreakPoint* commentary on the story, "Nearly eighteen centuries after the Plague of Cyprian, Christianity still prompts people to run toward the plague when virtually everyone else is running away."[14]

The Christian response to the Ebola crisis is a beautiful example of Christian healers using their gifts and calling to restore where a terrible disease is attempting to destroy. Twenty-first-century missionary doctors are following directly in the footsteps of first- and second-century Christian mothers, fathers, doctors, and neighbors.

Next generation Christians should hear that story and be moved to "go and do likewise."

Figuring out what it means to "go and do likewise" is not always easy.

Jim Liske, the CEO of Prison Fellowship Ministries, often talks of his visit to the ancient city of Ephesus. In the first century AD, Ephesus was a pagan town, dominated by the Temple of Artemis, one of the ancient Greek gods. The priests of the temple maintained a perpetual fire there in worship to the false deities.

Fire was, of course, a basic necessity of life for the people because it allowed for cooking, cleaning, and warmth. If the fire went out in a home, the residents were in big trouble. The only solution was to go to the temple with a ceramic bowl to get hot coals from the temple priests. The priests, of course, required a payment for tribute to appease the pagan gods and maintain the temple. The fire-keepers of this ancient temple were ancient Ephesus's equivalent of the power, water, sewer, and gas companies all rolled into one. And they were a monopoly. To get fire from another source, the priests taught, was an affront to the gods and risked their wrath.

Archaeology has unearthed how the Christians in Ephesus lived differently in that ancient city. When they noticed a home without fire, they would take hot coals to that family from their own fires in their own "fire bowls." This simple act of love of neighbor made a powerful statement. First, it provided lifesaving fire to a person who may have been too poor to pay a tribute at the temple. Second, it deprived the pagan temple of an important means of financial support. Third, it proclaimed to the world that the Christians in Ephesus were not afraid of the pagan gods.

When Liske tells this story, he concludes with a question: "What does it mean to be a fire-bearer today?" It's an interesting question. Though we have no record of those first-century Christians picketing outside the Temple of Artemis or successfully having laws passed in their favor, their acts of kindness toward their neighbors sped the demise of the Greek temple system and led to the rise of Christianity.

It is our prayer that the stories in this book will accomplish two things. We hope to inspire everyday Christians to "run toward the plague when everyone else is running away," and we hope to see the church today have the strategic wisdom to be fire-bearers in ways that are restorative and life-giving, and not merely reactionary.

CONCLUSION AND A TO-DO LIST

Each chapter in this book features stories to inspire, teach, and equip. After the stories, each chapter concludes with a section that summarizes the key ideas of the chapter and suggests a few things we can do to become a part of the work God is doing in our communities to restore all things to Himself. Because we both are avid readers who believe that "leaders are readers and readers inevitably become leaders," you will find some book recommendations among the list of "things to do." You can find the full references for the books we recommend in the bibliography in the back of the book.

So what is the "big idea" of this chapter? It is this: God is always at work in the world, actively "restoring all things to Himself." Those with "eyes to see" and "ears to hear" will look locally for where God is working and join wherever and whenever we can. We find the best opportunities to join God's work not by complaining loudly about what is going wrong at the top of culture but by meeting local needs within our communities from our areas of influence. When we look for the everyday stories of redemption all around us and join in, we're joining the Great Story of Redemption that is being accomplished by Jesus Christ.

Here are some ways to start:

1. Read "Telling the World Its Own Story" by Richard John Neuhaus (available online at http://www.colsoncenter.org/search -library/search?view=searchdetail&id=21199) and the book *How Now Shall We Live?* by Charles Colson and Nancy Pearcey to more fully grasp the idea of Christian worldview and our responsibility to the culture around us.

2. Using the questions given at the end of the introduction to this book, do an inventory of where God may be calling you to work in your sphere of influence.

3. Join us as we continue our journey through various areas of culture and human need and how God is using His people in these areas. In other words, keep reading! Better yet, invite a friend to join you.

2

Helping That Helps

Those who oppress the poor insult their Maker, but those
who are kind to the needy honor him.

—Proverbs 14:31 NRSV

There is bad aid and there is good aid. The bad aid is that
which creates dependencies, but good aid is that which
is targeted to create capacities in people so they are able
to live on their own activities.

—Paul Kagame, president of Rwanda[1]

Piety is no substitute for technique.

—Étienne Gilson

The Scriptures are clear: God cares deeply for the poor. Throughout
the Bible, we read that the rich have a special responsibility to help
those who are poor. In fact, some of the most memorable stories in
the Bible relate to the relationship between rich and poor: Elijah and
the Widow at Zarephath. Lazarus and the Rich Man. Zacchaeus. The

Good Samaritan. The Widow's Mite. This could quickly become a very long list.

Yet there is a difference between *caring about* the poor and *caring effectively for* the poor. Jesus's own understanding of poverty, in fact, is often misunderstood. His behavior and language toward the poor are complicated. For example, when Mary lavishly anointed Jesus's feet with costly oil, Judas rebuked Him for accepting her worship. "Why wasn't this oil sold and the money given to the poor?" Judas accused (see John 12:5). Jesus's response in verse 8 was surprising: "You will always have the poor among you, but you will not always have me."

A complete explication of this passage is beyond the scope of our discussion, but in some ways this story is a parable for our time. Judas was the keeper of the purse that was often used to help the poor, but he was also a liar and a thief. His concern for the poor was a false front to mask the much greater concern he had for his own power, wealth, and reputation. In other words, our motives matter.

Still, Jesus's rebuke of Judas in no way diminishes how much Jesus cared for the poor. He both declared in His words and demonstrated by His behavior how much He cared for the poor. But Mary's anointing was done to glorify Jesus. As the Westminster Catechism teaches, "Man's chief end is to glorify God, and to enjoy Him forever."[2] Jesus's response reveals this truth: We are never more fully human, never more fully "on purpose" in life, than when we are extravagantly worshiping God. If the money we have and give is not bringing glory to God, any benefit or relief it may bring is fleeting.

Implicit in this story is another point many find controversial. The most important aspect of poverty is not a lack of money. After all, Jesus Himself often had little or no money, and He told His followers they could expect a similar state. To a scribe who proclaimed loyalty to Jesus, He famously replied, "Foxes have holes, and birds of the air have nests, but the Son of Man has nowhere to lay his head" (Matt. 8:20).

When we look deeply at His exchange with Judas and Mary in light of the context of the rest of Scripture, we see that what Jesus is concerned about—and what we should be concerned about—is not material wealth but spiritual health. We should concern ourselves for the poor not primarily because they are poor but because they are human beings made in God's image, and so are we.

In no way are we suggesting that Christians shouldn't be generous to the poor. We should, in fact, be sacrificially generous. No one should out-give Christians. As the stories in this chapter demonstrate, it is beautiful when Christians live generous and redemptive lives.

But—as Jesus's own testimony confirms—effectively helping the poor is not measured by how much money we spend, and it is certainly not measured by how much money the government spends. So what does it mean to help the poor in meaningful and biblical ways?

Ultimately, the most effective poverty relief involves working side by side with people so they can flourish as humans made in the image of God. Any "help" we give the poor must take this truth into account. Otherwise we end up enslaving the poor in unending dependency and humiliation, while also trapping the rich in hypocrisy and narcissism.

The Tragedy of American Compassion

Not all help is helpful, and good intentions are not enough.

Many Americans first came to these insights through Marvin Olasky's book *The Tragedy of American Compassion*. The book came out in 1992, the same year Bill Clinton was elected president. It gained traction in 1994 when House Speaker Newt Gingrich, who engineered the GOP takeover of the U.S. Congress, made the book required reading for members of the House. Indeed, Olasky and *The Tragedy of American Compassion* deserve much of the credit for the sweeping reforms to the American welfare system that went into effect in 1996.[3] Even today we can learn much from the book as we attempt to understand what help is helpful and what help is not.

Olasky carefully documented the decline of Christian charity in the United States, specifically the grassroots and gospel-motivated network of churches and mediating institutions that cared for the poor. Local, faith-based solutions were—and are, where they continue—much more effective than government solutions. So what was behind the decline?

Olasky's book debunked the oft-repeated myth that the church had failed in its charitable responsibilities, thereby forcing the government to step in and fill the void. The true history of American compassion, Olasky said, is the story of a relentlessly expanding government that effectively crowded out faith-based, grassroots solutions to our nation's most vexing social problems. But, as Olasky argued, the large, increasingly bureaucratic, secular, and impersonal institutions not only failed to eliminate poverty, they often increased poverty by exacerbating its root causes. Furthermore, because power in Washington is measured by the size of one's budget and the size of one's staff, bureaucracies that serve the poor have a vested interest in an ever-expanding number of dependents. In other words, they are incentivized to increase the number of people who depend on them for services. Helping people find their way off welfare may be good for people, neighborhoods, and our country, but it is organizational suicide for those bureaucracies responsible for doling out welfare benefits.

In light of this, Olasky argued that for any help to be truly helpful, it must include three distinctive elements:

- First, it must challenge and equip people to participate actively in permanently solving their own problems.
- Second, it must recognize that poverty is fundamentally not a financial problem. Any material brokenness is rooted first and foremost in spiritual brokenness. Effective compassion will address the source, not just the symptom.
- Third, help must be personal, administered in such a way so as to recognize the inherent dignity of all people. For humans to truly flourish, personal dignity and relational integrity must be addressed and restored. This requires understanding that people are always in relationship with others, and that broken relationships of one type or another are most often a contributing cause of poverty.

Implied in all of this is that for help to be truly helpful, it should also be temporary. The goal of help should be to move people toward a restored self-sufficiency. When help is permanent—except in extreme cases of severe permanent disability—either the person "helped" or the organization doing the "helping" is doing something wrong. Making welfare and charity programs temporary for recipients ensures that bad programs don't persist and resources can be redeployed to good programs.

Help That Is Helpful

In their landmark analysis of effective charity, *When Helping Hurts: How to Alleviate Poverty without Hurting the Poor . . . and Yourself*, Steve Corbett and Brian Fikkert write, "[Forty] percent of the earth's inhabitants eke out an existence on less than two dollars per day."[4] All poverty is bad, but this kind of abject poverty is horrible. Christians should never cease to feel empathy and compassion whenever we encounter any bearer of God's image whose inherent dignity and worth are compromised by poverty. Our impulse should always be to "lean in" and help. We should never forget what Jesus Himself said: "Truly, I say to you, as you did it to one of the least of these my brothers, you did it to me" (Matt. 25:40). It was with this Scripture ringing in her ears that Mother Teresa worked with the dirtiest and most diseased in the Calcutta slums while referring to them as "Jesus, in His most distressing disguise."[5]

However, as we have already mentioned, the percentage of people living in abject poverty has declined dramatically and is perhaps at a low point in human history. The life span of Americans has nearly doubled in the past century, and almost every other nation on the planet has seen significant, though lesser, gains in this area as well. Indeed, one of the reasons the population of Earth has grown so much in the past century—from less than three billion in 1900 to more than seven billion today—is that humans tend to be healthier and therefore live longer now than at the turn of the twentieth century. Population expert Steven Mosher went so far as to say that the reason for the dramatic population growth during the last century was "not because we are breeding like rabbits, but because we no longer die like flies."[6]

This condition presents us with an incredible opportunity, one that is unprecedented in human history. While poverty and oppression are still much-too-present realities for far too many people, we have the opportunity to look critically on the various efforts to alleviate poverty and see plainly what has and what has not worked. Some even suggest that our generation has the potential to eliminate abject poverty around the globe.[7]

One of the most important lessons we've learned about alleviating poverty is that success should be measured not by how many people are being helped but by how many people now have the capacity to help themselves. According to Michael Miller of the PovertyCure project, aid distribution in developing countries, though well intended, has perpetuated abject poverty by creating cultures of dependency.[8] The primary cause of abject poverty is not the lack of resources but the lack of access to opportunity and institutions of justice. When access to these essential elements of wealth creation is restricted, poverty continues. When access is restored, people often are able to lift themselves out of abject poverty.

So with all this in mind, let's circle back: Poverty in America is real, but poverty in other parts of the world is often much more severe. The reason poverty has reached such extreme levels in other parts of the world is not that those countries are not receiving aid but that people in those countries often lack access to resources and the rule of law, and therefore lack the opportunity to lift themselves out of poverty. Thus, if we want our help to be helpful, we must give people not handouts but opportunities, as well as the freedom and skills to seize these opportunities. In other words, we ought not begin by asking, "How do we alleviate poverty?" but "How do we give opportunities for wealth creation and human flourishing?"

We can summarize in a single sentence one of the most important things people who study poverty have learned: The best way to eliminate poverty is by creating jobs. Specifically, societies are lifted out of poverty when the opportunities and skills for wealth creation are transferred to everyone in that society.

That's why those on both sides of the political aisle in our country agree that jobs are essential to any healthy economy. This conclusion should not come as a surprise to Christians. We can simplify the biblical picture of human work without, we hope, making it simplistic:

1. God is an intelligent and productive Creator.
2. Humans are made in the image of God and tasked with caring for His world.
3. Therefore, God is glorified and we are satisfied by intelligent, creative, and productive work.

Christians must go a step further. We must always go beyond asking, "What is working?" to "Is it good?" Christians must reject all pragmatic solutions that treat human beings as objects of pity or scorn. Any truly Christian solution must take into account the truths that every member of the human family is made in God's image and worthy of dignity and respect, and that the world is a place of moral norms that reflect the nature of God. Each of these realities points to the fact that work, when done well, is a good that is part of the way God created the human experience.

Work, before the fall, was not a burden but a gift. The fall made work more difficult (see Gen. 3:17–19) but did not remove the essential role work plays in reflecting the inherent dignity of humans. The gift of work remains a key way that God, in His sovereignty and grace, provides for us to flourish physically, relationally, and spiritually.

And so, work—according to the Christian worldview—ought not be forced or oppressive. That's why Christians throughout history often led the way in opposing slavery and harsh working conditions. As Paul wrote to Timothy, "The laborer is worthy of his wages" (1 Tim. 5:18 NKJV). It is also important to note that Old Testament Jewish law provided for debt alleviation and the freeing of indentured servants.

With these ideas in mind, we turn our attention to some organizations that are actively and effectively lifting individuals, families, and communities out of poverty.

Christian Women's Job Corps

The organization first founded as the Christian Women's Job Corps of Nashville[9] began as a work of the Women's Missionary Union, the women's ministry program of the Southern Baptist Convention. When the Nashville corps began in 1997, it initially served ten women. Today it serves more than one hundred women annually. The organization quickly grew, and to reflect its expanded reach, the leaders replaced Nashville in their name with "Middle Tennessee." Soon their incredible success spawned imitators around the country, and today more than two hundred Christian Women's Job Corps chapters help thousands of women in all fifty states. In fact, the CWJC of Middle Tennessee used the $10,000 prize it won as the 2006 *WORLD* Magazine Hope Award for Effective Compassion recipient to open new chapters.[10]

Each CWJC chapter operates independently under local leadership and a separate board of directors. CWJC is, in many ways, a classic example of the principles we've already discussed. Their various programs work with women's personal and spiritual needs, challenging them to participate in their own recovery process. CWJC doesn't offer handouts. Their motto is, "A hand up, not a hand out." Through GED preparation, life and job skills classes, mentoring, and Bible study, CWJC cares for employed but poor women, with the goal of helping to transform "body, mind, heart and spirit."

This means not allowing programs to grow beyond their capacity to be effective. To be accepted into one of their programs, women must pass a drug and alcohol test or currently be in recovery. They must attend Bible classes, and they must meet with a mentor weekly. Throughout the duration of their involvement, which typically lasts one to two years, they can only miss class three times without a legitimate excuse.

The work of CWJC reflects that key idea we've discussed in this chapter and throughout this book that we are all made in the image of our creative and diligently working God. Humans—to borrow the words of the great Christian missionary and athlete Eric Liddell—"feel God's pleasure" when we are both creative and diligent in our work.

Victory Trade School

This same idea is embedded in the work of the Victory Trade School (VTS) of Springfield, Missouri.

When Eric "Pork Chop" Wallace was profiled in *WORLD* magazine in 2011, he was twenty-three years old and yearning to work as a cook. However, in his hometown of Modesto, California, recovery from the economic recession was slow. So when his aunt told him in September 2010 about the opportunities being created by Victory Trade School, he boarded a bus for the 72-hour trip to Southwest Missouri.[11]

The young men who apply to Victory Trade School come from fifteen states and are drawn in part by its impressive track record of an 89.5 percent graduation rate (up from 17 percent when it opened in 2003) and a 100 percent job placement rate for its culinary arts graduates. Springfield-area restaurants are eager to hire VTS graduates.

Enrollees at Victory Trade School discover more than how to find a job. They learn how to discern a calling, and their faith in Christ is built up through regular worship and gospel preaching. Like the Christian Women's Job Corps, Victory Trade School focuses first on life skills, then on job skills. Students first complete a Christian discipleship program, then a one-month candidacy program tests the participant's ability and willingness to follow instructions. Only after successfully completing these first two steps may a participant enter Track One.

Track One students start every day with prayer at a family-style breakfast, where they read and discuss the Bible. They also must attend Sunday morning church services in the Christian denomination of their choice. Any students who haven't graduated from high school are required to earn their GEDs.

Victory Trade School began as a subsidiary of Springfield Victory Mission, a ministry that began thirty-five years ago when Everett and Esther Cook took free coffee and doughnuts or sandwiches to homeless people in Springfield's town square.

The Mission is an example of Christians running to, not away from, the problems of their local area. Springfield and the surrounding Ozarks vicinity, such as the West Plains, are home to many methamphetamine labs and users. The problems of West Plains were portrayed in the Oscar-nominated film *Winter's Bone*, which told the story of a seventeen-year-old girl, a victim of her dad's meth involvement. Former meth users who come to the Mission and enter VTS find a zero tolerance for drinking or drug use.

Springfield Victory Mission's executive director, Jim Harriger, admits the zero-tolerance policy is challenging to participants, some of whom have had lifelong addictions. But high expectations are also key to their success. Students are never asked to fight their addictions alone. Not only do they have the staff of Victory Trade School to help them, they also have the Holy Spirit working in their lives to—as Harriger says—"convict, convert, save, and sanctify."

Students who complete Track One and are interested in culinary arts enter Track Two and, upon graduation, receive certificates in seven areas recognized by the National Restaurant Association Educational Foundation. Students in Track Two learn food production, customer service, restaurant marketing, and cost controls.

The on-the-job training in Track Two comes via Cook's Kettle, a Springfield eatery popular with judges, lawyers, local construction workers, and others. VTS students earn wages and use the money to buy items that don't play to their weaknesses. Any tips stay in an account until graduation, providing one more incentive for these aspiring restaurant workers to stay in school.

Other VTS students staff the Branch Bistro, an upscale deli and catering service located on the ground floor of the Assemblies of God (AG) headquarters several blocks away. Visitors, as well as the 800 AG headquarters employees, can buy lunch there, and VTS students are often given the opportunity to cater the various AG events that happen around town.

The success stories are inspiring and diverse. One graduate came in with a master's degree, but it was the Christian discipleship training that helped him get back on track. Three weeks after completing the program, he secured a job teaching history at a local university. Another man who'd been suicidal came through the entry-level free lodging program at Victory Mission called Transitions. After completing a "Christian Twelve Steps in Twelve Weeks" program called 12/12, he graduated from VTS and gained a job.

Fruits of Labor

On a cool morning in early June, strawberry, asparagus, and pea sprouts stood in rows in a community garden in Lake City, Michigan. Dozens of Geronimo tomato plants and bell peppers grew inside a hoop house. Sprouts of parsley, sage, and basil spread their leaves in a greenhouse heated to 88 degrees Fahrenheit.[12]

Here at Friends Ministry, a 61-acre nonprofit in Northern Michigan, berries and eighteen varieties of vegetables grow in a community garden created to help the poor. Friends Ministry aims to revive a work ethic by hiring the unemployed as laborers in the garden in exchange for financial assistance. Along the way, they teach about both God and budgeting.

Some of these workers fulfill the hours required through "barter" contracts they've signed with Friends Ministry: Once they work in the garden 37.5 hours, the organization will directly pay a bill of up to $300, whether for rent, utilities, or a car repair. It works out to $8 an hour, though they are not technically employees. If they break a contract by failing to fulfill their scheduled hours, their bill goes unpaid.

The gardeners include volunteers who come here regularly to befriend the barter laborers and offer a word of encouragement or a listening ear. One, Don Hoitenga, carries gospel tracts in his shirt pocket and sometimes hands out Bibles to barter workers. "God bless you. Good to meet you again. Keep the faith," he told one after help-ing her transplant asparagus into a shallow trench.

Brian Cohee, a forty-three-year-old single dad who said he's been off drugs for three years, collects Social Security income for a head injury. In 2010 he huffed cleaning spray, passed out, hit his head on concrete, and underwent two brain surgeries. He said he doesn't yet attend church but prays more than he used to. He believes his head injury would make him a liability to a regular employer but thinks he might be able to run his own landscaping business. At Friends Minis-try he fired up a weed whacker and cut grass along the garden fence, working to pay off an electric furnace repair bill. "I've paid off court fees, I've paid off license fees, lawyer fees." He sometimes brings his kids along to teach them the value of hard work. "My five-year-old was even out here picking up rocks on a Saturday."[13]

Friends Ministry started in 1994 as a nondenominational outreach growing out of a deacons' ministry run by the Christian Reformed Church that offered prayer, transportation, or help with heating bills. It grew to include a banquet hall rental business (which failed) and a thrift shop (which thrived and brings in a third or more of Friends Ministry's annual revenue). It gives away or resells donated used cars and organizes summer volunteer church teams to mend roofs or clean up yards in the community.

In 2010 Friends Ministry added the garden in hopes of giving people with low income a dignified place to work in exchange for help. Today it sells the fruits and vegetables at a roadside stand and farmers' market.

When new clients arrive looking for help with a bill, executive director Mark Mortenson usually requires them to write out a bud-get. He often prays with them and invites them to surrender to God what they can't control: car problems, gas prices, physical pains. He provides spiritual counsel for overcoming alcohol or drug addictions and refers them to outside counselors for help with serious family problems or mental illness.

Friends Ministry does not hand out cash to clients but will give a free piece of furniture from the thrift shop and pay directly up to $50 for a legitimate need such as a heating payment, a GED testing fee, or work boots. For larger bills, clients must work off a garden contract. If their expenses exceed the contract limit, Friends Ministry con-nects them to other assistance agencies or helps them find subsidized housing if they are living beyond their means. Many clients get help with bills, then disappear the rest of the year. But some return to donate their time or money.

Clients often arrive blaming others for their problems or are sometimes lazy, so Mortenson challenges them to take responsibility. Once, when a worker was "lollygagging" instead of doing his job peeling the bark from cedar posts, Mortenson walked over, threatened to cancel his work contract, and said, "I want one log peeled every fifteen minutes. . . . If you can't do that, then go home." The worker peeled a log in fifteen minutes and, excited by his success, began teaching others how to do the same.

Mortenson's conclusion: "People respond when you love them enough to give 'em a little push."

Atlanta's FCS Urban Ministries and the Old Atlanta Stockade

Few individuals or organizations combine the principles we've discussed so far better than Atlanta's FCS Urban Ministries, and few have written more eloquently about both their successes and failures in helping the poor than Bob Lupton. Lupton's books, *Theirs Is the Kingdom* and *Toxic Charity*,[14] tell the story of FCS Urban Ministries and should be required reading for anyone who wants to know how to effectively serve the urban poor.

Lupton's expertise did not come easy. Having invested over forty years of his life working in inner-city Atlanta, any knowledge he has is hard-won. He first felt a call to minister to delinquent urban youth while performing military service in Vietnam. Upon his return, Bob, his wife, Peggy, and their two sons sold their suburban home and moved into the inner city, where they have lived and served as neighbors among those in need ever since. Their life's work has been aimed at rebuilding urban neighborhoods, transforming them into communities where families can flourish and children can grow into healthy adults.

One of the most compelling projects FCS Urban Ministries has ever undertaken was the conversion of what was known as the Old Atlanta Stockade. Today it is a place of healing, peace, and restoration in what once was one of the worst neighborhoods in Atlanta.

To fully understand the extent of the transformation, it's important to understand the history of the Stockade. Built in 1896, the Stockade was a prison. If you didn't know that, however, you might think it was beautiful. A large neoclassical and gothic facility, its guard towers look like the turrets of a castle. Its beauty makes it all the more ironic that the Stockade quickly became the largest prison in the state of Georgia and was, by all reports, a place of terrible injustice. The poor who could not pay their debts often shared cells with hardened criminals. Children as young as ten were imprisoned and fell prey to the worst kinds of abuse. According to some reports, the venereal disease rate among inmates was nearly 100 percent. When people started disappearing from the prison without a trace, family members and the general public rose up in protest. The prison closed its doors in the 1920s.

The building soon became a burned-out shell, and a blighted neighborhood grew up around it. The sordid reputation of the Stockade became even worse in the 1950s, nearly thirty years after the state had shut down the prison. The skeletal remains of fifty people were discovered by workers who were building Interstate 20 through the heart of Atlanta. They were what remained of those prisoners of a generation earlier who had "disappeared." Official government documents insist that only one person ever died at the prison, from tuberculosis.

By the 1980s, the old prison seemed destined to be an eternal blight on the city, even when closed. It had become an eyesore and was a haven for crime.

That's when it caught the eye of Renny Scott.[15]

In many ways, Scott had lived a charmed and privileged life. From an old-line Charleston, South Carolina, family, he had attended Yale, graduating and then continuing to a seminary education to become an Episcopal priest. When he married Margaret Howell, who was from an equally old-line Atlanta family, the wedding earned a mention in the society pages of the *New York Times*. But a funny thing happened to Renny Scott on his way to the top levels of the Episcopal Church: He had a radical encounter with Jesus Christ. He became an evangelical, holding to the core doctrines of Scripture even as the Episcopal Church was departing from orthodoxy. He eventually resigned his post as pastor of one of the largest and oldest Episcopal churches in South Carolina and moved his family back to his wife's hometown.

But he was not living in the tony neighborhoods of Buckhead, where a major thoroughfare, Howell Mill Road, was named for his wife's family. Instead, Renny and Margaret Scott chose to live among the poor, right in the shadow of the Old Atlanta Stockade.

Soon Scott had an outlandish idea that he brought to Bob Lupton and FCS Urban Ministries in the form of a question: Could a place of unspeakable horror and imprisonment become a place of hope and liberation? In other words, could the Atlanta Stockade, which had been the site of so much evil and destruction, become the center of a flourishing community for low-income people?

Together they decided to try, but the first step was to see if the project was even possible. Scott, Lupton, and FCS invited a group of architects to tour the facility. In one of the many miracles and near-miracles related to this project, the architects—from seven competing firms—decided to cooperate. They would donate their time to create architectural plans suitable for the challenge of converting the Stockade into apartments, a laundry, a store, and other facilities essential to a functioning and ultimately thriving community.

And that was just the beginning of what would become a large-scale effort of united Atlanta businesses, nonprofits, and individuals. During the fund-raising for the revitalization (another one of those "re" words!), Scott would sometimes ask people to donate $40,000 to pay for the complete restoration of an apartment. If you don't have that, he'd say, what about $4,000 for the appliances in the kitchen? Still too much money? Then what about $400 for a shower stall? If even that is too much for you to take on, what about $40 to buy all the nails needed for a single apartment?

"Helping people see that whatever they contributed was vital to the success of the project was key," he said.

When it came time to unveil the new facility, on Easter Sunday, the local newspaper donated a full page of advertising, and a local advertising agency designed a beautiful ad that featured an artfully shot photograph of the Stockade's guard tower rising into a clear sky in the early morning sun. That guard tower, though, now bore a cross, and the caption for the ad simply read, "He is risen, indeed."

That was twenty years ago. The converted Atlanta Stockade is now home to more than fifty families, and through the years it has helped thousands of people out of poverty and into the middle class.

Revitalizing America's Most Endangered City

It would be difficult to imagine an American city in worse shape than Detroit in the past twenty years.

For most of the twentieth century, Detroit was the envy of the world. The "Big Three" automobile manufacturers made their homes there, and the number of jobs and the amount of cash generated by these Detroit corporations is almost unimaginable. By the 1950 U.S. Census, Detroit had 1.8 million people and was the fifth largest city in the country, a rank it held for the census in 1960, 1970, and 1980. However, since then, its rank and population have dropped significantly. By 2010 it was well out of the top 10, at number 18, with barely over 700,000 people.

This precipitous decline is unprecedented in American history, and it has left many neighborhoods in Detroit essentially abandoned. Because Detroit owes its past growth to the automobile, and because the heyday of Detroit was during the construction of the interstate highway system, driving through parts of Detroit today can seem surreal. Interstates that are four, five, and six lanes wide—obviously built for heavy traffic—carry light traffic going well above the speed limit even during rush hour.

The demographic collapse has had a devastating economic effect on Detroit. As we have already suggested in earlier chapters, governments—whether they are local, state, or federal—only know how to expand. They do not shrink voluntarily. So when the people started leaving Detroit, city services did not initially shrink with them. Bloated bureaucracies continued to operate. The city rang up huge deficits. Thousands of abandoned homes and apartment buildings became havens for the homeless and for criminals. According to the *Detroit News*, owners of more than half of the city's 305,000 properties failed to pay their 2011 tax bills. Many of the people who had owned or lived in these buildings had simply fled with what they could carry with them, leaving the banks to foreclose or the city to condemn, sometimes both. Another indicator of how bad things got in Detroit is that an estimated twenty thousand stray dogs roamed Detroit's worst neighborhoods. In 2010, according to a Detroit postmaster, dogs attacked fifty-nine postal workers.[16]

The crisis in Detroit came to a head in 2013 when the state of Michigan took over control of the city. On July 18, 2013, Detroit became the largest city in the history of America to declare bankruptcy. The city of Detroit had more than $18.5 billion in debt.

In the midst of this crisis, Christopher Brooks serves as senior pastor of Evangel Ministries, a 1,500-member church in Detroit. It wouldn't be accurate to say that Brooks "stepped into" the crisis. He was already there. The history of Evangel Ministries is somewhat different from other large evangelical churches that start in the suburbs or move there when their urban neighborhoods deteriorate.

Rather than run away from the problems of the city, Evangel Ministries ran toward them. Evangel Church started in Mt. Clemens, Michigan, in 1964, and grew so rapidly that by 1970 it needed a new location. Conventional wisdom would have been for the church to buy a large piece of land in this affluent suburb and build a megachurch. Instead, the church moved into Detroit and by 2003 had a racially diverse congregation and staff. That's the year the white founding pastor, George Bogle, retired. He turned the reins over to the church's African American executive pastor, Chris Brooks.[17]

The church, now called Evangel Ministries, has thrived under Brooks's leadership. Still in the heart of Detroit, its main campus houses its central church as well as a fitness center, a radio station, two Christian academies, a Bible college, job training and placement centers, a food pantry, and a prison ministry.

Brooks has taken a page from Marvin Olasky's playbook and made spiritual growth a central part of all of Evangel's ministries. A particular event in the summer of 2007 crystallized his thinking. When Evangel members went into the surrounding neighborhoods to share the gospel through a summer-long program called Dare to Share, they found that many of their neighbors had strong objections to Christianity. These objections were not new to Brooks, who had studied apologetics at Biola University and at the Oxford Centre for Christian Apologetics. Brooks could "do apologetics" with the best of them.

"We realized that we needed to respond to not just the historic topics of theology and philosophy, but also to the pressing, present question: 'Does the Lord see what's happening in the hood?'"

Brooks's book, *Urban Apologetics*, tells the story of how Evangel enthusiastically embraced the questions and challenges that were being leveled at the truth claims of Christianity.[18] Brooks believes that the truths of Scripture, and the implications of those truths, apply to all, but the cultures from which we come teach us to see and hear some truths more easily than others. Brooks says it this way: "White evangelicals typically are drawn to the righteousness of God—the importance of right doctrine and right practices—whereas African Americans and minorities are drawn more to the justice of God. Yet Psalm 89 says the foundations of God's throne are righteousness and justice. We can't bifurcate the ethics of God into categories of righteousness—issues like abortion and human sexuality—or justice—issues like educational and economic equality."[19]

So Brooks works carefully to re-frame issues in ways that make them easier to hear. "The pro-life argument, for example, is more persuasive in our community if you approach it through the anti-youth-violence movement," Brooks said. "Our community has already been mobilized to stand against youth violence. It's a natural extension to say, 'Shouldn't we protect our children in the womb as well? Shouldn't the womb of a mother be the safest place for a child?'"[20]

Brooks is more than willing to address questions many in a different context may have never considered: Why should Christians care about restoring economic justice? Shouldn't the church just preach the gospel and trust that transformed people will take care of all the rest?

Well, yes . . . and no. "Christians believe that truth is a Person," Brooks said. "Truth is more than a proposition. Truth took on 'flesh and dwelt among us,' according to John, and we beheld him as 'the only begotten of the Father.' As he comes full of grace and truth, he comes healing us and addressing our woundedness. A truth that is not living, vibrant, and active is not fully expressed truth. Yes, there are intellectual aspects of truth, but for truth to be fully expressed, it has to be incarnated."[21]

Brooks is not primarily concerned about politics. He believes—as our mentor Chuck Colson often said—that "politics is downstream from culture."[22] The Great Commission is not about making converts, but about "teaching all things," and some of those things have political implications. For example, Brooks often makes the point that fatherless homes make it difficult for children to understand what it means to have a heavenly Father. "We are proclaiming a gospel that God is the Father who loves us, who sent his Son to die for us," Brooks said. "The very terms are hard to even relate to if you don't know a father. If you're an African American child growing up in a single-parent, female-led home, your mom is struggling to meet the bills. Who makes up for housing and food and all those things? The government does. Government becomes a quasi-father."[23]

Brooks said to change that reality, "We had better show them what a father is, what a family is, so that when we see analogies to family relationships in the Bible, they can relate. When John writes, 'What manner of love is this that we should be called the sons of God?' what does that look like? If I can see that in a visible example, the text will come alive."

It is perhaps no surprise that this son of Detroit, who has also studied C. S. Lewis, would bring the two together:

> I think about C. S. Lewis, who had the challenge of building the bridge between the culture of Oxford and Cambridge and the culture of the church. These cultures were worlds apart by his time, but he was bilingual, in a sense: able to speak the language of Oxford to the church and the language of the church to the intellectuals and naturalists.
>
> I hope there are Christians who can speak the language of righteousness to minorities. I think that is part of my call. On the other hand, I'm speaking the language of justice to those who haven't had to deal with justice issues. We need more bilingual Christians who can speak the languages of both justice and righteousness.[24]

Conclusion and a To-Do List

The gospel transforms not just our individual lives but also communities, towns, nations. When Jonathan Edwards preached the sermons in 1735 that are now credited with beginning the First Great Awakening, his community of Northampton, Massachusetts, saw not only souls saved but taverns closed, industry increased, and a civic spirit revived.[25]

The poor don't need handouts. Rather, they need opportunities to participate in the most effective anti-poverty program in the history of mankind: meaningful and dignified work. The poor don't need to be patronized. They need to know they matter to God and so does their work. Work, when done well, restores and makes plain the inherent dignity every human being shares. It reflects God's glory. By working, we imitate Him and live out in a very real sense who He has created us to be.

If your heart aches for those in poverty in America and around the world, here are several ways to participate in what God is doing to "restore all things" to Himself:

1. Hone your ability to understand the causes and solutions for poverty by reading Marvin Olasky's *The Tragedy of American Compassion* and *When Helping Hurts* by Steve Corbett and Brian Fikkert.

2. Be thankful for the opportunities you have to work, and communicate that thankfulness and dignity by mentoring someone younger in a true understanding of work and care for the poor.

3. Consider leading a small group using the Acton Institute's PovertyCure program.

4. Find a Christ-centered job training program in your area and volunteer there or make a financial contribution.

5. Talk with your pastor or someone else in leadership at your church to ask if someone in your congregation is in need of work. Help that person with résumé preparation, job skill training, or connections with employers.

6. If you are positioned to do so, expand opportunities by providing meaningful employment to others or by tithing corporate profits toward a program that helps the poor.

3

Capitalism for the Common Good

> The art of economics consists in looking not merely at
> the immediate but at the longer effects of an act or policy.
> It consists in tracing the consequences of that policy not
> merely for one group but for all groups.
>
> —Henry Hazlitt[1]

Capitalism has gotten a bad rap, and it's easy to see why.

Movies, television, literature, and virtually every other expression of entertainment culture have shaped our collective popular imaginations to consistently, you might even say relentlessly, see entrepreneurs as selfish, greedy, and ethically challenged, if not downright evil and rapacious.

Take, for example, the 1987 movie *Wall Street*. The villain in that movie is corporate raider Gordon Gekko, who—in a pivotal scene—defends his unscrupulous behavior by proclaiming, "Greed, for lack of a better word, is good. Greed is right. Greed works. Greed clarifies, cuts through, and captures the essence of the evolutionary spirit. Greed, in all of its forms . . . has marked the upward surge of mankind." The director of *Wall Street*, Oliver Stone, is a man of eclectic spiritual tastes. He spent time in the Church of Scientology, and he signed the Humanist Manifesto III, a document that is openly critical of Christianity. Currently he identifies as a Buddhist.

If Stone has trouble settling on a religious worldview, he leaves no doubt regarding his feelings about capitalism. The movie ends with Gekko getting his just deserts: going to jail for insider trading. It's ironic that Oliver Stone, who made the definitive movie critiquing capitalism, has a personal net worth of at least $50 million, mostly by making and selling movies.

And that's only one of the ironies. Lots of people apparently failed to understand the moral of *Wall Street*. Michael Douglas, the actor who played Gordon Gekko, told the *New York Times* that often "drunken Wall Street broker[s] come up to me and say, 'You're the man!'"[2]

It's not just liberals who want us to believe that capitalism is based on greed. Ayn Rand, whose books have sold more than thirty million copies, has become a hero to libertarians by teaching the same thing. Many fiscally conservative Christians have embraced her ideology without understanding the intensely anti-Christian worldview upon which it is based. Her philosophy of "objectivism" teaches that self-ishness is a virtue. "Capitalism and altruism are incompatible," she wrote. "They are philosophical opposites. They cannot coexist in the same man or in the same society."[3]

So is it true that capitalism is based on greed? Is it possible to be both a capitalist and truly virtuous? Ought Christians to support capitalism?

The Theological Roots of Capitalism

Let's acknowledge right away that greed, despite Gordon Gekko's affirmation, is not a virtue. It is, in fact, a vice. The Bible uses some version of the word *greed* about a dozen times, and not once is it described as a positive attribute. If we throw in the many biblical references to coveting, that list grows dramatically. And, again, every single usage of any form of the word *covet* in Scripture is negative. Jay Richards, in his book *Money, Greed, and God*, puts it this way: "This greed-is-good rhetoric is a big fat nonstarter for Christians. It is not like the Bible and the Christian tradition have been vague on the matter. Greed, or 'avarice,' is one of the seven deadly sins, and the Bible has nothing good to say about it."[4]

If greed is the basis of capitalism, as many assume, Christians cannot participate. But is it, really? We say no. In fact, we suggest that free-market capitalism, which we prefer to call the free enterprise system, is a system that, when properly understood and implemented, discourages rather than encourages greed. To understand what we mean, it is important to define what we mean by "free enterprise system." A free enterprise system must consist of the following elements:

1. Ownership of private property
2. Noncoercive trading of goods and services
3. Laws that provide a "level playing field" of access, opportunity, and legal protection for all participants

These elements promote community flourishing and are consistent with biblical ideals. First, God created humans to care for the creation. They were given the task of ruling over what God had made. This implies ownership. Second, humans were created free, with the capacity to make decisions in how they steward creation. They were not "programmed" to do things in a particular way. "You may freely eat," God told Adam. Third, there were moral boundaries within which they were expected to freely operate. In other words, though they had freedom, they could not do everything they wanted to do. God placed them in a moral universe, having written His laws on their hearts. Further, these three elements are reflected throughout Scripture, even after the fall.

While these three items above might be called the "systemic" qualities of a free enterprise system that encourages human flourishing, it is also important to remember the personal qualities necessary for this system to best work. While a system can encourage people to behave in virtuous ways, it cannot guarantee that they will. That's why Christian virtues, such as charity and stewardship, are so vital.

But there's also the "why" behind the work. Christian entrepreneurs throughout history have developed businesses to contribute something good to the world. Often, it's been a means of solving a problem, or simplifying a process, or increasing efficiency. Many Christians have even understood their contributions to be reversing the effects of the fall that has made so much of our work toilsome.

And this points to a fundamental difference between a free-market system and all others, especially socialism. Most economic systems treat human beings as consumers of resources. In a socialistic way of seeing things, the limited amount of resources in the world is under constant threat of being used up by consumers too greedy or too numerous for their own good. The resources, therefore, have to be carefully managed by state authorities.

Consumerism, a corruption of capitalism, also treats people as consumers. Descartes famously said, "I think therefore I am." The mantra in a consumerist society may as well be, "I shop therefore I .am." The "God-shaped" vacuum described by Blaise Pascal becomes a "stuff-shaped" vacuum that can only be filled by newer, more clever toys.

A healthy free-market economic system treats people differently. We humans certainly consume food and other resources. However, our creativity, diligence, and ingenuity—when not corrupted by vice or bound by improper regulation—offer more to the world than they take. They aren't a problem to be managed. They are the source of our best answers. In other words, the free-market system sees people primarily as producers, not consumers. This mirrors, of course, the vision of human capacity and dignity given in the Genesis creation account. "Be fruitful, multiply. Fill the earth and subdue it."

This productivity, when combined with charity and honesty, is a powerful redemptive force. Christian businessmen and businesswomen have changed lives and lifted entire communities out of poverty. They continue to do so today.

Truett Cathy and Chick-fil-A

One family well known for taking the notions of charity and stewardship seriously is the Cathy family, the owners of the Chick-fil-A restaurant chain.

The patriarch of the family was Truett Cathy, who died in 2014 at age 93.[5] Cathy began his career as a restaurateur in 1946, opening his first Chick-fil-A concept in 1967. But what distinguishes Truett's life isn't merely his business success but also his solid Christian witness throughout the span of his career.

The most obvious example of the company's efforts to operate according to the family's Christian convictions was their famous policy of closing every store on Sundays. But that policy is just one aspect of a company whose mission statement reflects the family's Christian commitment. While McDonald's aims to get a hamburger in the hands of everyone on the planet, Chick-fil-A exists "to glorify God by being a faithful steward of all that is entrusted to us."[6]

Chick-fil-A's "Closed on Sundays" policy—which the company was never bashful in promoting as part of its marketing messages—did not seem to hurt sales. Instead, the policy is one of many that helped create an uncommon loyalty among its customers. In fact, as the chain expanded from its base in Atlanta, new store openings became community-wide events. It is not uncommon to find customers camping out for days in advance of a new store opening.

The Cathy family also wants to use the profits from Chick-fil-A for the glory of God. One of the ways they do this is by making it possible for thousands of other families to have Chick-fil-A businesses. Other fast-food empires require a significant amount of financial capital to buy into their system. Chick-fil-A's initial investment is relatively small, but not everyone with the money can score a franchise. The company rigorously screens potential owner-operators for both skill and character. They also have created a pathway of mentoring and training for talented young employees to move from cashier and cook to management and ownership.

Their charitable activities also reflect their worldview. Through their WinShape Foundation, which is financially supported by tithing their corporate profits, they've opened long-term foster homes throughout the southern United States. Because of these efforts, hundreds of needy kids have grown up in loving, two-parent families, received the means to go to college, and even (at Truett's insistence) received matching funds for their first cars. The Cathys also opened summer camps for boys and girls and have given away millions of dollars in college scholarships.

They also started a marriage enrichment retreat at their Berry College conference center.

"Children," said Truett, "will never believe in the covenant of marriage unless they see it with their own eyes." In line with that belief, the Cathys have donated millions to pro-family organizations, which eventually landed their family and company in hot water with LGBT activists in 2012. They were accused of supporting "anti-gay" organizations, and their clearly written nondiscrimination employment policy did little to quell the controversy.

Gay rights groups organized protests on college campuses and at several Chick-fil-A locations. The mayors of Chicago and Boston even threatened to block new Chick-fil-A franchises from opening in their cities, a move that even the liberal American Civil Liberties Union opposed. Millions of Americans showed their support of the company in response, overflowing restaurants across the country during a grassroots-organized day of support. Many restaurants ran out of food that day.

The response of the family to the controversy, however, was far more personal. Truett's son, Dan, quietly began fostering a personal friendship with the national director of the gay rights group Campus Pride, Shane Windmeyer. The friendship dispelled Windmeyer's misconceptions about the Cathy family and their Christian beliefs. It surprised people on both sides of the issue when, in the *Huffington Post*, Windmeyer "came out" as a friend of Dan Cathy and Chick-fil-A, telling fellow activists to stop having a cow about the Cathys' chicken restaurant.[7]

Dan Cathy, Windmeyer admitted, wasn't the foaming, homophobic fundamentalist he'd expected. Instead, Cathy "expressed a sincere interest" in his life and "genuine sadness when he heard of people being treated unkindly in the name of Chick-fil-A." He never wavered on traditional marriage, though, says Windmeyer, but loved and respected him as a person, despite their differences.[8]

Dan Cathy's willingness to reach out and befriend an opponent is undoubtedly a reflection of the legacy established by his father and incorporated into the operation of the business. Truett spent his life putting others first, whether it was his family, his employees, or the countless lives he touched through his generosity. His legacy is worthy of imitation, not just in the fast-food world, but by Christians who want to know what it looks like to live out their faith in business.

Drake Enterprises

The Cathy family has become world famous because of their unique blend of entrepreneurial success and Christian philanthropy.

Phil Drake, on the other hand, is barely known outside of Macon County, North Carolina. But in the towns, hills, and valleys of this rural county on the west side of the state, he's put together the kind of entrepreneurial empire—some of it involving leading-edge technologies—that would make a Silicon Valley venture capitalist salivate.

The Cathy family had long-held Christian traditions, and their business was dedicated to Christian values from the beginning. Phil Drake's story is a bit more complicated. In fact, it resembles more the real life that most of us live.

Phil's father began Drake Income Tax and Accounting in 1954.[9] That business helped Drake's parents put him through Davidson College. After graduation, Drake taught high school math but returned home in 1976 to join his father's business. He helped lead the business from pencils, calculators, and ledger sheets into the computer age.

They were early adopters of technology, and the move was risky in an era when an IBM computer cost more than $20,000. The business went deeply into debt by mortgaging a piece of property to buy one, but Drake subsequently developed an accounting program to be used in his father's business and also sold to other accountants.[10]

The return on the investment was slow, and Drake quickly was overextended. According to a newspaper account written years later, "The Internal Revenue Service didn't get its due in the form of payroll taxes. One day a federal agent informed Drake the IRS planned to padlock the family's office door and seize their business equipment if the government didn't get its money. Drake didn't have that kind of cash. He instead drove to Asheville, retained an attorney, and filed for bankruptcy."[11]

That began a difficult season for Drake and his young family. It took him nearly six years to pay back his creditors, but the lessons learned during this time were important to his future success. Chief among them: Don't use borrowed money to grow your business.

The whole ordeal also strengthened Drake's reliance on his Christian faith. "This was a life-changing experience for me," Drake wrote of the bankruptcy in an article published by the National Christian Foundation, on whose board he serves. "I came to the place where I finally said, 'God, I've messed this up. From now on, I'll manage your business, and, Lord, would you manage mine?'"[12]

His software business proved to be, at least in part, an answer to his prayers. Today Drake's accounting software is an industry standard for small and mid-sized tax and accounting firms. More than thirty million tax returns are prepared on Drake software every year. The company has more than 350 employees, most of them in western North Carolina.

Drake never forgot what started his success. In 2004, he celebrated the fiftieth anniversary of the tax preparation service founded by his father by selling the company to its employees for one dollar. The gesture is a reflection of Drake's philosophy that business success is far more than merely creating personal wealth. It is also for providing opportunities so others can create their own success.

In addition to his core business of Drake Software, Phil Drake has a stake in at least fifteen other businesses, including a Christian book-store with two locations, a commercial printer, a public golf course and driving range, and BalsamWest FiberNet, which has built more than 225 miles of underground fiber in western North Carolina and provides broadband Internet access to the Eastern Band of Cherokee Indians. Most of his businesses are specifically aimed at adding things of value to his local community.

For example, one of the businesses Drake is particularly fond of is housed in a former Wrangler jeans factory in Franklin, where his mother once worked. That factory eventually shut down but was bought by Drake and converted into a 56,000-square-foot "Fun Factory" for kids that includes arcade games, rides, a bowling alley, batting cages, a go-cart track, and two restaurants. For Drake, it was a way of giving the children and teenagers in his community a place to enjoy while staying out of trouble. A few years later, he opened a fine arts center on the property. Today residents of Franklin enjoy an array of musical theater and other performances of a quality unheard of in other towns the same size.[13]

Teaching Entrepreneurship

The stories of Truett Cathy and Phil Drake are both interesting and inspiring, but their remarkable accomplishments might tempt us to believe they are not replicable.

Jeff Sandefer doesn't buy it. He believes you can both teach and learn entrepreneurship, but not without effort.[14]

Sandefer is founder of the Acton School of Business, a highly rated MBA program in Austin, Texas. And to make the point that what he's doing is serious business, he once told a student who wanted to work while attending Acton, "There is no time for students to work while attending Acton. Students work 80 to 100 hours or more a week attending class, meeting in peer groups, and preparing cases." The Acton website further reiterates this point: "Time-entrepreneurs don't insult each other by wasting it. . . . Here you'll get a transformational experience in less [than] half the time of other business programs. Your time's way too valuable to waste."

Sandefer made his first entrepreneurial dollars by seeing undervalued time: After a company hired him to paint storage tanks, he saw other paid-by-the-hour painters move slowly in the West Texas heat. So he set up his own business that paid by work done. Individuals who worked quickly could earn a lot, and so did Sandefer—though he was still in high school. He went on to gain a Harvard MBA and to found Sandefer Offshore (a profitable oil and gas company) and Sandefer Capital Partners (a half-billion-dollar energy investment fund).[15]

He taught part-time at the University of Texas before turning his energies there full-time. After building a top entrepreneurship program, he left because the university emphasized research over teaching. He also noted that many of the professors there—and at most other business schools—had never actually built a successful business.

Sandefer then did more than criticize. He created an MBA program that reflects business reality. Grading is on a forced curve, which means the lower-ranked students flunk out. Teaching is on a forced curve as well, with student evaluations of professors taken so seriously that the lowest-ranked loses his job.

But such policies are not heartless. Rather, they are designed to quickly and efficiently help students (and faculty) understand their gifts and passions. In fact, Sandefer said business is just a tool. "We believe in building profitable businesses, but know leading a meaningful life is much more important," he said. "Learn how to make money. Learn how to live a life of meaning."[16]

In fact, Sandefer teaches a class called "Life of Meaning," and it's required for all students.

Acton is not a Christian school, but its goals and purposes express a commitment to "cherish the arts, the wonders of the physical world and the mystery of life." It's committed to "economic, political, and religious freedom." Its website states without embarrassment, "We believe that the American Experiment, with all its faults, is the best hope on earth for protecting human liberty."

As for Sandefer himself, he believes entrepreneurship is heroic, and he wants each of his students to have this idea in mind: "I am on a hero's journey."[17]

Conclusions and a To-Do List

This chapter is related to the previous chapter but also different in that it focuses on entrepreneurs who see their work as an offering of good gifts and opportunity to the world. These creative Christians leverage resources (financial and human) to build community, address social ills, and teach vocation—the idea that all our work matters to God.

Many people struggle their whole lives to see how their worship on Sunday can inform nine-to-five workdays Monday through Friday. If the ideas and stories in this chapter capture your heart and mind, you can participate in what God is doing through work to "restore all things" to Himself.

1. Hone your ability to understand economics and think clearly about the goods brought by the market by reading *Money, Greed, and God: Why Capitalism Is the Solution and Not the Problem* by Jay Richards. Learn about the history of Christianity in developing communities by reading *The Victory of Reason: How Christianity Led to Freedom, Capitalism, and Western Success* by Rodney Stark and *Discipling Nations: The Power of Truth to Transform Cultures* by Darrow Miller.
2. Do your own work heartily, as to the Lord.
3. Dedicate forty-five minutes a week to creative personal or group thinking about innovation in your work, or consider starting a new business or investing in a new business idea.
4. Encourage young entrepreneurs to look for problems to solve and products or services people might need. Watch the television show *Shark Tank* together.

5. Identify and support the kinds of local businesses that contribute positively to the local community, especially those in the start-up phase.

6. If you are a supervisor, evaluate all hiring and employment policies to ensure those who work are cared for properly, that creativity and productivity are properly incentivized, and that everyone is treated with dignity and respect.

4

This Will Stop in Our Lifetime

The greatest destroyer of peace today is abortion, because it is a war against the child, and if we accept that a mother can kill even her own child, how can we tell other people not to kill one another?

—Mother Teresa

What is man that you are mindful of him, and the son of man that you care for him? Yet you have made him a little lower than the heavenly beings and crowned him with glory and honor.

—Psalm 8:4–5

A great evil haunts our civilization. The number of its victims is historically unprecedented.

Consider this: Nazi concentration camps hosted the extermination of seven million people. Communist and other totalitarian regimes in the twentieth century massacred one hundred million in various gulags and death camps. The Black Death plague of the fourteenth century may have killed two hundred million people. Add all these together, then double the number, and then double it again, and you approach the number of innocent children exterminated in the past century by abortion.

The Soviets first legalized abortion in 1919. Nazi Germany followed in 1935. The United States legalized it in 1973. China's "one-child policy," only recently and slightly modified, is mostly responsible for the thirteen million abortions that take place there *each year*—many of them forced.[1] Another ten million doses of abortion pills are sold in that country. Today, around the world, more than forty million abortions take place each year. That amounts to two Black Death plagues a decade or six Holocausts per year. Nearly sixty million unborn children have been aborted in the United States alone since 1973's *Roe v. Wade* Supreme Court decision.

Anyone who stands for peace, justice, and protecting the rights of the innocent should be on the front lines of the fight against abortion.

We opened this book by noting that "God loveth 're' words." In that introduction, we suggested that Christians spend too much time embodying certain "re" words, like *re*sist, while not engaging enough with the others that figure much more prominently in the New Testament: *re*deem, *re*new, *re*concile, and *re*store. But when it comes to abortion and the fight for life, *re*sistance must be one of the weapons in our arsenal.

As outrageous as the overall abortion numbers are, they only tell the tragic story of one of its victims. As many in the pro-life movement say, "Abortion leaves one dead and many wounded." Aunts and uncles, grandparents, and siblings are robbed of meeting, knowing, or perhaps even knowing *of* a close relative. Communities are missing citizens and neighbors. In fact, in some countries (Russia, to name but one of many), abortion has lowered the birth rate to the point that these nations face demographic collapse. The elderly in America are at risk due to an unsustainable Social Security system. We literally do not have enough young people to support the number of older people in the system.

But most of all, there are the wounded parents, especially mothers who must live with the abortion of their children for the rest of their lives. Nearly a half century of abortion-on-demand in this country and forced abortions in countries such as China now tell an indisputable story: Abortion takes innocent lives, hurts women, destroys families, and weakens countries.

Given these horrible realities, it seems almost flippant, or glib, to "pivot" from this story to tell positive, redemptive stories that have come out of the pro-life movement. But it is not. The stand taken by many in the Christian community in recent decades against this great evil has been courageous, caring, and increasingly strategic. And all of this is being done in the face of what often seems to be an undefeatable foe. Yet God tells us His strength is made perfect in our weakness (see 2 Cor. 12:9). And we see this principle clearly at work in the pro-life movement, especially in this country.

The Pregnancy Care Center Movement

How are Christians responding to this grave evil? Many entered the political process as lobbyists and candidates. Apologists have worked hard to develop intelligent, articulate, and reusable defenses of the dignity of all life, including the unborn. Journalists have told the various and diverse stories that have emerged because of abortion— stories of courageous women, selfish couples, wicked men, and racist organizations.[2] And yet perhaps no response to the tragedy of abortion has been more profound or effective than that by the everyday individuals who make up the pregnancy care center (PCC) movement.

After the *Roe v. Wade* decision legalized abortion-on-demand in the United States, many Christians struggled to determine an appropriate response. As remarkable as it seems today, some actually thought legalizing abortion would be an improvement over the status quo, which was an environment in which abortions, despite being illegal, were nonetheless common. Perhaps the legalization of abortion would allow them to be—as some on the side of legalizing abortion said—"safe, legal, and rare." But our clearest Christian thinkers quickly saw that idea as morally bankrupt and biblically unacceptable.

Dr. Harold O. J. Brown was among them. He founded the Christian Action Council in 1975. In the early days, Brown used his brain and his pen, writing about what he called "the abortion crisis." His colaborers in this effort were Christian apologist Francis Schaeffer and a man who would eventually become surgeon general of the United States, C. Everett Koop.

Soon, however, the Christian Action Council realized that tangible action was necessary, so it opened its first pregnancy care center in 1983.[3] In 1993, a remarkable young leader of the pro-life movement, Guy Condon, took over as president. He oversaw the change of the organization's name to CareNet, and under his leadership made the group an umbrella organization that helped start and support more than six hundred local grassroots organizations. On the night of November 11, 2000, Condon delivered the keynote address to the Capitol Hill Pregnancy Center in Washington, DC. As he was driving home, he died in an automobile accident. He was forty-six years old.

Though he was gone, the organization he left behind continued to grow. Today CareNet has more than 1,100 affiliated pregnancy care centers in the United States and Canada. It would be hard to find a better example of how a "mediating institution" has changed both the culture and the behavior of a country.[4] To understand the impact of these pregnancy care centers, consider the fact that when *Roe v. Wade* made abortion-on-demand legal in the United States in 1973, the number of abortions grew dramatically. Some Christians exercised two particular "re" words in those early days: they *reacted* and *resisted*. Thousands of evangelical Christians made headlines and got criminal records by protesting in front of abortion facilities. Abortion is a great evil, and the outrage of the abortion protesters was both understandable and necessary to bring public attention to this modern-day Holocaust.

But abortion facility protests are perfect examples of how merely reacting and resisting are not enough. The number of abortions continued to grow despite these protests. In recent years, however, a remarkable thing has happened. The number of abortions per year has started to decline, from a high of 1.3 million to less than one million today. Of course, even one abortion in a year would be a tragic loss of life, so please don't think we are saying that one million abortions a year is good. Still, we are seeing a trend moving in the right direction.

Perhaps even more telling is that the attitude of the country has made a quiet but unmistakable shift. According to the Gallup organization, in the mid-1990s about 35 percent of Americans believed abortion should be legal in all circumstances. Today that number is less than 20 percent.[5]

Are we saying pregnancy care centers alone are responsible for these remarkable changes in American culture? In reality, the causes are many and complicated. Demographics played a role. The widespread availability of birth control played a role. And, of course, ultrasound technology exposed us to the unseen world of life in the womb.

But, yes, we believe the pregnancy care center movement also played a vital role. Pregnancy care centers provide a compassionate face, hands, and feet to the pro-life movement. Every one of the 1,100 CareNet facilities has a board of directors, a staff, volunteers, and—most importantly—clients who have been helped. In the aggregate, these men and women now number in the millions, are spread all across the country, and know by their own experience that pro-life people are not judgmental hypocrites but compassionate caregivers.

Consider, for example, just one pregnancy care center: the Pregnancy and Family Care Center of Leesburg, Florida. Its very formation is an example of the idea that energizes this book: that we should not just react, resist, and reject; we should also restore, redeem, and renew. The pastor of the First Baptist Church of Leesburg,[6] Charles Roesel, came face-to-face with this choice when, in 1989, a woman in his church challenged him. "You talk tough about abortion, but talk is cheap."[7]

That woman was willing to put her money where her mouth was. She said she would donate $5,000 to help start a new ministry, so Pastor Roesel stepped up too. Today, the Pregnancy and Family Care Center serves more than two hundred clients per month. It provides diapers, clothes, toys, formula, and other necessities for mothers and families who choose to keep their babies rather than have an abortion. This church-based ministry has done such good work in the community that its parenting classes are now sometimes court-ordered in certain domestic cases.

And in keeping with a principle we introduced in chapter 2, the Pregnancy and Family Care Center is not only personal; it is both spiritual and challenging. Every year, men and women make first-time professions of faith during the counseling sessions. The Charlotte Pregnancy Care Center, in Charlotte, North Carolina, says more than one hundred women a year come to faith in Christ through their ministry. Other PCCs report similar results. In fact, CareNet says its affiliates have documented more than twenty-three thousand professions of faith in Christ. As Chris Brooks reminded us in chapter 2, "Truth is more than a proposition. . . . It has to be incarnated." Pregnancy care centers do just that.

Many pregnancy care centers follow Leesburg's "earn while you learn" policy. Rather than just give away stuff, the Leesburg PCC allows young families to earn what they need by completing parenting studies, Bible courses, counseling hours, and various other means of education.

But let's step back from Leesburg and Charlotte for a moment to do a bit of simple math. Charlotte's Pregnancy Care Center is somewhat larger than the one at Leesburg Baptist Church. Charlotte directly serves in longer-term relationships more than three thousand men and women each year and has more than thirteen thousand who use the center for "one-off" services such as pregnancy tests and ultrasounds. So just to make this math exercise easy, let's imagine that the average pregnancy care center serves one thousand people a year, multiplied by the 1,100 centers in the country. That equals 1.1 million people served each and every year. Each PCC also has a small army of donors and volunteers that keep them running.

Our point is this: These pregnancy care centers have, together, become an effective life-saving army of compassion, operating in outposts all across America. These centers are not just resisting abortion; they are rescuing the lives of babies, restoring the broken lives of their mothers and fathers, and rebuilding families and communities. It is a remarkable movement, and that's why we believe the clients, workers, volunteers, and donors of pregnancy care centers are truly the "secret ingredient" in the remarkable pro-life shift we've seen in the attitudes toward abortion in the past two decades here in America.

Save The Storks

Pregnancy care centers are perhaps the most well-known pro-life activists in the country, but they are by no means the only ones doing great pro-life work.

One of the most innovative and entrepreneurial organizations we've seen in a while is Save The Storks. Save The Storks is a grassroots, pro-life nonprofit that has a "simple mission": to seek to empower every abortion-minded mother to choose life and to share with them the good news of Jesus.

A key idea behind Save The Storks is this: When women see an ultrasound photo of their babies in their wombs, something happens inside of them. In fact, some surveys suggest that when abortion-minded women see these ultrasound photos, as many as 90 percent of them change their minds and decide to have their babies rather than have their planned abortions.

Because of the power of these photographs, the larger pregnancy care centers have purchased the machines for their facilities. But the cost of these machines is in the tens of thousands of dollars, and they require trained personnel to operate. Focus on the Family has created a grant program to help pregnancy care centers purchase the machines. To date, that program has helped more than one hundred organizations with more than one million dollars in grants.

But what about the rest? What about those women who are not aware of the local pregnancy care center in their town? That's where Save The Storks comes in. Using a bus equipped with a state-of-the-art sonogram machine and the ability to provide pregnancy tests, Save The Storks can meet with abortion-minded mothers in front of abortion clinics to show them images of their unborn children.

According to Joe Baker, who founded Save The Storks, "The majority of the women are not fully convinced that abortion is the best option, but rather they feel as if it is their only option." When a woman leaves the Save The Storks bus resolved to have her baby, Save The Storks immediately puts her in touch with a local pregnancy care center. According to Baker, "Save The Storks differs from protesters by offering resources to help these women in practical and tangible ways. As a result, approximately three out of five women Save The Storks sees choose life."

Incremental Changes

Americans United for Life (AUL) has often been called the "law firm of the pro-life movement." Founded in 1971, AUL is best known for drafting legislation that places restrictions on abortion or expands abortion alternatives, such as making adoption regulations easier to negotiate. AUL then works with pro-life legislators in states around the country to craft this "model legislation" in ways that work best in an individual state. At least one piece of AUL-crafted legislation has now passed in almost every state, and some states have passed many AUL-crafted laws. Some of these changes in the law are minor. For example, AUL has helped pass fetal homicide laws and unborn victims of violence laws that recognize unborn babies as human beings. At least thirty-six states have passed such laws so far.

The Susan B. Anthony List (SBA List) makes its pro-life voice known in the political and public policy arena. The SBA List raises money for pro-life candidates. In particular, it seeks to assist and promote female candidates. It spent more than $10 million in the 2014 political cycle, and its work in a few key states—especially North Carolina, Colorado, and Iowa—receives much of the credit for the U.S. Senate changing hands in the 2014 midterm elections.

All Have Value

As we have already said twice in this book, politics is downstream from culture. So while efforts on the political and legal fronts are vital, they will ultimately not be enough to turn a pervasive culture of death into a restored culture of life.

Instead, it will take changed hearts and minds. The main idea that will have to penetrate the hearts and minds of our nation is one that energizes this book—that we are all made in the image of God and therefore have inherent worth and dignity from the moment of conception to the moment of natural death.

Some stories, like that of Katie Blind, proclaim the truth about human value in ways arguments cannot.[8]

Katie has sung and danced her entire life, keeping her iPod close by and filled with music. Since she was a little girl watching her mom help produce plays at a local Catholic school, Katie, who has Down syndrome, has dreamed of performing onstage. So Katie and her mom, Joan Blind, jumped at the opportunity for her to perform in a musical with the Arts Inclusion Company (AIC).

Dianna Swenson founded AIC to provide performance opportunities for people with all ability levels. Swenson has a background in music and dreamed of singing opera professionally. But her dreams altered course when her son was diagnosed with cerebral palsy.

Many people like Katie come to AIC shy and reserved, afraid of standing out. But along with AIC's president, Meaghan Mozingo, and performance coach, David Beloff, Swenson helps them overcome the assumption that their different abilities define or limit them. "I hear it from all of them: 'Nobody gave me a chance,'" Swenson said.

Bias against those with Down syndrome is particularly acute. In Europe, approximately 92 percent of pre-born babies diagnosed with Down syndrome are aborted. In the United States that rate is somewhat lower, around 67 percent, but it is still tragically high.[9] Recently, outspoken atheist Richard Dawkins wrote that it is immoral to give birth to a baby with Down syndrome.[10]

"But Mr. Dawkins's argument is flawed," wrote Jamie Edgin, an assistant psychology professor at the University of Arizona, and Fabian Fernandez, a research associate at Johns Hopkins University School of Medicine, in the *New York Times*. "Individuals with Down syndrome can experience more happiness and potential for success than Mr. Dawkins seems to appreciate."[11]

Edgin and Fernandez argue that not only is Dawkins's moral reasoning badly flawed but the data don't support his assertions that Down syndrome children or their families suffer more than others or are less happy. In fact, consider these findings by Edgin and Fernandez:

> In 2010, researchers reported that parents of preschoolers with Down syndrome experienced lower levels of stress than parents of preschoolers with autism. In 2007, researchers found that the divorce rate in families with a child with Down syndrome was lower on average than that in families with a child with other congenital abnormalities and in those with a nondisabled child.
>
> In another study, 88 percent of siblings reported feeling that they themselves were better people for having a younger sibling with Down syndrome; and of 284 respondents to a survey of those with Down syndrome over the age of 12, 99 percent stated they were personally happy with their own lives.[12]

In short, these data confirm what the Bible says: "Children are a gift from the LORD" (Ps. 127:3 NLT). This verse doesn't say some children are a gift and some are not.

With all of this in mind, we can see something particularly beautiful about children with Down syndrome participating in the arts.

"Art is so central to their lives and a medium by which they share their thoughts, their feelings, their emotions," said Dr. Brian Skotko, co-director of the Down syndrome program at Massachusetts General Hospital. "It's a mechanism for so many to express themselves."

Skotko's sister, Kristin, who has Down syndrome, loves musicals, especially *The Sound of Music* film starring Julie Andrews. As a little girl, she sang the songs, danced, and dressed up like Maria.[13]

"For Kristin, it was a remarkable, emotional experience," Skotko said.

Two days after Katie, who is twenty-six, and her mother learned about AIC, they arrived at Swenson's house for what they thought would be a meet-and-greet session. Mozingo showed Katie down a hallway to a makeshift audition room. "Do you want me to go in with you?" her mother asked. "Nope, I've got it," Katie said.

In front of the auditioning committee, Katie kept her eyes downcast. "Hi, my name's Katie and I have Down syndrome," she said. The committee surprised Katie by asking her to sing something. Listening from the living room, Joan Blind assumed Katie would choose a simple song like "Happy Birthday." But Katie chose "This Is the Body of Christ," a song she had learned in her church choir. A week later, Katie learned Swenson selected her to sing Eponine's theme, "On My Own," in *Les Misérables School Edition*.

At AIC, "shadows" work with the performers, guiding them through performances. The shadows stand behind the performers, wearing black and modifying their volume to allow the performers to stand out as much as possible. Katie rehearsed twice a week with Swenson as her shadow. But Katie didn't stop there: For more than two months, her mother came home from teaching to find Katie practicing with her laptop, singing and listening to "On My Own" through headphones.

Many people with Down syndrome explore dance and fine art with the same dedication. In 2007, Colleen Perry, a marriage and family therapist, founded Free 2 Be Me Dance in Los Angeles, an adaptive dance class for children who have Down syndrome. Perry's instructors work with thirty kids in five different classes, teaching them ballet, hip-hop, and soon tap, encouraging artistic expression through routine-free dances. "My goal is to make sure that the students are having fun while engaging discipline and focus while learning sharing and friendship, which you won't get in a regular dance class," Perry said. "It's all about meeting the students where they are."

Many students arrive at their first dance speechless and shy, standing at the bar or staring at themselves in the mirror for the first few classes. But Perry encourages parents to keep bringing their children to class. By the fourth class, students often relate to something like a song and suddenly begin participating. "From then on, I know I have them," Perry said.

Some people with Down syndrome work to become professional artists. Gateway Arts in Boston provides opportunities for more than one hundred people with disabilities, including Down syndrome, to develop their artistic talents and profit from the sale of their work, Skotko said. They gain some independence while demonstrating their capabilities.

Oliver Hellowell's photography has gained popularity across the world through his Facebook page. According to his mother, Hellowell's Down syndrome offers him a unique perspective, a trait that has contributed to his popularity. Hellowell now attends college in England and aspires to make photography his profession.

Drama is especially natural for people with Down syndrome because many act throughout their lives, said Gail Williamson, director of Down Syndrome in Arts and Media (DSiAM), a casting liaison for people with Down syndrome.[14] From a young age, many people with Down syndrome perform social behavior they learn from therapists. But some, like her son Blair, also have an extra bent toward entertaining, Williamson said. She signed up Blair when he was eleven years old to appear in a commercial for the Special Olympics. Blair ran for four hours of film that were eventually cut to a 15-second segment. Williamson had never seen him so focused on anything.

From there, Williamson, who also works for a talent agency, committed to helping her son and others like him act professionally. "My son was on the air, finally," Williamson said. "And I saw the world changed for my son." Blair now sees himself as part of a larger community of people who have a variety of abilities.

Through all of these efforts, audiences are gaining a better understanding of a common disability. After people with Down syndrome began appearing on television shows like *Life Goes On* and *Sesame Street*, the public perception of the disorder began to change. Following those screen appearances, Skotko can trace a "seismic shift in the community's [perception] of what people with Down syndrome are capable of." The public is more aware of their abilities and offering them more opportunities to succeed. "They need opportunities to become flourishing community members like the rest of us," Skotko said.

Twenty years ago, a variety of misinformation circulated about Down syndrome, making a prenatal diagnosis frightening for parents.

But now, thanks to more frequent appearances in major productions, like Lauren Potter's role as Becky Jackson on the TV show *Glee*, society now sees people with Down syndrome thriving in their communities. Williamson has on file about four hundred people interested in acting. A few have autism or cerebral palsy, but most have Down syndrome. Some have landed big roles. "People with Down syndrome are extremely creative," Williamson said. "[Drama] helps define them and helps them grow."

Back to Katie Blind. After two months of rehearsing, Katie stepped into the spotlight wearing an olive green French Revolution–era costume. "Do your best. Everything's going to be fine. Just sing your heart out," her mother had told her. Swenson, clothed in black, stood behind her. Katie focused on the nearly two-hundred-member audience as her and Swenson's voices blended. By the last line, Katie sang on her own.

In the audience, Joan Blind watched and sobbed, thinking, "That's my daughter! That's my daughter!" As the audience erupted with applause, someone shouted, "Brava!"

Now, thanks to the opportunity to portray Eponine, Katie's confidence has soared. She dreams of pursuing acting and drama as a career, eventually debuting on Broadway. For now, Katie works as a secretary for the AIC board. And for a recent AIC production, *Arts Inclusion Presents Broadway in Concert*, Katie helped choreograph a dance and sang a duet before an audience of four hundred people.

"Playing Eponine turned my life around," Katie said.

Conclusions and a To-Do List

The positive developments in the pro-life movement are evidenced by the fact that young people are taking their places on the front lines in the fight for life. In fact, some surveys show that the Generation X and Millennial generations are more pro-life than their parents. This shift in public opinion is the result not just of standing against abortion but of standing *for* and *with* mothers and their babies. The pregnancy care center movement, which has spawned more than 1,100 pregnancy care centers all across the country, has created what we sometimes call not a grassroots movement but a "grass-tops movement" of tens of thousands of compassionate activists and leaders in local communities. This movement has a real chance of not only ending abortion in our lifetime but also of showing how other social movements can achieve their goals—not by simply resisting what is wrong but by rebuilding what was lost.

Like those we've discussed in this chapter, you too can participate in God's agenda of restoring all things by joining this movement that defends precious, unborn life.

1. Be ready to articulately defend the dignity of every human life by reading *Stand for Life: Answering the Call, Making the Case, Saving Lives* by John Ensor and Scott Klusendorf.

2. Commit to pray every day that abortion will end in our lifetime.

3. Seize any and every opportunity to support expectant mothers and fathers, particularly those in crisis or with unwanted pregnancies.

4. Volunteer your time, money, or expertise to a local pregnancy care center. Be ready to refer clients to them when the opportunity arises.

5. Vote for pro-life candidates and support pro-life legislation.

6. Consider adoption and foster care.

7. Get to know a family who has a child with Down syndrome. Learn their struggles and their needs, as well as the blessing those with Down syndrome bring to those around them.

5

Women at the Well

All places where women are excluded tend downward
to barbarism; but the moment she is introduced, there
come in with her courtesy, cleanliness, sobriety, and order.

—Harriet Beecher Stowe[1]

Jesus said to her, "Mary." She turned and said to him in
Aramaic, "Rabboni!" (which means Teacher). . . . Mary
Magdalene went and announced to the disciples, "I have
seen the Lord"—and that he had said these things to her.

—John 20:16, 18

Four women appear in the genealogy of Jesus Christ found in Matthew's Gospel. Though separated by time and place, what they share is this: Each of these women, in different ways and for different reasons, was vulnerable and socially unacceptable. They were women with questionable reputations.

Tamar, widowed and without means of support, seduced her father-in-law because he would not force his son to uphold his duty to marry and care for her as the law stipulated. She became pregnant by him. Rahab was a prostitute who aided the Jewish spies seeking her city's demise. God later rewarded her kindness to Israel by protecting her and her house from the collapse of Jericho. Ruth was a Moabitess, a foreigner who chose to remain with her mother-in-law even after both of them had lost their husbands (and providers). That meant they had few options and were vulnerable to both starvation and the lust of men. Ruth initiated a relationship when Boaz wouldn't. Because of her bold and perhaps questionable advances, the two women were redeemed.

And, of course, Mary—a pregnant teenager with no husband who chose obedience over reputation and birthed the Messiah.

Throughout history, women have been targets of abuse and exploitation at the hands of men and misogynist societies. Already seen as property and playthings, they become especially vulnerable when, like Ruth and Tamar, they are caught in difficult personal and social situations beyond their control.

The exploitation of women remains distressingly common today. Recently, *New York Times* columnist Nicholas Kristof, along with his wife, Sheryl WuDunn, documented the worldwide plight of women in a book titled *Half the Sky*.[2] A documentary series with the same title is based on the book. In addition to the trafficking, forced labor, prostitution, pornography, educational restrictions, and legal challenges that Kristof and WuDunn reported, millions of women around the world are under threat at an early age *simply because they are female*. In many areas around the world, and increasingly in the West, sex-selective abortion has reached epidemic proportions. According to one film, "It's a girl" are the three deadliest words in the world.[3]

Christianity is often accused of being an anti-woman religion. If one looks at some of the biblical texts from a twenty-first-century vantage point, it's easy to see why. In our post-feminist society, in which any language or actions that treat men and women differently are seen as cultural constructs and potentially violent, biblical teachings about women, originally written from the context of very different societies, can seem antiquated and harsh.

But that superficial analysis misses just how liberating the Bible is for women.

The idea that husbands are to *love* their wives (see Eph. 5:25) hardly seems remarkable today, but at the time it was an innovation.

Even today, when our idea of "love" has been reduced to romance and lust, the biblical idea that husbands are to love their wives as Christ has loved the church—selflessly, sacrificially—is still radically countercultural.

Perhaps even more remarkable is that early Christians actually obeyed this teaching. In one of the oldest surviving descriptions of early Christians, we are told that Christians "have a common table but not a common bed."[4] In other words, they shared their food freely, but not their wives.

It is notable that women, not men, were reported as the first witnesses of the resurrected Christ. Since women were not even considered reliable enough to testify in court in that day, first-century readers would have found this odd. For the Scriptures to report the narrative this way not only is evidence that it is true but furthers our contention that the Bible holds women in high esteem.

This is at least partially why we don't think the inclusion of Tamar, Rahab, Ruth, and Mary is merely incidental to Matthew's genealogy. It's significant that women, even those with shady pasts and cloudy presents, are part of God's redemption story. And of course, Jesus's treatment of the woman caught in adultery, the prostitute who anointed His feet, and the women who followed as He carried His cross also reflects that larger vision of the dignity and value of women that Scripture offers and requires Christians to embrace.

It's a vision that begins in the Garden of Eden. Before we even learn of the creation of woman or meet Eve by name in Genesis 2, we are told that God created both male and female in the image of God. "So God created man in his own image, in the image of God he created him; male and female he created them" (Gen. 1:27). Just as man was created in a way unique from everything else He created, woman was too. In fact, God crafted both Adam and Eve with His hands, while everything else was created by the fiat command of His voice.

Throughout Scripture, we read how women were used by God, honored, cared for, protected, and even exalted. Deborah and Jael are the heroes of Judges 4. The prophet protects the Shunammite woman and her son from famine. Mary's name will be "exalted forever."

There's no question that some Christian individuals and entire Christian communities have, in both teaching and practice, failed to uphold the biblical vision of the dignity of women. Whoever compromises the inherent value, worth, and dignity of women is guilty of grave evil. We see too much of this even in our day, often in well-intended attempts to resist hyper-feminist ideas about ministry, sex, marriage, and parenting.

But Christian history also tells of heroic protection and advancement of women by the church. Our favorite story in this vein also, by the way, helps us understand the incredible population growth within the church in its earliest days.

As the first Christians lived and formed the church, the Romans around them practiced "exposure." If an unwanted baby was born, it was common to get rid of the child by casting it outside. Exposed to the elements and to predators, it would die and leave the family with one less mouth to feed. Because males were suitable heirs as well as better providers and just more highly esteemed in that society, the babies most often subjected to death by exposure were girls.

Very quickly, Christians felt compelled to rescue these children and provide for them, as they would others who were destitute and without means of survival. It did not matter to them that most of the babies were female.

Interestingly, within a few decades, Baylor University sociologist Rodney Stark suggests, the cultural gender balance was out of whack. Because abortion was not tolerated among the early Christians, girls in Christian homes were less likely to be rendered infertile, like the women in Roman culture who practiced abortion, because of the primitive way the "procedure" was performed.

As Roman men looked for women to marry, the church had an ample supply. And so, by means of an unorganized missionary dating program, Roman men went to church. Stark reports evidence of a Christian "baby boom" within decades, all because Christians rescued those vulnerable female children.[5] The women of the church not only had been saved from death as infants but later had the opportunity to be parents, which also resulted in growing the church's population.

Times and methods have changed to meet the needs of the culture in which we live, but Christians remain at the forefront of championing the cause of exploited and abused women both here in America and abroad. By doing so, Christians continue one of the most redemptive trends in the history of the church to stop evil and restore human dignity.

A Way Out

When Megan Kane was fourteen years old, she ran away from home. By fifteen she was a mother. By nineteen, she was a stripper.[6]

Living in Memphis, Tennessee, she began dancing at a club known for live lesbian sex shows and a rampant drug culture. She found the attention and the money intoxicating. After making $300 her first night onstage, she wondered, "Why have I been struggling?" Soon she was making $1,300 on a good night, but with her newfound cash came a raging methamphetamine addiction.

At first, Megan justified her vice as a means to stay thin, but eventually she was downing a cocktail of prescription stimulants and caffeine followed by a bowl of crystal meth just to get out of bed in the morning. Her appetite disappeared. "I was completely empty," she recalled. "Nothing left inside of me." Within a few years, she faced felony drug possession charges.[7]

The prospect of serious jail time and losing custody of her daughter, Taylor, was the wake-up call Megan needed. That's when a news story for a recovery program caught her attention. The program was called "A Way Out," and within a year and a half Megan, then twenty-nine, had graduated from the program's new sixteen-week outpatient program. She received three years of probation for reduced charges and never lost custody of her daughter.

With new life in her blue eyes and a newfound ambition in her heart, Megan began to study nursing at the University of Memphis. The important thing, she said, is where she's going, not where she's been. Her new ambitions are to become a medical missionary and help refugees. "Sign me up for a hut," she said with a smile.

A Way Out has been rescuing women like Megan from Memphis's prostitution, stripping, and drug culture since 1992. The outpatient program, added in 2008, consists of sixteen classes, which the women attend four days a week. Through the classes, the women are helped in dealing with problems such as sexual addiction, depression, and setting and living within boundaries. "These women's spirits are broken and their souls are damaged, and they need time to heal," said director Carol Wiley. So A Way Out offers that time by providing material help. After a rigorous entrance interview, the women receive clothing, counseling, financial assistance, job training, and a Bible. Clients sign a lifestyle contract and are on probation for the first sixty days.

While the program works with the women for up to five years, most graduate after two. According to Wiley, almost none of the women return to the sex industry after completing the program.[8]

A Way Out teaches that knowing Jesus is essential to recovery. Cassandra Hudson had been through eight other drug rehabilitation programs before finding A Way Out. Now she has left her former life of drugs and prostitution, re-established a relationship with her son and daughter, and was able to have her nursing license reinstated. "Other programs tried to fix me and tell me something to do or to stop," she said. "But no one ever told me about Jesus. That's been the difference."[9]

As we have mentioned before in this book, and as we will see again and again, mentors play a key role in the restoration of these women's lives. The women have mentors for the entire length of their enrollment. Mentors have daily contact with their mentees and access to the women's counselors. Kay Montague has been a volunteer for eleven years. "They're pretty real and honest," she says. Mentoring is fun and rewarding, but, she admits, it can also be emotionally draining. "It's more like being a parent sometimes than it is a friend." Many of the young women still operate from an adolescent mind-set, because that's what they were when they entered their destructive lifestyle—adolescents.[10]

Since WORLD gave A Way Out its top Hope Award in 2008, this program that helps restore the lives of women has continued its sixteen-week intensive life skills classes, enabling many graduates to gain jobs as well as regain their families and their dignity. One of them is Megan Kane, the young woman introduced earlier in this section. Her dream of becoming a medical missionary has taken several giant steps toward reality: In 2012, she earned a nursing degree, and she is now married to a pastor.

Complete Dependence

Today, Reggie Littlejohn[11] is a committed Christian and the founder of Women's Rights Without Frontiers, an organization that has been leading the opposition of forced abortion in China.

But it wasn't always so.

"I grew up in a Christian home and at age 16 decided there's no God," she said. "So I wrote my parents a letter, sat them down, had them read the letter aloud, and told them I was no longer going to church."

And she didn't—all the way through high school and college. But in college an ancient literature course forced her to to read through the Gospel of John. "I had never read a book of the Bible start-to-finish before," she said. "When I read John, I saw who Jesus was—and this was not whom I was rejecting. So that moved me from being an atheist to being an agnostic."

She took a step closer to God when she got married at age twenty-seven. "Falling in love with [my husband] and looking into his eyes, I just could not believe that he had simply evolved from blue-green algae. It was just not possible." She was in Yale Law School and her husband was studying at Yale Divinity School. After she finished law school, she decided to wait a year before taking a job at a San Francisco law firm, and during that year had a son while also auditing a New Testament class at Yale. "It was the first time I ever read the entire New Testament," she said. "The whole message just blew me away. By the end of that I was a committed Christian."[12]

Even so, Reggie Littlejohn had more than God or even love on her mind. She joined that law firm and became a hard-charging litigator. However, because of her location on the West Coast, and a requirement to do pro bono work, she was exposed to refugees from China who were victims of forced abortions because of the nation's one-child policy.

That exposure had a profound impact on her. "I remember sitting behind my desk in my beautiful law firm surrounded by freedom and civilization, thinking to myself, *Right at this moment, on the other side of the world, women are dragged out of their homes, strapped down to tables, and forced to abort babies up until the ninth month of pregnancy.* I was utterly appalled."

She was already an intense and driven person, so her ambition for advancement in the law firm combined with her newfound passion for these Chinese women meant that sometimes she would sleep in her office at night. "At one point," she said, "I did not leave my office for 10 days, just working flat out. I was driven."

Despite all that time at the office, she managed to get pregnant again, but quickly suffered a miscarriage. "I was heartbroken. I called my mother and asked, 'Why would God allow me to become pregnant with a baby who would be loved and cared for wonderfully in this world—and then take that baby away?' My mother said, 'We will never know the answer to that question, but God does everything for a purpose. And I believe if you offer your suffering up to Him, He will use it.'"

When she had yet another miscarriage, her drive to help Chinese women intensified. Having a miscarriage, Littlejohn said, is "not the same as having someone break into your home, drag you out, and force you to abort a baby, usually without even anesthesia. But I know what it is like to lose a baby, so when I heard about forced abortions, my heart went out to these women in a way that it might not have if I had not miscarried my own babies."

The miscarriages were just the beginning of Littlejohn's suffering. The women in her family had a history of breast cancer, so in 2003—when she discovered lumps in her breast—she had bilateral mastectomies. While in the hospital, she became infected by the MRSA staph virus. Sometimes called a "super bug," it had a devastating effect on Littlejohn's body. "My hair was coming out in handfuls. My kidneys, my liver, my immune system were all affected, and I was disabled for five years," she said. "I went overnight from high-powered litigation lawyer to lying on my back and begging God to spare my life."

Those five years had a profound impact on her. "I went from being a driven person to someone completely helpless," she said. "God had to do that to me because I'm so stubborn. If He hadn't, probably I'd be a partner in a law firm right now and continuing on that path. Since I was not committing adultery or murder, since I wasn't stealing or lying, since I represented Chinese refugees on the side, I thought I was an exemplary Christian.

"[But] I saw in reading the Bible over and over again that almost my entire life was based on a violation of the first commandment, 'I am the Lord your God . . . you shall have no other gods before me.' Obviously I was not worshiping statues of Baal and Molech in my living room, but I was idolizing money, power, prestige, my boss, my house, my car. Everything I idolized, God took from me. I was left with complete dependence on Him. And He turned me from a life of focusing on making lots of money as an attorney to saving lives in China."

Littlejohn formed Women's Rights Without Frontiers to shine a light on China's one-child policy, a policy that has resulted in more than one hundred million abortions, the overwhelming majority of them baby girls. Today there are nearly forty million more males than females in China. The result is forced prostitution, sexual slavery, and widespread despair among the country's young people in particular.[13]

Her work has taken her to testify before the U.S. Congress, the European Parliament, the United Nations, and elsewhere, and she's seen results. China has relaxed its one-child policy. But Littlejohn says she has an "ongoing, intense frustration" with headlines like "China Abandons the One-Child Policy."

"China is heading for a demographic disaster," she said, "so leaders are slightly modifying the policy. If one member of a couple is an only child, the couple can have a second child. The exception is very narrow and will affect only 5 million couples. Even under this exception, those couples who can have two children will need to have a birth permit for their first child and their second child. If they don't have one, they are still at risk of forced abortion."

The bottom line, she says, is that there's still much work to do to protect the women and unborn babies of China—and everywhere else in the world. And she aims to continue fighting for them as long as she can.

CONCLUSIONS AND A TO-DO LIST

We often think of slavery as a faraway problem in a different time or different place. But all around us, women who are abused and exploited are being ministered to with the love of Christ and the hope of the gospel. These Christians are faithful heirs of a gospel that innovated a new level of care for women based on their equal footing as image bearers of God.

Here's how you can join this aspect of God's agenda of restoring all things:

1. Learn more about the plight of exploited and abused women by reading *The Slave Next Door: Human Trafficking and Slavery in America Today* by Kevin Bales and Ron Soodalter and *In Our Backyard: A Christian Perspective on Human Trafficking in the United States* by Nita Belles. Learn more about the most effective ways to help trafficking victims by reading *The White Umbrella: Walking with Survivors of Sex Trafficking* by Mary Frances Bowley.

2. Gather family and friends at your home or church to watch and discuss the film *It's a Girl* (http://www.itsagirlmovie.com/).

3. Learn more about the Christian understanding of love by reading *The Four Loves* by C. S. Lewis.

4. Commit to eliminating and blocking pornography in any form from your home. Consider taking the No Porn Pledge (http://www.nopornpledge.com/) and using the filtering software from a service such as Covenant Eyes (http://www.covenanteyes.com/).

5. Read through "21 Ways to Help" from the A21 Campaign,[14] and take action.

6. Learn to spot the signs of exploitation in your community, and support all legal means to end it.

7. Work within your church to create or support already existing safe havens and support networks for women trying to leave prostitution, pornography work, abusive homes, or other situations that exploit them.

8. Mentor the next generation on what it means to live out their God-given identities as male and female, as well as how to love one another.

9. If there are areas in your community where this type of brokenness is prevalent, find ways to be present there—prayer walks, outreaches to prostitutes and other exploited men and women, new businesses, or start-up churches.

6

Coloring Outside the Lines

The whole purpose of education is to turn mirrors into windows.

—Sydney J. Harris

Education is what remains after one has forgotten what one has learned in school.

—Albert Einstein

Fathers, do not provoke your children to wrath, but bring them up in the nurture and admonition of the Lord.

—Ephesians 6:4

Throughout history, wherever the church has gone, education has closely followed.

For a number of reasons, Christians are a learning people. First, Christians believe God that created the world and that the creation reflects the Creator. Therefore, to learn about the world is to learn about God. Second, because God is omniscient, or all-knowing, as we learn, we become more fully conformed to His mind and will. Therefore, we glorify Him by learning of Him and His world. To learn is an act of worship. Finally, we believe God has given humans the responsibility to care for the world. Our learning, then, has a *telos*, or a purpose. We learn so we can more fully become who we were created to be.

This clear sense of purpose has driven the incredible educational inventions and innovations pioneered by Christians throughout history. Indeed, educational imagination requires a clear sense of purpose. As T. S. Eliot wrote in *The Aims of Education*:

> If we see a new and mysterious machine, I think that the first question we ask is, "What is that machine for?" and afterwards we ask, "How does it do it?" But the moment we ask about the purpose of anything, we may be involving ourselves in asking about the purpose of everything.
>
> If we define education, we are led to ask, "What is Man?"; and if we define the purpose of education, we are committed to the question, "What is Man for?" Every definition of the purpose of education, therefore, implies some concealed, or rather implicit, philosophy or theology.
>
> In choosing one definition rather than another, we are attracted to the one because it fits in better with our answer to the question, "What is Man for?"[1]

If Eliot is right, education will always reflect the sense of purpose that dominates a culture. We see this in those countries where education's only or primary goal is to shape students into allegiant followers of the state.

It's also true that a culture untethered from a coherent sense of purpose won't be able to establish a solid vision for any educational initiatives. After all, without knowing what to shoot for, it's difficult to know where to aim. Ours is a culture that relativizes transcendent values and reduces human purpose to radically subjective and personalized outcomes. We ask ourselves, "What makes me happy now?" rather than "Who are we and why are we here?" Because we no longer have an answer to the question, "What are we for?" we have no answer to the question, "What is education?"

This problem is particularly acute in communities with a high rate of family breakdown and unemployment. People in such communities struggle to provide basic needs and have difficulty articulating for themselves, and presenting to their children, a compelling vision for learning and knowing. On the other end of the socioeconomic scale, education is too often correlated with the accumulation of wealth, material things, or a comfortable retirement. The idea with which we began this chapter—that learning, continually increasing our capacity to know, is a way of glorifying God—is as foreign to the rich as to the poor, perhaps more so.

So the roots of our educational problems run far deeper than socioeconomic disparity. Certainly, many schools in the poorest neighborhoods in America lack adequate resources, but decades of tax increases for better facilities and higher teacher salaries have done little to improve educational outcomes. And what of those communities with adequate resources that underperform? We agree with T. S. Eliot: The fundamental problem is one of purpose. Today both prosperous and impoverished communities find that without a clear "why" it's difficult to present a compelling "what" or an effective "how."

Attempts to decorate the process with altruistic language won't help, either. "To make the world a better place" certainly sounds better than "To make money," but ends up begging the question "For whom?" And "To better yourself" may be an inspiring answer to the "Why?" question, but only until it is time to decide which standard to use to measure "better."

These platitudes won't inspire a student trapped in a failing school in a broken community looking to a school lottery to escape a second-rate set of teachers. Students may suffer from grammatical and other scholastic impairments these days, but they aren't stupid. They quickly catch on to an overall lack of ultimate purpose undergirding their educational pursuits.

At least one Duke University student caught on to the ruse when he said, "We've got no philosophy of what the hell it is we want by the time somebody graduates. The so-called curriculum is a set of hoops that somebody says students ought to jump through before graduation. Nobody seems to have asked, 'How do people become good people?'"[2]

In essence, what the Duke student was asking was where all of this learning should lead and what sort of person it should lead him to become. Humans long for that kind of coherence, and education is the primary way society provides it for future generations. The word *university*, for example, means bringing a unity in understanding to the diversity of human experience, but that sense of purpose has long been lost, as Neil Postman pointed out decades ago:

> Perhaps the most important contribution schools can make to the education of our youths is to give them a sense of coherence in their studies, a sense of purpose, meaning and interconnectedness in what they learn. Modern secular education is failing not because it doesn't teach who Ginger Rogers, Norman Mailer and a thousand other people are but because it has no moral, social, or intellectual center. The curriculum is not, in fact, a "course of study" at all but a meaningless hodgepodge of subjects. It does not even put forward a clear vision of what constitutes an educated person, unless it is a person who possesses "skills." In other words, a person with no commitment and no point of view but with plenty of marketable skills.[3]

Education is not merely the process of skill acquisition. Exacerbating this problem in a secular society is the notion that education is the answer for everything that ails us. If it's poor, educate it. If it's antisocial, educate it. If it's intolerant, educate it. If it's criminal, educate it. No politician, local or federal, would ever downplay the importance of education and stand a chance to be elected. And so new things are tried and more money is spent, but rarely is the purpose of education reexamined or its actual effectiveness measured.

In reality, education without clear purpose is not only ineffective; it can also be dangerous. "If you take someone who steals railroad ties and give him an education," D. L. Moody famously said, "you've just taught him to steal the entire railroad the next time." Education without purpose is education without virtue. Some of the most evil and effective villains of history were the most educated.

Throughout history, Christians not only have seen education as a common good but also could explain *why* it was a common good. To know about God's world is to know about God Himself, and so learning is intrinsically good because it has a transcendent purpose. Further, from a Christian worldview, it can be clearly said that there is a moral order to the world. And so, for knowledge to be good, it must be properly ordered, with the technical understood in light of the moral. Indeed, the very first humans were corrupted by acquiring knowledge of something they were not made to know. Finally, learning reflects who we are in the deepest sense. We are made in the image of the One who knows all.

The brokenness of the educational system in America takes many forms. And like our forebears throughout history, Christians can be redemptive in this area. And many already are.

Cornerstone Schools

"There's nothing quite like a background in counter-insurgency to prepare you for building community in Southeast Washington, DC." So began *WORLD*'s account of Cornerstone Schools and its executive director, Clay Hanna.[4] Hanna is a former military officer who was executive director of the school in 2010. He says his work both in Iraq and at Cornerstone has been about "getting to a place of mutual trust" with communities that have "seen a lot of turmoil."

Christians who live on Capitol Hill founded Cornerstone Schools in 1998. It started with twenty-three primary students in the basement of Washington Community Fellowship. The school concentrates on both academic and spiritual needs as it seeks to "glorify God by serving families who are committed to the future of their child, but merely lack opportunities."

Today Cornerstone is a full preschool-through-twelfth-grade experience. It graduated its first high school class in 2013 and now serves about two hundred students from its facility in a former Catholic school building in Southeast Washington, DC. Its annual $7,000 tuition is a bargain in a town where many private schools cost upwards of $25,000, but most Cornerstone families still receive between $2,000 and $6,000 in scholarships. Although 64 percent of the students' families fall below the poverty line, the school offers no full scholarships. Cornerstone incarnates Marvin Olasky's idea that the help it provides should be challenging. "We believe everyone should pay something," Hanna said. "Educational success for a child requires parental involvement." In this spirit, Cornerstone asks its parents to volunteer a minimum of twenty hours of service a year and requires them to attend parent seminars.[5]

Maritza White is a supporter of the public schools and was personally committed to using them until a call from her babysitter one afternoon revealed that her son Michael had come home with a bloody mouth. According to White, the school had disciplined the boys responsible but had never bothered to call her. "He never set foot in that school again," she says. "I never felt I could trust them after that." When White visited Cornerstone to look it over for her son, the principal suggested she come to a morning chapel. "I was so undone by that service. The kids were worshiping and putting their hearts in it." She enrolled her son and now goes in to work a little late a few days each week to attend the chapel service herself.

Brookstone Schools

Cornerstone is not alone. In fact, in the past twenty years similar schools have been springing up all across the country. Consider, for example, Brookstone Schools in Charlotte, North Carolina. In 2007, Brookstone was in a small, yellow building near a pawn shop and a used car lot in West Charlotte.[6] But even then student artwork outside a third-grade classroom revealed that this school was different. Bright letters on long strips of blue, white, and green paper read, "Drugs are a bad thing to do," "Get high on God," and "Gangs kill people."

Brookstone was in a neighborhood with few businesses, and public schools that produced dismal results. Nearly 60 percent of students in the area's major high school failed state tests that year, and the school battled escalating violence. But at Brookstone, some 90 percent performed above grade level and behavioral problems were rare. Well-mannered children in neat uniforms sat quietly in classrooms and quickly obeyed teachers.

Since its founding in 2001, and WORLD's profile in 2007, the school has continued to grow, adding students and grades. It is now K-8, and it's come under the wing of the First Baptist Church of Charlotte, one of the city's largest churches.

What hasn't changed at Brookstone is its commitment to spiritual growth and academic excellence. It targets at-risk kids, and all the students are on a scholarship, though the school requires all parents to pay at least a nominal amount toward their children's education. As Director of Advancement Suzanne Wilson said, "The families value the education more, and get more out of it, if they have some investment in the process."

Private Christian Education

Cornerstone Schools and Brookstone Schools are just two examples of one of the most remarkable educational movements in human history: private Christian education.

Considering the fact that public school education in this country is virtually free (if you don't count the money we pay in taxes!), and the additional fact that public schools are located conveniently in almost every neighborhood and town in the United States, it is a wonder that private Christian schools find any takers at all. Despite these huge public school advantages, more than four million American children, approximately 1 in 12, attend religious schools. Another two million are homeschooled, part of a movement that takes many innovative forms. And as the stories of Cornerstone and Brookstone highlight, Christian schools are often as racially and economically diverse as public schools.

When you take into account that neither private Christian education nor homeschooling even existed in this country to any great degree as recently as fifty years ago, it is easy to see why we consider the rise of private Christian education such a significant phenomenon.

Christian schools, of course, are not perfect. The faculty, administrators, students, and parents in these institutions are fallen humans, too, but—to put it delicately—some schools are much better at accounting for human frailty than others. We both travel around the country and speak often in Christian schools, and we can say that the quality varies widely. But that is to be expected in any fledgling movement, and we celebrate the heroic, sacrificial efforts of Christian educators and homeschoolers who are doing much to restore our culture literally from the bottom up.

Gap-Year Experiences

Even after attending one of the better Christian schools or receiving a handcrafted education from a homeschooling parent, students still encounter a world largely indifferent to Christian values.

As we will discuss more fully in chapter 9, "Loving God with All Your Mind," the secular college campus especially can undermine Christian commitment. Professors and the overall environment at secular universities are often antagonistic to the understanding of education articulated here: that the purpose of education is to know about God and His world.

That's one of the reasons so many Christian students and their families are now choosing gap-year programs when they graduate from high school. Typically taken during the year between high school and college, these programs are a relatively new phenomenon in the United States but are common in other parts of the world. In fact, in some countries it is the norm for students to take a year between high school and college to learn and mature. Yemen, for example, requires that students take a year off between secondary school and college.

One organization offering a Christian gap-year experience is the Impact 360 Institute, located on a beautiful property in Pine Mountain, Georgia.[7] Impact 360 is one of the many programs that owes its existence to the Cathys, the family behind Chick-fil-A whom we introduced in chapter 3.

The mission of the Impact 360 Institute is to equip members of future generations to become Christ-centered servant leaders. Each academic year, up to forty students from across the nation are selected to attend based on leadership potential and their desire to grow in faith and understanding of God's purpose for their lives.

The program includes intensive classroom experiences, with courses on Christian apologetics, philosophy and theology, and public speaking. Impact 360 also includes experiential learning experiences. For example, during a weeklong course on Christianity and poverty, students spend the night at a homeless shelter. A study of the Old Testament includes preparing and eating a meal composed exclusively of ingredients from biblical times.

Impact 360 is not the only such experience. Summit Ministries, with which both of us have had a long association, provides intensive two-week summer programs in worldview and apologetics and, for those who want to go deeper, Summit Semester, a semester-long course of study in the mountains of Colorado. For the academically driven, Summit offers a semester-long study experience at Oxford University.[8]

John Jay Institute

Even gifted, committed kids from great families and great schools can rise to greater levels of learning and leadership via a capstone experience. That's what the John Jay Institute provides.

Named for the American Founding Father John Jay (1745–1829), the John Jay Institute is an educational and professional civic leadership organization based in Philadelphia.[9] The Institute's mission is to "prepare principled leaders for faith-informed public service."

Alan Crippen founded the John Jay Institute after also founding the Family Research Council's Witherspoon Fellowship. He says, "The John Jay Institute undertakes nothing less than a renaissance of the animating ideals that inspired America's founding."

It is tempting and not altogether inaccurate to call the John Jay Institute a "gap year" program, but their students have finished an undergraduate degree and plan to venture on to graduate school or a vocational career. A *Huffington Post* reporter recently described his visit to the John Jay Institute, whose students, called "fellows," live expense-free in a mansion outside of Philadelphia:

> The young women and men in this year's class of fellows represent a broad array of traditions within Christianity. The composition of the group was just one of several surprises that I found that afternoon. Sitting around the table were individuals who identified as Anglican, Non-Denominational, Roman Catholic, PCA [Presbyterian Church in America], Southern Baptist, and Russian Orthodox. Along with denominational affiliations, some used words like "Evangelical" and "Charismatic" to describe themselves. With an age range spanning about fifteen years, some of the fellows came directly after college, one is taking off time from law school in Texas, another is finishing up a dissertation, and another left a teaching job to enroll in the program. One very winsome student just completed a year serving in missions, while another just finished a master's thesis on Liberation Theology. Among this diverse gathering is even a popular rock star from Slovakia.[10]

This diverse group spends an academic semester in Philadelphia before departing for "externships" at Washington think tanks, congressional offices, or state legislatures around the country. During the semester in residence, they eat, study, and worship together. They cook their meals together and develop community rules. If anyone breaks the community rules, the community metes out consequences.

The program is selective and small, but its goals are not. Crippen wrote on the group's website:

98

Financial corruption and economic collapse, the growth of the state, family breakdown, educational failure, a vulgar and dehumanizing culture are just some of the consequences of the loss of the public virtues and character traits once considered necessary for sustaining American self-government. The current crisis is not merely political; it is cultural—which is to say religious and spiritual at its root. Our times demand men and women of high principle, personal integrity, and undaunted courage who are grounded in the spiritual and intellectual tradition of the past and have the inspirational vision, prudential wisdom, and practical insight to lead our society into its future. Such leaders have shaped civilizations. They can renew and revive the American promise in our time.

Restoring Public Schools

Though our focus in this chapter has been on private education, in no way are we calling for Christians to abandon public education. Even if you send your children to Christian schools, you are still sending your tax dollars to the government, and public schools are also producing the citizens who will make up our communities and our future. We all, therefore, have both a right and a responsibility to participate in the process of public education in our communities.

One community that took this responsibility seriously is SouthLake Church in Portland, Oregon.

Back in 2007, Kevin Palau, president of the Luis Palau Association headquartered in the Portland suburb of Beaverton, called on church leaders in the area to participate in a day of service to the local schools.

The leaders at SouthLake Church liked the idea and asked to take on nearby Roosevelt High School. Roosevelt was once one of Portland's most outstanding schools, but when SouthLake partnered with the school, it was failing and slated for closure.

"We'll be much more successful at this if we own it," said Kristine Sommers, SouthLake's outreach director at the time.[11]

And "own it" they did. About a thousand volunteers showed up for a first day of service organized by the church. "Something happened that first day," Sommers said. "So many people came up to me saying we can't stop here, we need to do more. It was very catalytic for SouthLake because we'd never had that kind of ongoing local outreach. Now it is what defines us, to a great extent."[12]

Since 2007, SouthLake has had a daily presence at Roosevelt. Seventy-five regular volunteers, plus hundreds more who participate in special events, regularly stock a clothes closet for students. In reality, the word *closet* fails to do justice to an outreach that now serves about 350 people who come each month for clothes that are donated by SouthLake members and others. In 2013, an anonymous donor gave the "closet" $20,000 for clothing racks.

SouthLake also started a student mentoring program and annually holds special events at Thanksgiving and Christmas. Church members pack out the gym and stadium for Roosevelt High School Rough Rider basketball and football games.

"A lot of people think you have to go overseas to do a mission trip, to make a huge difference," SouthLake's current outreach coordinator, Heather Huggitt, told the *Portland Tribune*. "This was a different concept, look in your backyard at a local school."[13]

The SouthLake-Roosevelt High School partnership became the subject of a feature documentary called *UnDivided*, and the proceeds from the documentary are funding an effort, Be UnDivided, that aims to recruit churches to partner with schools across the country. The Be UnDivided website includes guides for creating clothes closets, food pantries, and other programs—including lists of materials needed and descriptions of volunteer positions.

The goal of the project is ambitious. What began as a season of service became an ongoing expression of faith and sparked a movement to enlist three hundred thousand churches to serve one hundred thousand schools nationwide.

Conclusions and a To-Do List

School teaches us to color "inside the lines." Often people who are successful in school—people who learn to color inside the lines—become teachers and administrators. But some visionary and entrepreneurial educators are in the process of painting their own pictures, and not merely "coloring in" the pictures given to them by the current educational establishment. In this chapter, we met visionary leaders who are addressing problems in education in a restorative way. They ask not only what makes a "quality education" according to the standards of education experts. They also ask the question, "Why?" Why are we educating ourselves and our children? To what end? Only when we can answer that question with something like the first words of the Westminster Catechism—"Man's chief end is to glorify God, and to enjoy Him forever"—will we see reformation and renewal in American education.

But what is your role in this restorative process?

1. Read *The Fabric of Faithfulness* by Steven Garber to understand the idea of learning and why it matters to Christians; *Education, Christianity and the State* by J. Gresham Machen to articulate the role the church can play in education; and *The Abolition of Man* by C. S. Lewis, which offers an anthropology on which to base learning.

2. Gather a group of interested Christians to watch the film *Waiting for Superman* (http://www.takepart.com/waiting-for-superman/film) to better understand the problems facing America's public school students. Then watch the film *UnDivided: The Unbelievable Love Story of a Church and a Public School* (http://www.undividedthemovie.com/) to see what one church did to change the lives of students and the trajectory of a school.

3. Visit the website www.beundivided.com for ideas on how your church can join a nationwide movement of churches assisting public schools.

4. Identify problems in schools local to your church community and commit to meet them.

5. Start a mentoring program to connect Christian adults with local public school children.

6. Research, identify, and support the para-educational programs developed by Christians that are training future leaders.

7. Consider starting a charter school in your community to meet the specific needs there.

7

Justice That Restores

The degree of civilization in a society can be judged by entering its prisons.

—Fyodor Dostoyevsky

The real legacy of my life was my biggest failure—that I was an ex-convict. My greatest humiliation—being sent to prison—was the beginning of God's greatest use of my life. He chose the one thing in which I could not glory for His glory.

—Charles W. Colson[1]

Bless you, prison, bless you for being in my life. For there, lying upon the rotting prison straw, I came to realize that the object of life is not prosperity as we are made to believe, but the maturity of the human soul.

—Aleksandr Solzhenitsyn, *The Gulag Archipelago*

The rule of law is one of the key pillars of civilization.

Indeed, most historians count the codification of the Ten Commandments as one of the turning points in human history. Though secular historians do not believe the Commandments came from God, they nonetheless admit that the establishment of a system of laws—and the laws of the Jewish people are among the first such in recorded history—permitted the rise of civilizations.

As believers, we want to see a Christian worldview reflected in all spheres of culture. From the church to the government, from schools to prisons, we should seek to evaluate all things through the lens of Christian truth. This would also include how we, as a society, handle those who break laws. What does the status of our criminal justice system say about our culture?

To help us answer that question, we turned to Heather Rice-Minus, a policy analyst for the Justice Fellowship, the division of Prison Fellowship Ministries that seeks to address the injustices in our justice system. They accomplish this goal by promoting "restorative justice," a concept pioneered by the late Chuck Colson.

Restorative Justice: A New Paradigm for the Criminal Justice System

A fundamental problem of our current criminal justice system, according to Rice-Minus, is that it treats crime as "a violation of the state, not the victim."[2] That single misunderstanding perverts the goal of the criminal justice system: "The legal system is adversarial, pitting defendants against the state and promoting 'winning' over identifying the harmed party's needs and the responsible party's obligations."

This assessment can sound abstract, but consider this: According to Rice-Minus, the vast majority of defendants enter into a plea agreement with the prosecutor instead of going to trial. Victims are hardly ever consulted in the process. As a result, in the estimated seven million violent crimes committed per year, less than 3 percent of the victims receive financial compensation of any kind.

On the other hand, we excel at throwing criminals in jail. The United States has more prisoners per capita than any other nation in the world. Seven million people in the United States (roughly 1 in 34) are currently under the supervision of our criminal justice system. This means, according to Rice-Minus, that "sadly, nearly two million children know the loneliness that comes from having an incarcerated mom or dad."

Because the vast majority of these people will eventually make their way back into society, approximately 25 percent of all Americans have a criminal record. That stunningly high number means that approximately 25 percent of the adult population of this country face significant obstacles when it comes to looking for work or—for that matter—even passing a background check to be a volunteer in many churches.

It might be tempting to say that such consequences are the just consequences of breaking the law. They are certainly consequences, but are they just?

Richard Viguerie is fond of saying, "I was conservative before conservative was cool."[3] Having worked for Barry Goldwater in the 1960s, Richard Nixon in the 1970s, and Ronald Reagan in the 1980s, his conservative bona fides stack up to anyone alive today. "I was a law-and-order guy," he says. "I was just fine with a lock-em-up-and-throw-away-the-key approach."

But Viguerie, now in his eighties, says, "Our current approach to crime is neither Christian nor conservative." He objects to a system in which the punishment often doesn't fit the crime and in which the victim's needs are completely left out of the equation. "As Christians we should be offended, and as conservatives we should be outraged. The prison system is the largest government program in the country. If you are a small-government conservative, the size of the prison system in this country should be appalling to you."[4]

Rice-Minus and Justice Fellowship believe that restorative justice offers a better vision forward in addressing these problems. "Restorative justice recognizes that crime is not just an offense against a government. It damages the security and well-being of the victim and the entire community." She cites Isaiah 32:18 as a biblical basis: "My people will live in peaceful dwelling places, in secure homes, in undisturbed places of rest" (NIV). This verse, she maintains, "gives us a glimpse of the ancient concept of shalom, a peace that encompasses tranquility, wholeness, safety, prosperity, and relational harmony. Crime impairs our ability to experience shalom."

So what exactly is restorative justice? Restorative justice "prioritizes participation of those who are harmed by crime, promotes accountability of those who are responsible, and cultivates community engagement," she says.

In the status quo criminal justice system, the government and the defendant are the direct parties in an adversarial process, while the harmed party and the community are largely observers. But restorative justice transitions the government from "playing the victim" to being a facilitator of justice. Thus, the person harmed and the person responsible for the harm become the direct parties involved in the justice process.

Resources are redirected toward providing opportunities to meet the victim's needs and promote accountability. The government engages the larger community as a partner in addressing the needs of the direct parties in ways that the state cannot. It also serves the communities' needs for education and public safety.

The church can play a vital role in this process. "Thanks to ministries like Prison Fellowship," Rice-Minus says, "many churches are meeting the Matthew 25 call to visit the prisoner. Unfortunately, an intentional effort to assist victims of crime as demonstrated in the parable of the Good Samaritan is not as established. People harmed by crime have physical, emotional, and spiritual needs. The government and the community, including and especially the church, shoulder a joint responsibility to meet these needs."

One key way restorative justice can make a difference is by prioritizing restitution to the victim ahead of fines and fees to the courts. That might mean actual prison or jail time should be reduced or eliminated in favor of allowing the perpetrator to work and pay restitution to the victims.

Rice-Minus says restitution might not be merely monetary. She tells the story of the mother of a murdered son. She asked the murderer to send a card signed with "I remember him" each year on her deceased son's birthday. "Allowing for individualized restitution personalizes the harm and illuminates human dignity and value," Rice-Minus says.

Making amends involves purposeful ways to make up for harms caused by wrongdoing, such as apology, service, and payment. In the current criminal justice system, monetary restitution may be ordered, but often there are no additional expectations or opportunities to make amends. Of course, the government and community cannot force anyone to authentically take responsibility for the harm they have caused, but they can provide the opportunity and expectation to do so.

Angel Tree

Organizations such as Prison Fellowship and Justice Fellowship play a vital role in calling the church back to its biblical responsibilities to both prisoners and the justice system. Prison Fellowship has done nothing less than launch a global movement. The ministry begun by Chuck Colson in 1976 has now spread to more than a hundred countries. Angel Tree, an outreach to children of inmates and their families, started in 1997, attempts to connect with some of the 2.7 million American children who have at least one parent in prison. That connection takes the form of mentoring and summer camps, with an emphasis on Christmastime gift giving. In 2014, Angel Tree provided about 350,000 Christmas gifts to the children of prisoners.

The gifts are not merely given to children by churches and volunteers, however. The gifts are given by churches and volunteers to children *on behalf of their incarcerated parents.* As Angel Tree volunteers will tell you, these children are thrilled to know they have not been forgotten by their parents. The structure of the program aims to reconcile children and their parents who are separated because of incarceration.

There's a story behind each one of those 350,000 gifts, but we will tell just one before moving on. It is the story of Chris and his son, Christopher.[5] By age sixteen, Chris was kicked out of school. His parents divorced, his mom died of cancer, and, as Chris says, he "shook his fist" at God. And before he landed in prison with sixty-nine felony charges, he'd fathered a son, Christopher.

Although Chris gave his life to Christ in prison, he fretted about his son. Chris says, "He knew his dad had to be a real scoundrel." Chris had no way to show his boy that Jesus had changed him.

Until, that is, someone slid an Angel Tree pamphlet through Chris's cell door. Chris signed up Christopher for Angel Tree, and by Christmas, Christopher had a brand-new basketball. An excited Christopher called his dad, and all he could talk about was his basketball. The wounds began to heal.

After his release, Chris won custody of Christopher. Chris is now a business owner. He's started a transitional home for ex-prisoners and is fully reconciled with Christopher—who, by the way, is growing in Christ and doing an apprenticeship at a local church.

Administer Justice

A restorative justice ministry of a somewhat different kind is Administer Justice, run by a lawyer named Bruce Strom.[6]

Growing up as a pastor's kid, Strom watched his father draw a meager salary and make hospital visits in the middle of the night. Strom decided to pursue a law career so he'd never struggle to make ends meet.

Life went according to his dreams. He graduated from law school, married, and started a successful legal firm. Strom charged clients 25 percent extra per hour if they called him at home—on top of his regular $300 per hour fee. He argued a case all the way to the U.S. Supreme Court and won. Back home, he was a respected church leader and gave generously from his income.

Yet Strom became angry about one area he and his wife couldn't control—seven years of infertility. "God owed me," Strom said of his thoughts at the time. "I mean, I was doing everything right. And it just didn't seem fair." But the seeming injustice of infertility started him thinking about injustice in the lives of the poor. "Their pain was different than mine, but their pain was just as real."

Strom's wife had twin boys in the summer of 1999. Eight months later, Strom founded Administer Justice (AJ), a non-profit providing free legal services to the poor of Kane and DuPage counties, suburbs just west of Chicago. Since then over forty thousand people have come to the organization seeking legal help. The elderly, single parents, and orphaned and homeless children are frequently victims of fraud and abuse but often don't understand the law or can't afford a lawyer.

Administer Justice helps those who often have nowhere else to turn. Its services are free for anyone with an income under 125 percent of the federal poverty line. Administer Justice has a staff of twelve but a network of over 250 attorneys who volunteer to advise or represent clients as part of their pro bono work. For clients with slightly higher incomes, AJ offers free consultations and will represent them in court at a reduced rate. Administer Justice is explicitly Christian but doesn't require volunteer attorneys to profess Christ.

Clients come to the organization's headquarters in Elgin, Illinois, for help with tax disputes, identity theft, foreclosures, custody disputes, divorce mediation, immigration law, and more. Administer Justice doesn't attempt to represent most clients in court, but instead focuses on coaching them to represent themselves. Often they simply need counsel in overcoming fear of their situation, interpreting a notice filled with legalese, and understanding what steps to take in response.

For example, twenty-four-year-old Jose Robledo of Carpentersville had a problem: An ex-girlfriend had custody of their four-year-old son. He had fallen $660 behind on child support payments while temporarily unemployed and hadn't seen his son for a month. He wanted to establish a new visitation agreement or petition the court for full custody, and an attorney outlined for him the first step he needed to take: acquire his ex-girlfriend's address so she could be sent a legal statement.[7]

Much of the advice Administer Justice offers is similarly unspectacular but incredibly helpful for many who have nowhere else to turn. When a client arrives at AJ for an initial consultation, he or she receives a folder with a handwritten note of encouragement, a list of area churches, and Bible verses such as "Cast all your anxiety on him because he cares for you" (1 Pet. 5:7 NIV). When clients are distressed, Administer Justice staff members sometimes pray with them or encourage them to consider how God may be using the circumstances to bring about some greater good in their lives.

They have plenty of challenging opportunities. One of AJ's first clients was a Brazilian immigrant who had mothered a son with her fiancé, a U.S. citizen. When the fiancé died in a car accident, his family took the boy and placed the mother under a voodoo curse. She came to AJ in tremendous fear, but after Strom explained the worthlessness of a voodoo curse and the power of God's love for her, she professed faith in Christ. A simple phone call to police got the child back.[8]

In another case, Administer Justice attorneys discovered an employer pocketing medical insurance premiums of immigrant workers. In a third case, a man stopped for a traffic violation was inexplicably arrested and stuck with a $16,000 IRS bill. Someone had stolen his identity. AJ also runs a low-income tax clinic with the help of an IRS grant. People sometimes arrive with unopened IRS letters they're too scared to read.

In 2012, Administer Justice served people from twenty-seven countries of origin. Kimberly Spagui, a staff attorney who also runs a private practice, handles the organization's immigration clients, many of whom come to Administer Justice for help with tax or custody disputes. AJ lawyers learn their status while gently probing their situation. AJ can help undocumented immigrants obtain a visa if they have a relative in the United States or are victims of abuse or trafficking. Spagui also works with trafficking victims who often "come in lawfully with a visa, under a promise that they're going to be working in a certain place. And then they end up working in a sweatshop . . . or in the sex trade."[9]

Administer Justice continues to grow. In 2013, it served more than six thousand people through its programs, and Bruce Strom formed the Gospel Justice Initiative to replicate what Administer Justice is doing in communities all across the country.[10]

Surrogate Parents

As we mentioned earlier in this chapter, one of the most heartbreaking problems of the current criminal justice system is the number of children who are left as virtual orphans while their parents are in prison. The best estimates we have are that more than two million children have at least one parent in prison at any given time.

One Colorado community decided to do something for these victims.

Fremont County is—in many ways—proud of its prisons. The county has thirteen of them, nine state and four federal institutions that the largest town in the area, Cañon City, welcomes as a boost to the local economy. The prisoners, bused in under guard, serve their terms in this otherwise picturesque part of the country and—for the most part—return home, usually to Denver, Colorado Springs, or Pueblo, the state's largest cities.

But several of these prisons house women, and many of these women leave children on the outside. That is where Loren Miller comes in.[11]

In 1990, Miller took a one-year leave of absence from his job at a Bible college in Pennsylvania to obey what he believed was a call from God. He moved his family to Colorado. Initially, both he and his family were a bit befuddled, because the call was no more specific than that: just a small, still voice in his heart telling him Colorado needed him.

When he arrived, he began to look for the reason God had called him more than halfway across the continent. He learned that when a woman gives birth while incarcerated, Colorado, like most states, automatically places her children in foster care. Since the deadline for reclaiming their children typically falls while the mothers are still in custody, most will never have the chance to be reunited with their babies. Thinking there had to be a better way, Miller founded New Horizons Ministry as a Mennonite mission.

In 1991, the ministry took power of attorney over its first infant. Since then it has cared for more than 142 children. Today, if a mother gives birth in prison, she can assign power of attorney to New Horizons. New Horizons then sends over a nanny that same day to pick up the baby. The nannies are typically young women nineteen or twenty years old, who come from one of the Mennonite communities with which Miller has developed a relationship. The infant is raised in a loving, Christian home. The nanny and baby visit the mother in prison every week, giving the mother a chance to see her baby grow. Upon the mother's release, the baby is returned to her, giving mother and child a second chance at being a family.

The nannies are not on their own; they live together under the supervision of houseparents, such as Merv and Barb Helmuth. A retired electrician from Iowa, Merv is in his fifties. His own children are grown, so it's easy to see why he's still amused to be once again living in a house with infants. "It feels like starting over again, being around all these small children."

The Helmuths live at "Hannah's House" in Penrose, Colorado, a half hour from Cañon City, with their daughter Karen and Harmony Headings, two of New Horizons' nannies. Merv wears a neatly trimmed gray beard with no mustache, in the Mennonite style. The women wear head coverings, also in the Mennonite tradition. The only sign that this is, in fact, not a Mennonite family are the three Hispanic babies sitting on laps or in high chairs. This is a typical New Horizons nuclear family.

The young women are the primary caregivers for eighteen-month-old Samuel, thirteen-month-old Angel, and seven-month-old Isaiah. Every Wednesday the household loads into a van and makes the two-hour drive to the Denver Women's Correctional Facility so the mothers can visit their children. These visits are central to the New Horizons mission, which aims to keep families together and give the women ties to the outside world that help to keep them from re-offending.

Prisoners eagerly await the visits that give them a chance to hold and feed their babies, and the nannies anticipate the visits as well. "I never thought I could love a prisoner the way I do Samuel's mom," Karen Helmuth says. "A lot of these moms have never felt love."

This is the relationship triangle at the heart of the New Horizons work. Nannies care for children, giving them love and attention at a crucial time in their development. Nannies and houseparents mentor prisoners, loving them while also teaching them about parenting. A prisoner gets a chance to love her child in a secure environment, knowing that not only will the child be waiting for her upon release, but a New Horizons extended family will help her through the reintegration process.

Angel is sound asleep in his high chair, all his energy devoted to digesting his just-eaten slice of cake. His mother, already released, is finding it tough on the outside, and Merv and Barb have stepped in to help care for her son while she tries to get her act together.

The Mennonite emphasis on family explains why so many are willing to leave their homes "back east" and come to Colorado.

"It's hard enough giving up your children to be married, but having to give up a newborn to a stranger—I can't relate to that, I can't imagine it," Barb Helmuth says. "So when I'm caring for a child, I try to be the same role model that I would want to be for my own children."

After a year or more of caring for a child, it can be difficult for a nanny to hand the baby back to his or her mother. Joana Beachy, a nanny at Polly's Place, another New Horizons facility, still remembers the day she picked up "her" baby from the prison hospital. "I remind myself every day that they aren't my children. You just have to keep reminding yourself and trust that God will give you the grace to let go. It's not something that's going to be easy."

In the early years, Department of Corrections regulations stated that the child would be handed back to the mother immediately upon release, with additional regulations limiting prison volunteers from initiating contact with released inmates. So when a mother was released, she collected her child and moved on, often leaving New Horizons behind. But through years of working diligently with the state, New Horizons has been able to relax those rules. Now mothers entering the program sign a contract that gives New Horizons the ability to reintegrate the child slowly into the mother's life.

Reintegration starts with outside visits, then moves up to overnight visits before the mother is eventually allowed full custody. The mother must first demonstrate that she has reliable housing, employment, and child care, and New Horizons helps mothers through that process with a facility called The Oasis. Here, mothers can regain their footing away from bad influences in their hometowns. They live with houseparents, and eventually with their own children, attending Bible studies and parenting classes, learning how to be a family again. "We need to break the kind of thinking they take into prison," Miller says.

The last arc of the circle is the New Horizons thrift store in downtown Cañon City. The facility opened in 2005, and a sister branch opened in Pueblo in 2008. The thrift stores raise money for the ministry but also provide jobs for recently released mothers. Sherelle Brown works at the thrift store alongside Mennonite volunteers.

Brown gave birth to her son Macaiah in the Denver Women's Correctional Facility. When she found out she was pregnant, she was serving a three-year sentence for theft and possession of a controlled substance. Macaiah lived with a New Horizons nanny while Brown served twenty-eight months of her sentence. The weekly visits with Macaiah helped her stay focused on her release. She was paroled before The Oasis opened, but New Horizons staff found her a residential program in Cañon City and gave her a job at the thrift store.

"[Without New Horizons] I'd probably be back in prison. I didn't have to walk all by myself," Brown says. "Nine times out of ten, I'd be back in jail." Now she has full-time custody of Macaiah (though the Helmuths still occasionally babysit him) and is taking classes in medical billing and coding at a technical school. "I never thought I'd be telling my brother about my college classes. Usually when you get out of prison, you have to start all over. I wish a lot of other people could have the same opportunity."

With her family intact, Brown is looking forward to her future. "I want to get a house, get a career established." She grins and points at the store manager, Nelson Hoover, who sold his construction business to run New Horizons' thrift stores. "I want Nelson's job!"

Conclusion and a To-Do List

Crime threatens all communities, but it need not have the last word. When victims and perpetrators are reconciled, communities can be healed and made even stronger. There really is no other framework, other than the gospel, that provides the resources for those who have been deeply hurt by others to be reconciled.

If you would like to join God's reconciling work of the incarcerated and their communities, consider the following:

1. Read *Justice That Restores* by Chuck Colson, which offers a framework for understanding restorative justice, and *As We Forgive: Stories of Reconciliation from Rwanda* by Catherine Larson, which tells what a gospel approach to forgiveness and reconciliation has brought to a country torn apart by genocide. (The book is a companion to the award-winning movie *As We Forgive*, directed by Laura Waters Hinson.)

2. Lead a group study and discussion through the principles of restorative justice found at http://justicefellowship.org/building -restorative-justice.

3. Sign up your church for Prison Fellowship's Angel Tree program. Be sure no child in your community who has an incarcerated parent is forgotten this Christmas.

4. Work with the local Department of Corrections to develop or support a ministry to those being released from prison. Often very simple acts like providing transportation or mentoring in basic finances can make the difference between successful re-entry and recidivism.

5. Found or volunteer at a local help group for families with incarcerated family members. Offer job training, counseling, transportation, child care, financial advising, or legal assistance.

6. Consider becoming a volunteer at a local prison and developing a relationship with an inmate that can last beyond their incarceration.

8

Forgiveness Heals, Time Doesn't

> How can you love those who have stolen from you, assaulted or abused you, or tried to blow you up and completely destroy you? How can you forgive those who have kidnapped, tortured and killed someone you love? Yet this is where reconciliation has to begin.
>
> —Canon Andrew White[1]

> But let justice roll down like waters, and righteousness like an ever-flowing stream.
>
> —Amos 5:24

Though "racial reconciliation" has been a buzz phrase in the evangelical church since at least the 1970s, 11:00 a.m. Sunday morning remains, to borrow the famous words of Martin Luther King Jr., "the most segregated hour of Christian America." And even though America has made obvious progress since the days of slavery and Jim Crow laws, recent events make it obvious that we still have an explosive race problem in this country.

The book *Divided by Faith: Evangelical Religion and the Problem of Race in America* took the position that Christians are often guilty of failing to address the race problem in America. In some cases, the authors say, white evangelicals fail even to understand it.[2] Thus, white evangelicals seem quick, according to these authors, to turn deaf ears and blind eyes to the grave concerns of their black evangelical brothers and sisters.

It's easy to dismiss racial concerns when one witnesses race-baiting and attention-grabbing antics from high-profile religious leaders of the far left, such as Al Sharpton and Jesse Jackson. But men such as Chris Brooks (whom we met in chapter 2) and Anthony Bradley[3] also tell stories of the personal and systemic racism they have experienced. Such men are harder for us to dismiss. We know them personally, consider them friends, and know they share and even exceed our commitment to historic Christian orthodoxy. They and other men like them have a history of being measured, thoughtful, and biblical in their behavior and public utterances.

In some circles, *Divided by Faith* sparked a conversation that continues to this day. We need to have that conversation, but for it to move forward we must agree on what's at stake.

First, racism in any form is an assault on the inherent dignity we all share as image bearers of God. An assault on the image of God is an assault on the God in whose image we are made.

Second, racism is most obvious when it is personal, but it can also be systemic. One reason many Christians dismiss the concerns of Christian brothers and sisters of another race is they have a singular idea of what racism looks like. Very few people today resemble the hooded bigots of the Ku Klux Klan or the angry, violent Black Panthers. With these caricatures in mind, it's easy to think that racism is no longer a problem. But racism can also take the form of oppressive regulations, denied access to resources, discriminatory hiring practices, and other social norms that prevent some from enjoying the opportunities of others. Over the past half century, the United States has—at least as a matter of law—virtually eliminated these systemic barriers. However, affirmative action and other measures that were intended to be restorative have come under criticism as having unintended and detrimental consequences.[4]

But that doesn't mean we have eliminated systemic racism. We all have blind spots on this issue. As Carl Ellis explained, those in a dominant population tend to see problems at the individual level ("I'm not racist, and no one I know is racist") but overlook problems that persist at the systemic level. On the other hand, those in the sub-dominant population are more clearly able to see systemic problems ("Look at how much we must overcome!") though are tempted to underestimate personal responsibility.[5] Because of these tendencies, an important step in the process of eliminating racism is listening carefully to each other, keeping in mind that sin mars our ability to see and hear as well as we ought.

Third, racism thrives in environments in which it is perpetuated and abetted by silence. We may not be the cause of the evil, but as Dietrich Bonhoeffer said, "Silence in the face of evil is itself evil: God will not hold us guiltless. Not to speak is to speak. Not to act is to act."[6] Scripture always describes love as an intentional action toward another, not merely the passive absence of hate. When we can love our neighbor, we must speak and act.

Fourth, there is no way forward without forgiveness and reconciliation. We cannot wait for "time to heal all wounds," because it doesn't. Like any of our relationship fractures, the longer this divide goes unaddressed in communities of faith and in the larger culture, the deeper it will continue to grow. There's no way around it. The only way to get past it is to go through it.

The good news is that this is yet another area where Christians, with the robust resources of biblical understanding, can lead culture to a better place. We have solid grounding for the inherent dignity of all people. Scripture offers an understanding of human fallenness that explains, but does not justify, the evil in our hearts and actions. And we have a God who loves and forgives us and asks us to love and forgive others.

The even better news is that evangelical Christians are often leading the way when it comes to racial reconciliation, and we offer as Exhibit A the role pastors are playing in one of the most racially divisive situations of recent years: Ferguson, Missouri.

Churches Step into Ferguson's Pain

In November 2014, the morning after a St. Louis County grand jury decided not to indict police officer Darren Wilson for the death of

Michael Brown and rioters destroyed portions of Ferguson, Missouri, Pastor Rodrick Burton drove to New Northside Missionary Baptist Church, minutes from Ferguson, to pick up the church van and a few cleaning supplies.[7] Congregants texted him, asking what they could do, and he told them it was time to help their neighbors: cleaning up businesses damaged by rioters and helping transport people who felt unsafe out of the area in the church van.

At South City Church, worship and outreach coordinator Michelle Higgins kept soup warm and the church doors open for anyone—including protesters, off-duty police, and fearful community members—to find a space for prayer and rest. The church was stocked with medicines, sleeping bags, hot food, and prayer services, but some just needed a moment to sit in silence as the jury's decision "spoke deep, deep hurt to their souls," Higgins said. Other churches in the city similarly prepared for the aftermath of the grand jury decision by creating care centers.

Higgins is an African American who has lived in St. Louis her whole life. The church she serves, a part of the theologically conservative Presbyterian Church in America (PCA), is predominantly white, though it has a black senior pastor. When she heard Darren Wilson would not be indicted, she knew there would be violence. "All the blood rushed out of my body," she said.

Later that night, she and ten other Christians from nearby PCA churches joined a largely peaceful protest in South City, about ten miles south of Ferguson. A predominately non-black crowd shut down Highway 44 and blocked a main intersection. During a lull in the momentum, Higgins said, a few opportunists set a garbage can on fire and vandalized buildings, but other protesters stopped most of the unruly behavior. Law enforcement responded by tear-gassing the entire crowd.

In Ferguson, protests were more destructive and violent and included gunshots as well as the burning of businesses. Burton, an African American, believes that clergy at St. Louis churches should focus on both the protesters' "sin of retribution" as well as the sins of the government.[8]

While he doesn't know what compelled Wilson to shoot, he said, "I do know that Christ is consistent in that we are supposed to pray for our enemy and we are supposed to forgive."

In the discussions and meetings he's participated in during the approximately one hundred days between the shooting and the grand jury decision, Burton said he saw pastors egging on the "idolatry of protest." As a result of the unrest, many businesses were destroyed in Ferguson, including those owned by African Americans. He said, "If businesses don't come back, the property value goes down, which means less money in the school district. Then they won't be able to teach and educate kids," continuing a cycle of poverty.

Dawn Jones, who formerly lived just up the street from where Brown was shot, said she was "trying to scrape up the words" to explain how she felt. "I'm so disappointed and angry it scares me," said Jones, an intern at South City Church. "My nephew is black and I'll have kids one day who are black. If I have a son and he walks to the store, will he come home? It's a hopelessness I've never experienced before. I'm constantly reminding myself that my hope is in Christ. It's an all-day battle."

In the midst of all the tension, Higgins believes the church has the responsibility to "model the unity to which we are all bound, always striving to be that family you wish everyone else would be, and that means worshiping and repenting together." At the multi-ethnic South City Church, leaders welcome everyone regardless of their views about the grand jury's decision. "We've been repeating, 'God's truth is greater than your opinion,'" Higgins said. And in the last few months, she's seen the church start living more like a family.

Burton also sees the fruit that has come from such dark times, specifically the conversations about race in St. Louis that have been silenced for so long. Burton pointed out that for many churches, "most of the thoughtful contextualization for the mission field is rarely applied to brothers of color" in their own city. He finds it encouraging to see people discussing racial reconciliation in their congregations as well as in their homes with friends and family members.

Higgins stresses that Christians need to be present to provide ultimate answers. "When we clothe ourselves in the gospel and we walk into the midst of blocked highways and deep pain and heavy tragedy, just by being there we can communicate this profound theology that is the answer to all of their problems."

Mediating Institutions in the African American Community

The efforts of Higgins and Burton are, of course, admirable. But there is also the heavy lifting done in the time between the crises, when the cameras are turned off and the crowds go home. That's when the hard, ongoing, unheralded work of relationship building, education, and faith formation takes place.

One of those groups is the Black Family Preservation Group, an organization created "to raise awareness of adverse conditions impacting the stability of African-American families."

The group's founder is Sharon Brooks Hodge. She said the most significant threat to black families is not systemic racism, but the lack of "stable, two-parent homes," which she called the "best environment for raising children."

With a budget of less than $250,000 per year, the organization has programs in Ohio, Pennsylvania, Arizona, North Carolina, South Carolina, and Virginia. Among those programs are a marriage preparation program aimed at predominantly black churches and marriage enrichment programs for black families. Several of these programs are focused on prisons.

"My message differed from most other 'responsible fatherhood' conference presentations," Hodge said. "They primarily encourage non-custodial fathers to be involved in their children's lives or provide advice for mastering the art of co-parenting."

Such advice is, she said, unfortunately needed in a culture where most black children are raised in homes without a father consistently present. However, the ultimate goal should be to encourage marriage and encourage those who are married to stay together. "My message is not intended to castigate those who are single or divorced," she said. Rather, it is to "give voice to the uncomfortable truth: Marriage provides the best environment and foundation for raising children. If a boy grows up without a father, he may never learn how to be a husband. He may never realize that married men are healthier, wealthier, and happier than unmarried men."

The Black Family Preservation Group is not, of course, alone. The Gloucester Institute, based in Virginia, trains young black leaders. The organization's director, Kay Cole James, was the director of the U.S. Office of Personnel Management under President George W. Bush. These and many other "mediating institutions" are helping to shape the attitudes, beliefs, behaviors, and assumptions of all races in ways that are providing a helpful way forward.

The Story of Tom Tarrants

Thirty-four people died in the LA Watts riots in the 1960s when racial tensions escalated. In the 1990s Los Angeles police beat an African American named Rodney King. Two white officers were acquitted (and two convicted) in the incident, and subsequent riots killed more than fifty people and injured two thousand more. The events in Ferguson in 2014, though they did not result in multiple lives lost, were tragic.

Time and again a racially charged situation makes the headlines.

But is it possible to hope that things can change? After all, we have already shown how pastors like Rodrick Burton are powerful instruments of peace in racially charged situations. We do not want to be glib or to sugarcoat the hard work that still needs to be done to build trust between the races in this country, but neither do we want to deny the gospel and say there is no hope of reconciliation. As evidence of how the grace of God can work in even the darkest of hearts, we offer the story of Tom Tarrants.

Tom Tarrants was once billed as "the most dangerous man in Mississippi,"[9] and not without cause. Born and raised in Mobile, Alabama, during the years of racial segregation, Tarrants bitterly opposed the move toward racial equality in the 1960s, directing his hatred toward Jews, whom he believed were involved in a communist plot against America and whom he viewed as God's enemies.

As a young man in his early twenties, Tarrants aligned himself with Sam Bowers, a man who was later convicted for his part in the murder of three civil rights workers in Philadelphia, Mississippi, the story fictionalized in the movie *Mississippi Burning*. The FBI referred to Bowers's group, the White Knights of the Ku Klux Klan, as the most violent right-wing terrorist group in the nation.

As an operative for the White Knights, Tarrants was involved in some thirty bombings of synagogues, churches, and homes. On June 29, 1968, Tarrants and an associate from the White Knights terrorist cell were planting a bomb at the home of a successful Jewish business-man in Meridian, Mississippi. Things did not go as they had planned. A police SWAT team, working with the FBI, was waiting for them.

The gun battle that ensued killed his associate and left a police officer badly wounded. Tarrants himself was near death, with four gunshot wounds, two of which had been inflicted at point-blank range. When he arrived at the hospital, doctors said it would be a miracle if he lived another forty-five minutes.[10]

Tarrants did live. It took months for him to recover, and he was eventually convicted of a wide variety of federal crimes and given a thirty-year sentence to be served at the Mississippi State Penitentiary in Parchman—a prison that had the reputation of being one of the most violent in the nation.

Despite Tarrants's close brush with death, he was unrepentant. In fact, he began planning his escape, and after six months he and a group of prisoners made a successful break. They fled to a hideout, and it was here that Tarrants had another brush with death. The criminals took turns as lookouts. Five minutes after Tarrants's shift as lookout ended, the FBI raided their hideout, killing the man who had relieved Tarrants.

Back in prison and now an escape risk, Tarrants had many privileges suspended. His only diversion was reading. Out of boredom, he started reading a Bible. The words of Jesus struck home: "What will it profit a man if he gains the whole world and forfeits his soul?" (Matt. 16:26).

Although he had attended a Southern Baptist church as a child, Tarrants realized he was not a Christian, and that his life had been a contradiction to biblical teaching. Alone in his cell, Tarrants gave his broken life to Christ. He wrote about that conversion experience in the prologue to his book, *The Conversion of a Klansman*:

> I was overcome with a sense of my sinfulness—not just for prejudice, hatred, and political violence, but for my whole life-style. All my life I had been living for myself—what pleased me, made me feel good, made me look good to others. The feelings, needs, desires of other people were always secondary to what I wanted. Indeed, the whole world revolved around me and this showed itself in the outward sins of my life.
>
> As I came to see myself as I really was—as God saw me—I was crushed, and I wept bitterly. How hideous and wretched I was. Then, seeing my need so clearly and knowing there was only One who could meet it, I surrendered myself to the Lord Jesus Christ as fully as I knew how. A tremendous weight was lifted from me, and I began to feel at peace at last.[11]

Tarrants renounced his racism and hatred and committed his life to the service of Jesus Christ. The realization that he had only narrowly escaped death when he was apprehended convinced him that God had another purpose for his life. Later, Tarrants found out that the wife of an FBI agent involved in his capture had been praying for his salvation for years. After his conversion, the FBI agent and his wife, along with others who had been the targets of his hatred, were instrumental in securing his release after eight years in prison.

Tarrants earned college and seminary degrees and served in various ministry positions, including a co-pastorate at the nondenominational evangelical Christ Our Shepherd Church in Washington, DC. Once a crusader for hate, Tarrants now, as president of the C. S. Lewis Institute, headquartered in Washington, works to reconcile the races and to reconcile all men to God through a relationship with Jesus. He eventually coauthored a book on racial reconciliation with African American leader John Perkins.[12]

CONCLUSIONS AND A TO-DO LIST

As recent events in American culture have made clear, we still have a race problem in this country. Many Christians have allowed the issue to become politicized and fail to listen to voices within our own community that are helpfully presenting a way forward. The only worldview with the resources necessary for the level of forgiveness required is Christianity. Christians can lead the way in racial reconciliation.

That's why we were much encouraged by this comment from New Orleans Saints tight end Benjamin Watson, who went to social media in the aftermath of the Ferguson riots to proclaim:

> I'm encouraged, because ultimately the problem is not a SKIN problem, it is a SIN problem. SIN is the reason we rebel against authority. SIN is the reason we abuse our authority. SIN is the reason we are racist, prejudiced and lie to cover for our own. SIN is the reason we riot, loot and burn. BUT I'M ENCOURAGED because God has provided a solution for sin through his son Jesus and, with it, a transformed heart and mind. One that's capable of looking past the outward and seeing what's truly important in every human being.[13]

Here are some things you can do to help advance racial reconciliation in your own community:

1. Read *Divided by Faith: Evangelical Religion and the Problem of Race in America* by Michael O. Emerson and Christian Smith and *He's My Brother: Former Racial Foes Offer Strategy for Reconciliation* by John Perkins and Thomas Tarrants.

2. Initiate a serious discussion in your church about whether it is an agent of racial reconciliation in the community and how it can become more involved. Use the article "Why You Should Still Care about Ferguson *Despite* the Facts" by Ed Stetzer as well as the linked series of articles by several guest authors (http://www.christianitytoday.com/edstetzer/2014/november/why-you-should-still-care-about-ferguson-despite-facts.html).

3. Annually bring church congregations of predominantly different races together for joint worship services.

4. Pray faithfully for those cities in our country and around the world that struggle with racial tension.

5. Intentionally get to know individuals and families of a different race. Share meals and ask questions about mutual blind spots that negatively affect others.

9

Loving God with All Your Mind

The people who are most bigoted are the people who
have no convictions. . . . It is the vague modern who is
not at all certain what is right who is most certain that
Dante was wrong.

—G. K. Chesterton[1]

Intellectuals are especially prone to self-deception, seeing
themselves as the standard-bearers of the cult of origi-
nality, having emancipated themselves from all the con-
straints of tradition, community and obligation.

—Vinoth Ramachandra[2]

In chapter 6, "Coloring Outside the Lines," we discussed how Christians have historically been champions of education. Christians have
also been champions of discovery. We believe not only that God gave
His image bearers stewardship over the world He made, but that
He also reveals Himself through it. That belief gave our Christian
forebears the motivation they needed to drive their exploration in the
sciences and the arts.

"I was merely thinking God's thoughts after him," Johannes Kepler wrote. "Since we astronomers are priests of the highest God in regard to the book of nature, it benefits us to be thoughtful, not of the glory of our minds, but rather, above all else, of the glory of God."[3]

In today's university environment, however, Christians who bring their convictions with them to the academy are not always welcome. The idea that higher education is an open-minded and tolerant place of exploring ideas is, in many ways, a myth. A secular worldview dominates most academic disciplines. That worldview dogmatically keeps Christian ideas outside the classroom door.

For some in the university, in fact, it's personal. A 2007 study conducted by the Institute for Jewish and Community Research, a study looking for anti-Jewish bias, found instead that 53 percent of college and university faculty surveyed held "unfavorable feelings" toward evangelicals.[4] It's one thing to dismiss ideas or to disagree with someone's conclusions, but not liking them because of their convictions is another.

Studies also demonstrate that college faculty identify as secular, nonreligious, and liberal far more than the general population, even more than "the most conspiratorial conservatives might have imagined," wrote Howard Kurtz in a 2005 *Washington Post* article. The study on which he was reporting was coauthored by three political science professors from different universities, and found that 72 percent of the college faculty they surveyed self-identified as liberal, 51 percent rarely or never went to church, 84 percent were in favor of abortions, and 65 percent thought the government should ensure full employment, a position Kurtz called "left of the Democratic Party."[5] One thing that made this study particularly striking, according to Kurtz, was that according to a Carnegie Foundation study, only 39 percent of college faculty had identified as liberal *just twenty years earlier.*

As the stories we tell in this chapter make clear, some Christian convictions are particularly intolerable to secularists. The sexual revolution, for example, has spread beyond advocating personal freedom in our sexual choices (which has been destructive enough) to advocating personal freedom in choosing our identities based on sexual preferences. Anything short of full affirmation of all sexual choices, explorations, and identities can quickly make one persona non grata on the secular college campus. Also, the issue of the origins of human life is subject to a strict neo-Darwinian orthodoxy. Opposition to abortion and support for the Judeo-Christian values that gave rise to Western civilization are minority views that generate scorn on many college campuses.

Not walking in lockstep with the orthodoxy of secularists on these issues can threaten a promising academic career, and so many Christian professors struggle to integrate their faith with their areas of academic study. Unfortunately, this means current generations of students are not exposed to all views, including some of the best ideas Western civilization has to offer. The university setting, then, becomes captive to politically correct views, even if those views are not, well, correct.

But there are courageous professors in secular academic settings who take their faith as seriously as they do their scholarship. Moreover, because "all truth is God's truth,"[6] they rightfully understand that both their faith and their academic prowess can mutually inform one another and lead us to a deeper understanding of whatever we are studying. It's a risky move in terms of career advancement, departmental promotions, and publishing contracts; but they realize their allegiance belongs to truth, and to the God of all truth, more than it does to academic societies or politically correct fashions of the day.

Fine, you ask, but how is this redemptive? It is not uncommon for Christians to think academic quibbling is antithetical to faith and may even get in the way of the more important matters of the heart. This view is fundamentally wrong, however, and forgets the repeated exhortations in Scripture about the importance of the mind. "And [Jesus] answered, 'You shall love the Lord your God with all your heart and with all your soul and with all your strength and with all your mind'" (Luke 10:27).

Ideas matter because truth matters. And the health of a culture, as well as the state of its receptivity toward the message of Christ, is largely dependent on which ideas are embraced as true. As Princeton theologian J. Gresham Machen said:

> False ideas are the greatest obstacles to the reception of the gospel. We may preach with all the fervor of a reformer and yet succeed only in winning a straggler here and there, if we permit the whole collective thought of the nation or of the world to be controlled by ideas which, by the resistless force of logic, prevent Christianity from being regarded as anything more than a harmless delusion. Under such circumstances, what God desires us to do is to destroy the obstacle at its root.[7]

And many Christians have taken Machen's challenge to heart. Consider, for example, the remarkable impact Christian philosophers have made in a discipline that, as recently as the start of the twentieth century, had all but dismissed the existence and relevance of God. Philosophers such as Nicholas Wolterstorff, Francis Schaeffer, Dallas Willard, Eleonore Stump, William Lane Craig, and especially Alvin Plantinga have made Christianity once again a force to be reckoned with in the field of philosophy.[8] The impact of this work has been nothing short of resurrecting sub-disciplines within philosophy that were dying, challenging the anti-Christian strongholds that were defining much of modern philosophy[9] and inspiring rising generations of philosophers who are serious about their faith and their academic task.[10]

The same is happening in other universities and academic disciplines. And we'd like to introduce a few of the individuals now.

Good Deeds Punished

To understand just how relentless and, at times, even vicious the attack on Christians in higher education can be, just take a look at a recent incident involving University of Texas at Austin (UT) professor Mark Regnerus.

An important component of pro-homosexual propaganda is the notion that children raised by homosexuals turn out as well as children raised by heterosexuals, but Regnerus undercut that notion with a study published in *Social Science Research* journal.[11]

Regnerus used one of the largest data sets ever amassed for such a study. He found that children raised by homosexual parents tend to have more problems than children raised by married heterosexual parents in virtually every one of more than forty categories examined. When the children grow up, they have problems with impulse control, depression, and thoughts of suicide. They are more likely to need mental health therapy and identify as homosexual themselves. Regnerus concluded, "The empirical claim that no notable differences exist must go."[12]

The study received nationwide media attention and an immediate backlash from pro-homosexual quarters. Activist blogger Scott Rose complained to UT President Bill Powers that Regnerus's study made "gay people look bad, through means plainly fraudulent and defamatory."[13] He also said the Witherspoon Institute and the Bradley Foundation, which provided $750,000 to fund the study, are "anti-gay political organization[s]."

But Regnerus has defenders in the academic community. Byron Johnson, co-director of the Baylor University Institute for Studies of Religion, decried the "witch hunt" and said, "Typically, when [academics] disagree with research, we do our own." Notre Dame sociologist Christian Smith argued in *The Chronicle of Higher Education*, "Whoever said inquisitions and witch hunts were things of the past? A big one is going on now. . . . In today's political climate, and particularly in the discipline of sociology—dominated as it is by a progressive orthodoxy—what Regnerus did is unacceptable. It makes him a heretic, a traitor—and so he must be thrown under the bus."[14]

It will not be easy for the administration at the University of Texas to get rid of Regnerus because he has tenure. But this story shows how hard it is for Christians—or even for those non-Christians who value intellectual diversity and freedom of thought—to express themselves if their views run counter to prevailing ideologies.

Mark Regnerus provides a model for Christian scholarship at the secular university that we hope many other young Christians will follow, and he isn't alone in his fight against politically correct restrictions on pursuing truth in the groves of academe.

Doubting Darwin

Sociology isn't the only department where anti-science ideology rules. In fact, some of the most anti-science ideology comes from a place you'd least expect it: the science department.

University of Washington professor David Barash unintentionally allowed us to see how ideology trumps science in secular university science departments when he wrote an opinion piece in the *New York Times* that said he gave all of his students what he called "The Talk." In that talk he said he "evicts God" from his science class with his explanation about "evolution and religion, and how they get along. More to the point, how they don't."[15]

Barash is obviously anti-God, but how is he anti-science? Because, according to Stephen Meyer, author of *Darwin's Doubt*, "he's either ignoring or willfully ignorant of the huge problem that exists in evolutionary theory."[16]

Meyer is director of Discovery Institute's Center for Science and Culture. Barash gives his talk because, Meyer says, "it's irresponsible to teach biology without evolution." But according to Meyer, a growing number of leading evolutionary theorists are now saying neo-Darwinism is dead and those who continue to teach it are not keeping up with the latest scientific research.

"Even Darwin was plagued by doubt about his own theories," Meyer said in a recent interview.[17] Of particular concern is the Cambrian Explosion, a period when most of the major life forms on earth developed, all in a relatively short period of time. Scientists have known about the Cambrian Explosion since the 1840s. When Darwin wrote his most influential work in the 1850s and '60s, he was well aware of it. In fact, he cited the Cambrian Explosion as a significant argument against his own theories. He hoped, though, that further developments in science would reconcile the disconnect between his theory and the scientific evidence.

In fact, further discoveries have made Darwin's theories increasingly untenable, according to Meyer. It is, simply put, impossible to get from simple life forms to more complex life forms via "the Darwinian mechanism of natural selection and random mutation," Meyer said. Those like Barash, who still cling to neo-Darwinism, "seem to be stuck in the 1970s and completely unaware of what's going on in the field and the problems evolutionary theorists encounter as old ideas fail to explain new discoveries."

Yet these outdated views remain common in the science departments of modern universities. That's why, Meyer said, "it's important [for parents] to prepare [their] kids for that mind-set before they get there."

Mike Adams against the Machine

Few professors have faced the sort of prolonged opposition encountered by Mike Adams, a professor of criminology at the University of North Carolina at Wilmington. It's a story worth telling in detail.[18]

Adams's journey began in 1993 when UNC Wilmington hired him as a professor, a young atheist with a newly minted PhD. "They loved me back then," he said. In fact, they loved him so much that he received Faculty Member of the Year honors not just once—a rare enough accomplishment—but twice.

But whether or not someone believes in God does not change the fact that He does indeed exist. And the Holy Spirit, whom poet Francis Thompson called the "hound of heaven," was in hot pursuit. Adams's work as a criminologist took him in 1996 to the prisons of Ecuador, where he saw terrible human rights abuses, including evidence of torture. Adams said, "I wanted to be outraged, but on what basis?" As an atheist and moral relativist, he had no basis for saying torture or anything else was moral or immoral. He came to the conclusion, though, that such behavior was, in fact, immoral and that there must be a God or some divine presence that imprints that sense of right and wrong on every human mind and heart. "That experience did not convert me to Christianity," Adams said. "But it did convert me to theism."

Three years later, in 1999, Adams's research as a criminologist took him to death row, where he interviewed a mentally challenged man awaiting execution. The prisoner quoted Scripture to him. "I realized that this mentally challenged man knew more about the Bible than I did," Adams said. He decided to start studying the Bible and Christianity, not at first for the purpose of conversion, but just to fill that gap in his education. But two things happened. First and most important, Adams came to believe that the Bible is true, that Jesus is real, and that he was a sinner in need of a Savior. The former atheist professor converted to Christianity in 2000.

But something else happened. Mike Adams's experience with the mentally challenged death row prisoner made him realize it was possible to go through high school, college—even so far as to get a PhD from a leading university—and be almost totally ignorant of the Bible and Christianity. It began to seem impossible that such a "blackout" of Christian values in higher education was totally by accident. So in 2002, Adams said, "I made a decision to start speaking out about the systematic abuses of free speech on college campuses and the tremendous double standards that were going on. I wrote for about four years." His columns appeared in print and on-line in a variety of publications, and he even wrote a book on the subject: *Welcome to the Ivory Tower of Babel*.[19]

By this time, Adams had tenure, but he was not a full professor. On September 15, 2006, the university denied him promotion to full professor, saying he was deficient in every criterion evaluated: teaching, research, and service. Adams said that after he read the letter denying the promotion, he looked up. "I was staring at my 1998 Professor of the Year award and looking at my year 2000 Professor of the Year award that I had won before I converted to Christianity. I called the Alliance Defending Freedom (ADF) and made a decision that day that we were going to fight."

But Adams admitted he had no idea, at the time, how difficult the road ahead would be. He said, "Our case was mostly a circumstantial case: They loved me when I was one of them, but I converted and they didn't love me anymore. There was some evidence of retaliation, but we began with what was simply a circumstantial case."

Nonetheless, on April 10, 2007, Adams and his ADF attorneys filed a lawsuit in federal court in Greenville, North Carolina. The court system in such cases can take years, and in this case it did. In March 2010, after three years of discovery and testimony, Judge Malcolm Howard threw out Adams's case. That day, Adams admitted, was "one of the worst days of my life, because when that decision was rendered, that was eight years into my career as an activist talking about the First Amendment on college campuses. I am holding myself out as this expert on campus free speech and we suffered this crushing defeat. It was embarrassing. By that evening it was on all of the headlines on the evening news: 'UNCW professor loses lawsuit against university.'"

Adams said he did not sleep that night. The next morning, he took a call from one of his ADF attorneys, Joseph Martins. Martins told Adams, "I'm very sorry this thing happened. But I want you to know, this isn't defeat. This is providence."

Adams was dumbfounded. He admitted that in his sleep-deprived state he had some unchristian thoughts in the face of Martins's apparently glib cheerfulness. "I am glad that was a long-distance phone call, because if Joe Martins was in that room, I probably would have punched him."

But Martins was right. ADF understood the importance of this case, so they decided to appeal. But for the rest of the day, Adams was in a funk. He was embarrassed by the loss in court, and he was also troubled by Martins's faith—or, more accurately, his own lack of faith. Martins's words kept coming back to him: "This isn't defeat. This is providence."

Nonetheless, Adams composed himself and went onto campus that morning, even though, he said, "I thought my career was over. No one wants to hear what Mike Adams has to say about the First Amendment anymore."

But just as his self-loathing reached a low point, his phone rang. A young man named Tim said he was calling from Rhode Island. "We want you to come to our college to give a speech on the First Amendment," Tim said.

Adams asked where Tim was calling from.

"This is Providence College," Tim said.

Adams could not believe his ears. "Where are you calling from?"

Tim repeated, "This is Providence."

Adams still did not believe what he was hearing. He thought his attorney was playing a cruel practical joke on him. "Is this Joe?"

"No. It's Tim. From Providence," came the answer a third time.

Adams said that phone call was a turning point for him. "I decided for the first time that no matter what happened, everything was going to be okay," he later said.

And it was, though it would take several more years. Adams and his ADF attorneys did indeed appeal. After a seemingly endless series of hearings and motions, and numerous attempts by Adams to settle, the case ended up back in Judge Malcolm Howard's court. He set a trial date: March 17, 2014. Both sides had exactly six hours for opening statements, direct examination, cross examination, and closing arguments. After all the legal wrangling, Adams said, "It was to be a simple trial."

After four days of arguments and one hour and 50 minutes of deliberation, the jury came back into the courtroom. The foreperson handed the verdict form to the clerk, and the clerk read the verdict.

Adams is a trained criminologist who has been in many courtrooms. Nonetheless, he was so overwhelmed by the moment, he had to turn to his attorneys and ask, "Does that mean we won?"

They said, "Yeah, we won."

What Adams won was about $50,000 in back pay and promotion to full professor at UNC–Wilmington. Alliance Defending Freedom attorneys ultimately received $710,000 to reimburse them for the time and expenses they incurred during the seven-year trial.

But there was far more to the win than financial compensation and personal satisfaction, something that became clear to Adams a couple of weeks after the trial, when he spoke at a Baptist church in Raleigh, North Carolina. "I was walking out of the church and the most incredible thing happens," Adams said. "An elderly black man grabs me by the arm and he just looks down at me. He's about 6 foot 4 and he looks down at me and he says, 'I just want to thank you for that thing that you done for our people.'"

Adams said the comment "really caught me off guard." But as Adams looked into the face of a man who lived through segregation, the great civil rights struggle of his era, they both realized that Adams's fight—for religious liberty—is one of the great civil rights issues of this era. What this elderly black man knew better than most is that when Mike Adams fought for his rights to exercise his religious and free speech liberties, he was fighting for all. When the man grabbed Adams's arm, he was really locking arms with him. As Adams put it, "We are all involved, black and white, in an epic civil rights struggle in the United States of America."

But these ideas, Adams said, came later. "When people compliment me on what I've done, I feel awkward," he said. So he replied to the man, "The Lord's been raising me up to do this thing since 1993. When He brought me in as an atheist, He knew what my fate would be."

That elderly black man knew God's sovereignty is deeper and richer and more powerful than even Adams understood then. Adams said, "He looked at me and stuck his finger in my face and said, 'No.' He said, 'The Lord been raising you up to do this thing since you was a little boy.' And he turned and he walked off."

Today Adams tells this story in speeches on college campuses. He often concludes by saying:

> I see a lot of young people, and let me tell you that if you follow Christ in this secular, post-Christian culture, your battles are going to be epic and your struggles are going to be great; never think that you're not here for a reason. You're not here by chance. You're here because the Lord's been raising you up to do something great since you were little boys and little girls. This is not chance. This is providence.

Conclusion and a To-Do List

Higher education in this country is, in many ways, captive to anti-Christian ideology and intolerance. Even so, some courageous

Christian professors are quietly leading a counterrevolution that is slowly taking ground in the groves of academe. By some estimates, a full half of the PhD candidates in philosophy in this country are evangelical Christians, mostly due to the life and legacy of Dr. Alvin Plantinga at Notre Dame. In addition to the stories we've already told, other brilliant Christian minds have achieved positions of influence in the ivory tower schools, such as Dr. Robert George at Princeton University, Dr. Jean Bethke Elshtain of the University of Chicago, Dr. Mark Noll of Notre Dame, Dr. Glenn Sunshine of Central Connecticut State University, and many more. And we each know dozens of promising young scholars who will potentially emerge as witnesses for Christ in the academy.

Here's what you can do to join in God's redemptive work taking place right now in the halls of higher education:

1. Read *Jesus Christ and the Life of the Mind* by Mark Noll and *Love Your God with All Your Mind: The Role of Reason in the Life of the Soul* (2nd ed.) by J. P. Moreland.
2. Commit to reading one challenging book each year that will stretch you and sharpen your ability to think well.
3. Identify and encourage the promising young minds in your church or community. Help them understand the potential of their God-given abilities and that it can be spiritual to be smart!
4. Encourage every college-bound student in your sphere of influence to be prepared for the intellectual challenges to their faith that are coming. Send them to a worldview and apologetics training program like Summit Ministries (www.summit.org) or buy them a copy of *Welcome to College* by Jonathan Morrow.
5. Recognize the ministry that college professors and academics have, acknowledge it in front of the church, and commit to pray for them regularly.

10

It Doesn't Define You

Washed and waiting. That is my life—my identity as one who is forgiven and spiritually cleansed and my struggle as one who perseveres with a frustrating thorn in the flesh, looking forward to what God has promised to do.

—Wesley Hill

And such were some of you. But you were washed, you were sanctified, you were justified in the name of the Lord Jesus Christ and by the Spirit of our God.

—1 Corinthians 6:11

You will know the truth, and the truth will make you free.

—John 8:32

No issue has been more divisive in the Christian church and in the culture at large than homosexuality. After splitting some of America's largest and oldest Protestant denominations at the end of the twentieth century, it threatens today to split evangelicalism as well. The former consensus on the issue within evangelical churches has recently eroded in the wake of high-profile shifts by pastors with children who are same-sex attracted, young-evangelical bloggers tired of being on the cultural outs, and high-profile academics and ethicists.

In the larger culture, same-sex marriage has become a defining political issue both here and abroad. The initial undefeated run of voters passing state amendments defining marriage as only between man and woman was stopped and reversed by legislative bodies and activist judges. The move by elected and unelected officials to usher in same-sex marriage has been tsunami-like since President Barack Obama famously evolved on the issue. More Americans now live in states where same-sex marriage is legal than in those where it is not, and it seems all but inevitable that it will soon be legally imposed on the rest of the nation as well.

This issue, even more so than others, is a classic example of how stories are often more effective than arguments in swaying minds and hearts. For example, we now know that the murder of Matthew Shepard in 1998 was more likely a meth-induced act of rage than the result of hatred of homosexual people. Still, the original narrative is the one that shaped the national debate and remains firmly embedded in the popular imagination.[1] We've heard so many stories of harmful or failed "reparative therapy" that we tend to discredit the true (and often courageous) stories of those who have successfully left a homosexual lifestyle for heterosexual marriage or celibacy. We call these stories courageous because those who tell them often face ridicule and discrimination from the very gay activists who seek sympathy with their own stories of ridicule and discrimination.

We believe that all deserve a full and open hearing. Even more, we believe that by telling and hearing the stories of those who have left the homosexual lifestyle, we can arrive at a deeper truth about human identity that is largely suppressed in the contemporary debates about sexuality. Their stories demonstrate that we are far more than our appetites and inclinations, and to reduce identity to sexuality is antithetical to human flourishing.

At the root of our cultural confusion about sexuality is an idea with a long intellectual history. Secular thinkers like psychotherapist Sigmund Freud, Planned Parenthood founder Margaret Sanger, and postmodernist Michel Foucault proclaimed that any norms about sexual behavior are nothing more than social constructs of a culture with religious hang-ups.[2] This view assumes our world is not created by God, and therefore no particular human sexual relationship is better than any other. Time-tested realities—such as confining sexual behavior within the covenant of marriage to ensure mutual commitment as well as security for any children of the union—are dismissed as antiquated impositions that no longer apply in our "enlightened" age.

But if human sexuality is designed by God, then how we express our sexuality is more than a matter of religious preference. Instead, it is embedded in our humanity, and how we behave matters both personally and collectively. And, if the rest of the biblical story is true, our inclinations and passions will be impacted by the human sinfulness we all share.

We realize that many, especially those who do not share our Christian convictions, find this view difficult to accept. But any who claim Christ as Lord and Savior must take seriously the vision of humanity presented in the Scriptures. After all, the same Scriptures that describe Jesus and what He accomplished begin by describing this vision of the creation and fall of all of mankind. One of the implications of the fall is this: that the intensity of our inclinations does not morally justify our actions. All we think, do, feel, and say must be measured by the truth communicated in the Word of God.

Of course, we should expect to see the truth of Scripture reflected in the world in which we live. And we do. There is an obviousness about human sexuality. Sex is good and necessary, for without it, the human race would surely die out. And when sex is protected within marriage, and serves more than our individual choices, it's better for all of us, especially women and children.

In fact, as sociologist Pitirim Sorokin suggested, few things are more important to the long-term health of a society than what it thinks about human sexuality.[3] And Christianity offers a rich view of our humanity in which sexuality alone doesn't define us. Instead, our identity rests in the eternal truth that God has created every human being in His image.

To fully present all the arguments for the position we've just espoused is beyond the scope of our conversation. To get the full picture, we've recommended some helpful books at the end of this chapter. But if the biblical picture for human sexuality is indeed true, we fail miserably in our efforts to love our neighbors if we let stand the myth that sexual orientation is all or most of one's identity and justifies (or even demands) behavior. Love without truth is simply not love. Many have faced and overcome challenges with sexuality, and our sexually broken culture needs to hear their stories.

An Unlikely Convert

One such story belongs to Rosaria Butterfield.

At twenty-eight years old, Butterfield wrote in the first sentence of her book *The Secret Thoughts of an Unlikely Convert*, "I boldly declared myself lesbian."[4]

At the time, she was a graduate student who "cared deeply about relationships. I even authored at least one article on the subject of morality and moral living. I was steeped in worldviews that buttressed a sense of equality and the high value of personal experience."[5]

Butterfield said, "I had wonderful relationships with many of my female colleagues—deeper, resonating relationships. For me, coming out as a lesbian was the same way I might come out as someone who loves her dog or feeds her cat in the morning. It didn't seem spectacular. It didn't seem very extraordinary. It just was."[6]

By age thirty-six, she had completed her doctorate and was well established as a professor at Syracuse University. But the responses she received to a critique of the Promise Keepers movement she wrote in a local newspaper began what would eventually be a move to an entirely different worldview. Most responses easily fit either in her fan mail tray or in her hate mail tray, but the letter from a pastor, Ken Smith, didn't. It wasn't affirming, nor was it nasty. Instead, it asked questions she couldn't answer.

"I couldn't dispose of this letter. I tried to, but at the end of the day I would fish it out of the recycling bin and put it back on my desk. It had some questions that no one had ever asked me in my life. At the end of the letter the pastor asked me, please, to give him a call. The title of the church was Syracuse Reformed Presbyterian Church, and I assumed reformed meant enlightened. An anthropologist colleague of mine said a meeting would be 'good for your research! Call him back!' So I did."[7]

What were the questions in the letter that haunted her?

"One had to do with the nature of the Bible as a library, not just a book, that it contained every genre I used to teach from. He asked

138

questions about my well-being. He asked, do I believe in God, and if so, what do I think He thinks of all this? He wrote in such a gracious way, and I was intrigued by it."[8]

When she accepted the pastor's invitation to dinner at his home, Butterfield was impressed by something else: Pastor Smith had no air conditioning.

Butterfield fancied herself a "progressive" at that time, and she assumed that evangelical Christians "felt entitled to a dominion over the earth," which she considered "hateful, violent, unhelpful, unkind." Her view of air conditioning in upstate New York was that it was environmentally unfriendly, wasteful, and expensive. But the Smiths, she said, "had fans and served a vegetarian meal, which I appreciated because I felt at this point that the eating of meat was a violent activity, and I didn't want to be a part of it. Their home and their culture didn't seem so different from mine. That put me at ease."[9]

And then there was that prayer before the meal.

"I had heard lots of prayer before. I was the heathen who got to overhear the prayers of many people at gay pride marches and in front of Planned Parenthood. I was going to hold my breath and get through the prayer, and then I could have a chance to get to some of my research by talking with this family. But it wasn't like that at all: It was a very conversational prayer, a prayer that included asking God for forgiveness of sins, and in a very specific way. It wasn't a terribly lengthy prayer, but it had some details in it that made me think about myself, like forgetting to bring a meal to someone. Basic everyday things, but he was noticing them, and they were big enough to ask a holy God to forgive him."

Surprisingly, Pastor Ken and his family didn't "share the gospel" or invite Butterfield to church, and to her, it was important that they didn't.

"I trusted them because they did not do those things. I knew the script. But Ken and his wife, Floy, were not talking to me as if I simply were a blank slate: 'OK, here is someone who clearly needs the gospel; let's make sure we get to these points before we let her leave our house.' They seemed more interested in having a long relationship with me."

And they became, in Butterfield's words, "genuine friends."

"When I wouldn't answer an email or didn't show up, or they hadn't heard from me in a month, Ken would come over, or Floy would drop off a loaf of bread. We had many things in common—Floy and

I both love to bake bread, and we like the same literature, which was astounding. And because I was a researcher, I started to read the Bible."

Ironically, Butterfield researched the Bible for a book she was writing on the religious right.

"I needed to read the book that had gotten all these well-meaning, good-intentioned, but naïve and foolish, people offtrack. And so I was doing that, was reading the Bible the way a glutton approaches a bag of Oreo cookies, and I needed some scholarly help."

She didn't read bits and pieces of the Bible. She read big chunks of it. "Some powerful things happen when you read the Bible many, many times in a year, from Genesis to Revelation, and in multiple translations," she said. "I really encourage Christians to do that, and not to read the Bible as though you're reading your horoscope. I don't think it's really meant to be read like that."

And the Bible did its work. In Butterfield's own words:

> My friend Jay at that point was a transgendered woman—biologically male, but had taken enough female hormones to be what's called chemically castrated. Jay followed me to the kitchen, put her large hand on my hand, and said, "Rosaria, something is changing you. This Bible reading is changing you, and you need to tell me what is going on with you, because I am worried I am losing you."[10]

But at that point, Butterfield was not ready to change. "I like my life, I like my girlfriend, I like my house thank you very much, I even like my wonderful career," she said.

Soon, though, the Bible and other religious books she had started reading had her in the parking lot across from Pastor Ken's Presbyterian church.

"I had my Starbucks coffee and my *New York Times* and maybe an article I was working on in my truck with the gay and lesbian bumper stickers on the back," she said. "I would park and watch these enormous families pour out of 15-person passenger vans. The kids just kept coming and coming, and it was astounding."

Then one Sunday, she went from the parking lot into the church.

> I woke up one morning, emerged from a bed that I shared with a woman, got in my truck with my bumper stickers and my butch haircut, and showed up at the Reformed Presbyterian Church. What strikes me, looking back, is what this church had been doing: praying for me

faithfully, faithfully. Ken was sharing with this church our friendship and our relationship, and the members were genuinely on their knees praying for me. It's easier to simply be disgusted by a person like me than pray for me. I also brought friends. The church went from being a cleaned-up homeschooling church to suddenly a church with ministry to a lot of broken people.[11]

Pastor Ken's hospitality, the prayers of his church, and her close reading of Scripture eventually brought Butterfield to a place of repentance and conversion. It was initially not easy for her. "Conversion put me in a complicated and comprehensive chaos," she said. "I had some really burning questions for people. I would go up to my homeschool mom friends and say, 'Look, I have to give up the girlfriend: What did you have to give up to be here?' I heard amazing things that made me realize I did not have any more to give up than anyone else. I learned there were other people in my church who struggled with sexual sin, with lust, with faithlessness . . . and they told me that! They took the risk of no longer looking all cleaned up to me."

Butterfield said she thinks the witness of the church to the LGBT community, as well as to everyone else, would be much more effective if we were more hospitable and more honest.

> I'm grateful that I never heard anybody say, "God has a perfect plan for your life." No, they said, "Rosaria, count the costs, this is going to be brutal, this is going to be bloody." When I said, "Look at all these hurting people," nobody said, "Serves them right, boy, are they a bunch of sinners." Instead, people in church rolled up their sleeves and said, "OK, how can we help? How can we get to know your friends?"[12]

Out of a Far Country

If we had met Christopher Yuan before the gospel transformed his life, we might have been tempted to think of him as beyond God's reach. In fact, for a while, Yuan thought the same thing about himself. But his story is an example of one of the ideas that energize this book: When we are at our weakest and most vulnerable, God often shows up most powerfully.

Like Rosaria Butterfield, Yuan's story teaches us that things are not always what they appear. From the outside, both of them appeared to be happy and successful. Butterfield was a young "rising star" in the "hot" academic field of gender studies. And Yuan looked to be the picture of success. He was a brilliant young man who raced through college on his way to dental school. A fitness fanatic, he was—there's no other way to say it—beautiful. And he was "out and proud," the center of attention in his circle of equally beautiful gay friends.

But Yuan's fitness obsession and his success in school masked deep pain and self-destructive behavior. Looking back today, Yuan cites a number of factors that led him to embrace homosexual behavior and come out as gay in his early twenties. An early exposure to pornography "awoke in me feelings that shouldn't have been awoken," he said. Growing up in a Chicago suburb Asian and with no aptitude for sports led to bullying and name-calling. He heard other boys call him "sissy" and "fag" from an early age, and he began to wonder if those names might be accurate.[13]

Yuan said his coming out "devastated my mom. She and my father weren't Christians, and she thought an ultimatum could bring me to my senses. She said, 'You must either choose the family or choose this.' I left home. Then I got involved in drugs and started selling drugs in Louisville, Kentucky."

Yuan's parents were struggling with other issues too. They were on the verge of divorce after thirty years of marriage. "My mother bought a one-way Amtrak ticket to Louisville: She was going to say good-bye to me, then end her life," Yuan said. "But someone gave her a little pamphlet that she read on the train. It explained how we're all sinners, and yet in spite of our sins, the God of the universe still loves us. She realized God could still love her and she could still love her gay son."[14]

Yuan's mother, Angela, dove deeply into her newfound Christian faith. Soon Christopher's father also became a Christian. His parents called off the divorce and began working on their marriage. They also decided to move to Louisville to be near their wayward son.

But they did not know how wayward he was. Yuan had started selling drugs to support his fast-paced lifestyle. "I was supplying drugs to dealers in over a dozen states at that time," Yuan said. "They had no idea the depth to which I had gone, but they knew I needed to know Christ. They prayed for that miracle, that God would do whatever it takes, which for a Chinese mother is a scary bold prayer to make. She knew there was nothing she could do or say to soften my heart to make me a follower of Jesus, that it needed to be truly an act of the Living God."

Yuan's drug dealing caught the attention of authorities, who arrested him and seized all his drugs and his money. He was facing ten years to life in federal prison. Ultimately, he received a sentence of six years but soon after received news of a different kind of life sentence: He was HIV positive.

Yuan found a Gideon Bible in a garbage can in prison, and he started reading it. Soon he had shaken his drug addiction, but as he would later put it, "What I was holding to was my sexuality." He went to the prison chaplain, but "to my surprise he told me the Bible doesn't condemn homosexuality and gave me a book explaining that view. I took that book. I wanted to find biblical justification for homosexuality. I had that book in one hand and the Bible in the other, and every reason in the world to accept what that book was claiming. I wanted to have God and a gay relationship, but as I read through the Bible and read that book, it was clear to me that the book presented a clear distortion of God, His Word, and His unmistakable condemnation of homosexual sex."

All this time, Yuan's mother was praying for her son. That prayer was not that he would get out of prison and get back to a socially respectable career, but rather that he would be in prison for the "right amount of time."

Given their background and history, Yuan knew his mother had changed when she could say, "It's not important for my son to become a doctor." Her goal, rather, was that "Christ must be preeminent over all things." Yuan said she even "pleaded with the judge, 'Don't give my son too long of a sentence, but don't give him too short a sentence. Just give him just the right amount of time for him to turn his life over to God.'"

And that's exactly what happened. After spending three years in prison, he was released, received a master's degree in biblical exegesis, and (as of late 2014) has nearly completed a doctorate in ministry.

Yuan's life is redeemed, but not perfect. He remains HIV positive, though with modern medicine it is likely that he will live a long, healthy life. Still, his story is a powerful testimony of just how far God can and will reach to redeem His children.[15]

Transformed

Because Rosaria Butterfield and Christopher Yuan have written powerful books, many thousands of people have come to know their stories. That's good. But it is tempting to say, "Yeah, people like Butterfield and Yuan have spectacular stories, but they are not representative." Some gay activists go even further and attempt to discredit such stories.

Our research and experience, however, have shown us there are thousands, perhaps tens of thousands, of people with stories similar to Yuan's and Butterfield's. Indeed, something remarkable is happening. All across the country, grassroots organizations are springing up to help men and women with same-sex attractions live their lives consistent with biblical principles.

One of these ministries is Living Hope, run by Ricky Chelette in Arlington, Texas. Chelette's own story is like some of the thousands belonging to individuals that he and his ministry have helped over a twenty-five-year history.

"At the age of eighteen, graduating near the top of my class, [I] gave the commencement address at my graduation," he said.[16] But inside, he said, "I was more miserable than I had ever been in my life. From all outward appearances I was on top of the world. I was a 'good boy,' earned great scholarships, didn't cuss, smoke, or drink, was student council president and teenager of the year, but internally my world was a nightmare."

Despite his successes, he felt like a "frightened boy, desperately crying for someone to affirm me." Those feelings of inadequacy and fear were in part the result of years of childhood sexual abuse that had "produced in me a seemingly uncontrollable desire for the affections of other men. The abuse started when I was young, and at first, I didn't know it was really wrong. I was so young, and I adored my abuser. For me, it was simply 'normal.' The abuse continued almost weekly for over a decade. He was deeply invested in me, said he loved me, and knew exactly what buttons to push to manipulate my emotions and garner my cooperation."

But as he grew older, Chelette developed the "overwhelming sense that what I had been doing was wrong and what I was feeling was not what I wanted to be feeling." The result: "I tried to kill myself. I wanted all the pain to end and for someone to finally see that I was hurting beneath the charade of my accomplished life."

That suicide attempt, with drugs, was unsuccessful. So Chelette decided to try an approach that would be more effective. "I grabbed a pistol and put it in my mouth to blow out the back of my head. I had decided it would be quick, painless, and final."

Chelette had, however, heard the gospel. And the words of one of those gospel presentations came back to him as he prepared to pull the trigger of that pistol. "When I first heard it, I had no interest in this gospel or this Jesus," Chelette said. "I was the 'good kid.' I was already far better behaved than the 'Christians' I knew. But in this moment, my behavior was not what rang true in my heart. As I contemplated the words of the preacher about this Jesus who died on a cross for my sins and who wanted to give me a new heart and a new beginning, it seemed like the only option in the world. I pulled the gun out of my mouth and cried out into the darkness, 'I don't know if You are real, or if You are there, or if You did what they said You did on the cross to take away my sins, but if You are, if You don't do something in me right now, I'm going to pull this trigger and blow my brains out.'

"In that moment, the Jesus I so doubted accomplished the work He had died to show me. In that moment, something changed in me that completely transformed my life and thinking to this day. In that moment, the gospel of the Lord Jesus Christ, His death, burial, and resurrection on behalf of evil, broken people like me, became a reality. In that moment, change happened in ways I could never have imagined."

Chelette still had much growing to do. "When I stood that evening, I still had the same family and the same abuser who would again and again try to do things with me, I still had the same strained relationships and those feelings of otherness. But I also knew I had a heavenly Father who would never leave me or forsake me, and someone who promised to be a Father to the fatherless."

That event happened more than thirty years ago, and for most of the years since, Chelette has been leading Living Hope Ministries, a group that has helped thousands more achieve "sexual and relational wholeness through Jesus Christ."

The Great "I Am"

Stories such as those of Rosaria Butterfield, Christopher Yuan, Ricky Chelette, and the thousands of other men and women who have been transformed are a source of great hope and should be a cause of celebration in the church.

Unfortunately, though, they are too often a source of division or fear. Gay activists attack such stories because they are, of course, an affront to them. They want us to believe their homosexuality is "how God made them" or—if they don't appeal to God—simply, "This is who I am."

But that position fails to take into account an important part of God's Great Redemptive Story, the story that makes up the backbone of this book: that while God made the world "good," man's rebellion means we now live in a broken world. That means saying "This is how God made me" is theologically flawed. God made the world good, but sin has marred that goodness. To say "This is who I am" does have some truth in it. We are all who we are. But who we are now is not who God intends us to be. We are all sinners in need of a Savior. The stories of Rosaria Butterfield, Christopher Yuan, and Ricky Chelette are our own stories. Only the details, the individual sins, are different. We should celebrate them as examples of what Ricky Chelette said about his own story: "God can do the impossible."

CONCLUSIONS AND A TO-DO LIST

Our culture has fully embraced the idea that sexuality is the most important part of human identity, and therefore our attractions determine who we are and justify our behavior. The church, however, can offer hope and healing and a more robust understanding of identity than that offered by a culture that actively seeks to define people down. In the future, there will be even more opportunities for the church to offer to a sexually broken culture a larger vision of human dignity, as well as the very good gifts of chastity and lifelong married love. The question is, will we be faithful to God's Word and ready to love our neighbors?

Here are a few ways you can join God's work to restore the sexual brokenness all around us:

1. Be very clear on the biblical picture for human sexuality and the Bible's view on homosexuality by reading *Washed and Waiting*

by Wesley Hill. Be very clear on how to love and respect those in the LGBT community by reading *Loving My (LGBT) Neighbor* by Glenn Stanton. And be very clear about the continuing challenges to the definition of marriage by reading *Same-Sex Marriage: A Thoughtful Approach to God's Design for Marriage* by John Stonestreet and Sean McDowell.

2. Stop telling gay jokes, and stop using slogans like "Love the sinner, hate the sin" or any others that confuse the issue by singling out certain sexual sins over others or by implying that same-sex attractions are someone's identity.

3. Start a conversation in your church to prepare members and leaders to ensure that the church has settled on and clarified its views on homosexuality, transgender, and same-sex marriage.

4. Develop a plan at your church and with your family for how to treat any LGBT visitors or friends with love and respect.

5. Be intentional about reaching out to singles, helping them properly understand and pursue chastity, and teach them a robust theology of human sexuality and marriage.

6. Be intentional about forming trusting and loving friendships with those in your life who identify as LGBT.

11

Not the Least of These

I can tell you this. This former Nixon "hatchet man" has learned more about love from Max than anyone else.

—Chuck Colson, speaking of his autistic grandson

[The disabled] embody the wisdom of God in ways that interrogate, critique, and undermine the status quo.

—Amos Yong

But when you give a feast, invite the poor, the crippled, the lame, the blind, and you will be blessed, because they cannot repay you. For you will be repaid at the resurrection of the just.

—Luke 14:13–14

Why would a good God let this happen?

It's one thing when this question is, as it so *often* is, asked by a skeptic bent on creating doubt in others about God's existence. It's another thing when asked by someone in deep physical or emotional pain. Perhaps you've even found yourself asking this question, wondering honestly, "How can *anything* good come of this?"

From a secular mind-set, pain and suffering can do nothing but prohibit our various and self-chosen pursuits of meaning and happiness. Ultimately, this mind-set has brought our culture to a place where the most vulnerable among us find their lives in danger from a very bad idea. This idea sounds loving and compassionate and goes by the popular nomenclature "death with dignity."

On November 1, 2014, Brittany Maynard—young, intelligent, and facing debilitating and extraordinarily painful days with terminal brain cancer—chose to end her own life with assistance from a physician. She had recently moved to Oregon from California, where a so-called "death with dignity" law allowed her legally to ask someone who had at one time taken a vow to "do no harm" to end her life, as she said it, on her "own terms."

But sometimes the victim of this mind-set has no say. According to Dr. Peter Saunders of the Care Not Killing alliance, "In the Netherlands . . . dementia patients are euthanized, mobile euthanasia clinics operate and the 'Groningen protocol' allows euthanasia for disabled babies. In Belgium, organs are harvested from euthanasia patients and 32 percent of all euthanasia deaths are 'without consent.'"[1]

At times, ending another's extreme suffering can *feel* like the right decision. A few weeks after Maynard's suicide, a British mom received permission from a High Court judge to euthanize her severely disabled twelve-year-old daughter. In her request to the High Court, the mother said, "My daughter is no longer my daughter, she is now merely just a shell. The light from her eyes is now gone and is replaced with fear and a longing to be at peace. Today I am appealing to you for Nancy, as I truly believe she has endured enough. For me to say that breaks my heart. But I have to say it."[2]

To read of that level of a mother's desperation in the suffering of her daughter is, of course, heartbreaking. But using the same justification, the lives of many others are taken to avoid suffering or even to avoid a disability of inconvenience. For example, in some countries, nearly 90 percent of children prenatally diagnosed as possibly having Down syndrome are aborted. In the United States, that number is about 67 percent.[3] Anyone with friends and family members with Down syndrome knows the significant challenges that come with it, but also knows the joy many of these children and adults bring to others as well.

Many mothers of children with Down syndrome report on the pressure they received from their doctors to abort and of criticism from friends, family, and even strangers for choosing not to abort. And, remember, dozens of other conditions prenatally diagnosed create similar conflicts, not to mention many permanent disabilities and terminal conditions that do as well. As Saunders says, "The right to die can so easily become the duty to die."

This is why so many organizations that represent people with disability are emphatically opposed to physician-assisted suicide. As Joni Eareckson Tada, whose story we tell in this chapter, wrote in the *Wall Street Journal*, society's goal should be to help "disabled people live independent lives with dignity," not to encourage them—or as we see in Europe, force them—to die.[4]

Undergirding the "death with dignity" movement are euphemisms that need to be clarified and exposed.[5] First, "ending your own life" is called suicide. That's what it is. The church, seeing all lives as valuable and all people with inherent dignity, has rightly rejected suicide in any and all forms as ultimately wrong.

Also, the idea that we should be able to choose suicide to live and die "on our own terms" is really a concept signifying nothing. It is, in fact, an illusion. If we were truly in control and able to live life on our own terms, wouldn't we choose not to contract a fatal illness or suffer greatly in the first place?

In a culture in which we are consistently tempted by the illusion of autonomy, we have to constantly remind ourselves of what the Christian poet John Donne wrote: "No man is an island, entire of itself . . . any man's death diminishes me, because I am involved in mankind, and therefore never send to know for whom the bell tolls; it tolls for thee."[6]

And, of course, our decisions about life, particularly those of this magnitude, are never done alone. Suicide affects others. Every time the intentional taking of a life is justified by our verbal gymnastics, it moves our culture toward an acceptance of something that ought not be. That, in turn, affects all of us.

Let us be clear: The impulse to avoid suffering and spare loved ones the pain of watching is more than understandable. It's human. But the idea that we can and should be able to go to any lengths to avoid pain and suffering, and at all costs, assumes that nothing good can come from pain and suffering. And that just isn't true.

At the center of the Christian worldview is Jesus Christ who, through His suffering, brings redemption and, through His death, brings life. And the biblical account of our human condition reveals that each of us is, in certain ways, disabled by sin and the cosmic impact of the fall, though not all disabilities are as obvious as others. Throughout history, Christ followers have been asked to walk in the footsteps of the Savior into suffering, sometimes to rescue others and sometimes because it was the path ordained by God.

In this chapter, we come face-to-face with some of these Christ followers in our day. They inspire us with their perseverance and courage, but they also instruct us in how the restoring work of Christ is present in even the most difficult of personal situations. From them we learn that a world without them would be poorer indeed. That, truly, we need to see it is possible to suffer with dignity, and that attempts to remove all disability and suffering from our world are born of a utopian fantasy that would be far worse for all of us. In our fallen condition, we are tempted by arrogance and safety and autonomy, but in reality we are in desperate need of reminders that we are mortal, fallen, and dependent on God for rescue and others for love.

Today, especially in this culture, we need these stories.

Suffering Is Sacred

It's possible that no one in recent years has more effectively personified the power of suffering to give meaning to a life than Joni Eareckson Tada.

"Joni," as she is almost universally known, was a talented teenager who enjoyed hiking, horseback riding, and swimming. Then, at the age of seventeen, she dove into Chesapeake Bay after misjudging the depth of the water. She broke her cervical vertebrae and became a quadriplegic from the shoulders down. After years of rehabilitation, religious doubt, and struggle, she told the story of her life in a 1976 autobiography that became an international bestseller. That book also launched her career as a speaker and activist for the disabled and the voiceless, including the unborn.

We should disclose straightaway that we are huge fans of Joni. She combines the vulnerability of her plight as a disabled person with a first-rate intellect and strong leadership skills that have allowed the ministry she founded, Joni and Friends, to become one of the largest Christian ministries devoted to helping the disabled in the world.

We should also say that Joni married well. Her husband, Ken Tada, has been a strong partner with Joni in her personal and professional life.

All of which is to say that she has become something of an icon in the Christian world. Now that she is in her sixties, it is common for her to receive lifetime achievement awards such as the one she recently received from the National Religious Broadcasters for her decades-long radio ministry.[7]

For her own part, though, Joni seems a bit embarrassed by all the attention. "Maybe I'm not seeing the forest for the trees, but I'm so focused on God's calling on my life, which is to share His love with special needs families and to promote a biblical worldview on disability globally. I forget about all the other things that might be happening and the perceptions people might have. I'm honored, though, that my life might serve as a role model of encouragement to other brothers and sisters in Jesus."

A key part of Joni's message to the church is that we should embrace suffering as a part of living. "All too often, we want to erase suffering out of the Christian's dictionary. After 47 years of living as a quadriplegic in a wheelchair, perhaps people look at my smile and they can see that it is hard-won. Maybe that gives me credence when I speak from this wheelchair about the sufficiency of God and His Word and His grace."

One of the ways Joni exhibited grace under fire recently was when the Academy of Motion Picture Arts and Sciences rescinded its Academy Award nomination for the song she sang for the movie *Alone Yet Not Alone*. The Academy felt the songwriter had bent the rules by emailing friends, alerting them to be on the lookout for this Christian film that might otherwise have been lost in the shuffle of big-budget Hollywood productions. But Joni refused to act like a victim, choosing instead to keep smiling and use the controversy to talk about her life and work.

Among the issues she speaks out about are abortion, euthanasia, and stem-cell research. Her message: All life has value. "Recently in Belgium and Western Europe, legislators passed a law that extended their adult euthanasia laws to children under the age of 12 with incurable conditions, which could, incidentally, include disabling conditions." Joni called it "outrageous and ridiculous" that children are rightfully banned from access to tobacco, pornography, and alcohol, "but minors can have access to three grams of Phenobarbital in their veins to kill themselves. It's ridiculous."

She added, not mincing words, "What concerns me is this continuing culture of death is promoting the premise that one is better off dead than disabled. It doesn't matter what age you are, whether you are unborn, whether you are an infant, whether you are elderly. And of course as a quadriplegic, living in a wheelchair for 47 years, this is a message that I think is straight from the pit of hell."

Joni said she loves the church, and her ministry works actively with churches around the world, but she also said, "The church still is a little schizophrenic on this issue. We as Christians here in the United States don't know what to do with suffering. Surveys have shown that many Christians feel physician-assisted suicide as an end of life option is not all that bad of an idea," though she calls the idea "abhorrent."

She said it's not just the church who is conflicted. "We want to erase the word *suffering* out of the dictionary. We're going to ibuprofen it, drug it, institutionalize it, do everything but live with it. And yet people with disabilities have to live with it each and every day."

She also says being disabled has much to teach us about being dependent on God. To make that point, she explains her own morning rituals.

> It is so hard living with quadriplegia and pushing 65 years old. When I wake up in the morning, my eyes are still closed, my head is on the pillow, and I can hear my girlfriend in the kitchen running water for coffee. I know she's going to come into the bedroom in a moment. She's going to give me a bed bath, do my toileting routines, exercise my legs, strap on my corset, pull up my slacks, put on my blouse, sling me into a wheelchair. Then she will push me to the bathroom, brush my teeth, brush my hair, and blow my nose. I haven't even opened my eyes yet and I'm already exhausted. I'm thinking, "I have no strength for this. God I am so tired of being a quadriplegic. I'm so tired of this. I have no ability to do this today, but I can do all things through you if you strengthen me. So would you please empower me today? Infuse within me today the grace needed to help me to open my eyes and face the day with a bright attitude, your attitude." I tell you what, when I pray that way—and it happens almost every morning—by the time

my girlfriend does come into the bedroom with that cup of coffee, I've got a smile sent straight from heaven.

And it's not just Joni's own relationship with God that grows by dealing with her disability, but those around her too. "I know in the morning before I wake up my eyes, I could choose to be complaining. I could choose to become demoralized. I could choose to think that I'm a burden on others," she said.

> But I refuse to do that because God's Word tells me the truth. The truth is every time that girlfriend of mine gets me up in the morning, she is enlarging her eternal estate. She is gaining a greater capacity for service and worship and joy in heaven. She gets to experience that by helping me. Looking at life that way helps me be courageous about my own experience with a disability. God can use me every time I ask for a drink of water. Every time I ask for someone to empty my leg bag, they have a chance to serve sacrificially, and that is helping them.

A Church-Based Ministry

Joni Eareckson Tada's life has been dedicated to helping the local church embrace suffering both as a means of spiritual growth and as a way to love neighbors who need extra love to navigate life.

One of the churches that has taken her up on that challenge is McLean Bible Church in the Washington, DC, suburbs. Jackie Mills-Fernald leads Access Ministry there, and she says she is on a quest to help her church be a welcoming place for those with disabilities.[8]

Because kids and families with disabilities face additional stresses, and because being in public adds to that stress, she said, often people see persons with disabilities, especially children, at their worst. "People see a kid melting down and think, 'C'mon, can't you parent better than that?'

"The effort began more than a decade ago with four students in children's ministry who needed a level of help we couldn't provide at that time," explained Mills-Fernald. "Now we have 25 different programs at two campuses serving 500 families with disabled members, using 600 volunteers. We have moved from just making Sunday mornings work to supporting families with a holistic approach addressing physical and spiritual needs."

What does all that mean for a parent of a disabled child? Often it means regaining a healthy perspective after a time of respite. The Access Break-out and Breakaway respite services offer five hours of fun activities for a reasonable fee with two nurses on-site to administer medication and care for this more fragile and accident-prone population. Experienced professionals manage the dreaded moment of drop-off: Therapy dogs at the check-in line hold the attention of children as their parents register. Those who won't let go are offered the chance to "have Mason walk you in." Escort service from a genial shepherd is rarely declined.

Aundrea Foster is now on staff with Access but remembers well her first encounters with the program as the mother of a son with autism looking for help. Volunteers "were welcoming and smiling and glad to see us. We were so used to getting stares because our son was melting down." She said the ministry probably saved her marriage. "I know the staff could see it in my face the first time we came. We were in a dark place as a family. Our spirits were broken. We had basically stayed in the house for two years following our son's diagnosis. Knowing he would be safe for a couple of hours made all the difference."

Foster's assertion that the ministry may have saved her marriage is not hyperbole. Parents of special needs children have a greater than 80 percent chance of divorce.

Access also offers a yearly conference, a monthly community lecture series, and an array of parent support groups, mentoring programs, friendship clubs, and Sunday morning classes. Its four-week summer camp for disabled kids and their siblings comes without the sticker shock of a typical special needs camp, but with Access's characteristic compassion. "I kept waiting for that call from the camp saying, 'Um, this isn't working out,'" Foster said. "Our son had a bunch of bad days and finally I said to his counselor, 'If you want to pull him out, that's OK.' She just looked at me and said, 'No. That's not what we do here. We will find a way to work it out.'"

Foster was so taken aback that she told her husband, "I want to see what this church is all about." On a Sunday morning they put their son in a Beautiful Blessings class and, Foster says, "For the first time since he was a baby we were able to sit in a pew and worship together."

Dealing with Life's Hard

None of us are immune from suffering, and suffering can sometimes find us when we think things are going great.

Kara Tippetts and her husband, Jason, were in just that position. They were well educated, outgoing, and had four beautiful children and a thriving new church that Jason started and serves as pastor. But soon after moving to Colorado Springs in 2011 to start that church, Tippetts discovered she had breast cancer. Despite aggressive treatment, the cancer spread throughout her body.[9]

Kara describes herself as a terrible sick person. She hates being sick, so it might have been easy for her to retreat into self-pity. Instead, she decided to begin a blog about her experiences that she calls "Mundane Faithfulness." Her remarkable transparency soon won her as many as twenty thousand daily page views. A publisher discovered the blog and helped her release her first book, *The Hardest Peace: Expecting Grace in the Midst of Life's Hard*.[10]

The subtitle of the book at first feels incomplete. You almost want to finish the sentence for her: "life's hard stuff" or "life's hard times" or something. But Kara left the title intentionally ambiguous. "I am not trying to win at having the hardest story," she said. "I'm trying to get us all to look for God's grace in the midst of any 'hard.' Though my hard is cancer, each of us faces hard every single day. We have an expectation of what life would be, and yet it becomes unmet."

Soon after Kara and Jason moved to the west side of Colorado Springs to plant a church, the Waldo Canyon fire came, in Kara's words, "screaming down that ridge." She points from the front porch of her house to a blackened ridge to the west. The Waldo Canyon fire made national news as the largest fire in the history of Colorado. More than 330 homes were burned to the ground. But it was also an opportunity for the Christians of Colorado Springs—a town home to hundreds of prominent Christian ministries—to respond.

"That was the side of town that we had chosen to do the church plant. It was very clear to us that it was a door opening," Kara said. "And people came out of those doors, talking to each other about what happened. It was really a beautiful moment of God opening the doors for community in the brokenness of that."

Tippetts didn't know it then, but God was also preparing her for something else. "Ten days after that is when I found the lump and learned I had breast cancer."

With four small children and a life she loved, she was not about to roll over and let the cancer win. She and Jason chose to fight aggressively: a double mastectomy, reconstruction, and then radiation. "We started our church plant in the midst of radiation," she said. "God has just been blessing our work. There's just a real sense of brokenness in our community, so we have this really beautiful church with people who know that we need to do this. There are seven of us in our community with cancer, in our small little community of about 200 now."

But with the blessings came more trials. In fall 2013, Tippetts discovered the cancer had spread. She was diagnosed with stage four metastatic cancer, which means the cancer had gone into her blood and moved to her vital organs. She had a radical hysterectomy. Her story, she said, is one of "cancer growing and Jason and I looking for Jesus in the midst of it."

She said her blog has helped her—and many—look for and find Jesus in the midst of suffering. The name of the blog, "Mundane Faithfulness," comes from a quote by the reformer Martin Luther: "What will you do in the mundane days of faithfulness?"

"My husband had preached on that idea often," she said. And she said that as a mother she felt she had lived out this idea of remaining faithful not in the big, heroic moments, but in the small and mundane moments. "As a mom, most of my days are like Groundhog Day. Every day is the same: laundry, dishes, dinners. How do you see Jesus in the midst of it and how do you not just get through it, but live well?"

But when you have cancer, sometimes doing just the mundane things becomes heroic. The chemotherapy makes Tippetts nauseated, "like car sickness," she said. The drugs she takes to help rapidly grow white blood cells cause great pain. "Jason and I will be going out to an event at night, and he'll say, 'Do you feel good?' And I look at him and I say, 'Nope, let's go.' I just have to learn to live, even when I feel horrible."

You might think Kara would be resentful toward God. After all, she had a great husband, great marriage, great kids, a calling in her life—and then this cancer came along and threatened to rip it all away. It would be easy to say, "Why, God? Why?"

But Kara has a different perspective. She says suffering is not the opposite of or the absence of God's goodness. In fact, it may be a sign of it. "Look at how our salvation was made. It was through the suffering of Jesus. Philippians says we get to partner with Jesus in suffering, so it's a calling of us all. I think we forget that. I think somewhere we have blended this American culture into our faith and forgotten that suffering is very much a part of what we're all called to."

Recently Kara recounted an episode with her second-born son, Harper. "He wanted to know if his mommy was going to die of old age or cancer." It was a hard question, and at the point he asked it, an impossible question to answer. So, she said, "We just lay in bed and cried together. I said, 'Harper, will Jesus be good to us in either answer?' We just cried. But we believe that truth."

The Ultimate Sacrifice

Father Thomas Vander Woude, pastor at Holy Trinity Catholic Church in Gainesville, Virginia, has a special place in his heart for children born with Down syndrome. He believes their lives are sacred, and he actively works to defend them. In fact, a parish campaign to save one such life grabbed national headlines.[11]

In 2013, Vander Woude got wind of a young couple in another state whose unborn child had been diagnosed with Down syndrome. The couple made the decision that, as we discussed in chapter 4, around 67 percent of American parents in their shoes make. They decided to abort their baby. Because the pregnancy was almost six months along, they had just days before the legal cutoff for abortions in their state. But Vander Woude had other ideas.

He contacted the parents and asked them to agree to a deal. If he could find adoptive parents for the child before the legal deadline to abort, they would allow the child to live. The couple agreed, and so Vander Woude and a volunteer sent messages via the church's social network accounts, pleading for a family willing to agree to adopt the baby.

Over nine hundred people responded, some from as far away as England and the Netherlands, ready to make the life-changing decision to adopt a child with special needs. As the torrent subsided, Vander Woude placed three of the families in contact with the expectant parents and an adoption agency for interviews. The child was saved. But to understand this story, and why these children are so special to Vander Woude, you need to know another story. Vander Woude has a brother with Down syndrome, Joseph, who is at the center of another story that makes the first one all the more poignant.

In 2008, Joseph fell through a decaying septic tank in his family's backyard. The filth submerged Joseph over his head. In a heroic act of self-sacrificial love, Father Thomas Vander Woude's father, Thomas Sr., leapt into the septic tank and literally sank below the filth, holding Joseph above his head until help came. Tragically, in saving his son, Thomas Sr. drowned.[12]

Five years after Father Thomas Vander Woude officiated at his dad's funeral, he, too, saved the life of a child with Down syndrome. You might say he got his pro-life views honestly, inheriting them from his father. We think he made both his father and his heavenly Father proud.

C. Jimmy Lin and the Rare Genomics Institute

Sometimes God calls us to share in His suffering, like Joni Eareckson Tada and Kara Tippetts. Sometimes He calls us to make an incredible sacrifice, like Thomas Vander Woude Sr. Each path demonstrates to a skeptical world that we really believe what we say we believe.

But sometimes God calls us to fight back against the darkness with our gifts and abilities. That's what C. Jimmy Lin is doing.

On his way to both a medical doctor's degree and a PhD, Lin learned something that broke his heart. Those seeking a cure for those relatively few well-known diseases have big public relations machines and huge funding behind them. But the overwhelming majority of diseases that afflict humans are less well known, and the researchers fighting these diseases are not well funded. Yet, in the aggregate, these so-called "orphan diseases" afflict tens of millions of people. In fact, Lin says there are more than seven thousand orphan diseases afflicting more than 350 million people.[13] Many of these diseases are so rare that the people who have them can't even get reliable diagnoses, much less effective treatment.

"There are millions of kids wandering from place to place that no one is really helping," Lin said.[14]

Motivated by his Christian faith and compassion for those who suffer from these orphan diseases, Lin, and his colleagues, created the Rare Genomics Institute (RGI).

The Rare Genomics Institute uses crowdfunding to help people with rare diseases sequence their DNA. The price of sequencing one's DNA has fallen dramatically. It took more than $3 billion and fifteen years to sequence the first human genome. Today you or I can have our DNA sequenced for about $7,500. RGI selects people to feature on its website, and supporters donate the money for a genetic sequencing. Partnering with top medical institutions, RGI helps custom design personalized research projects that address any genetic abnormalities that might be contributing to or causing these rare diseases.

In 2012, RGI announced its first crowdfunded gene sequencing. That process uncovered the cause of a disease afflicting Maya Nieder, then four years old. The girl was nonresponsive, and her doctors were not sure if she could hear her parents when they spoke to her. When Lin's team posted Nieder's story online, donors gave $3,500 toward the sequencing and Yale University contributed the rest. The results, RGI said, pointed to a flaw in a gene crucial to fetal development. A research team is looking into gene therapy for the girl and others like her who may be afflicted with a similar genetic flaw.

While a cure was not yet available for Maya's family, Lin's team was able to confirm that Maya was not cognitively impaired. Years after their daughter became nonresponsive, these parents discovered that she could in fact hear them every time they told her they loved her. And they are able to use adaptive technologies so she can learn and develop.[15]

To date, hundreds of people, mostly children, have been profiled and funded by the RGI site. "The Bible is clear that we are to look after orphans," Lin said. "Orphan diseases may not have been what the Bible was talking about, but if we can help cure some of these orphan diseases, we might be able to help a few orphans along the way."[16]

CONCLUSION AND A TO-DO LIST

Each and every one of us is disabled by sin. Each of us will experience life's hard. Most of us don't wear our disability on the outside like

Joni Eareckson Tada or the children whom Jimmy Lin seeks to serve and help, but we all are—in one way or another—disabled by sin.

For children with Down syndrome and other prenatally diagnosable conditions, our culture is a dangerous place, attempting to systemically eliminate them from our world. The same is the case for many who suffer as the movement toward embracing euthanasia gains steam. But our world will be poorer if we lose those who demonstrate to us what it means to "suffer redemptively."

God's redemptive work among those with disabilities clearly pictures His heart for His people. If you would like to join this work, here are some next steps:

1. Read *Dancing with Max* by Emily Colson and *The Hardest Peace* by Kara Tippetts to learn more about God's redemptive work in suffering. Read *Christian Bioethics: A Guide for Pastors, Health Care Professionals, and Families* by C. Ben Mitchell and D. Joy Riley to determine ethical positions on bioethical questions.

2. Begin a study group in your church using the curriculum *Beyond Suffering* from the Christian Institute on Disability from Joni and Friends.

3. Visit the Rare Genomics Institute website and consider supporting their work.

4. Initiate an evaluation process at your church to ensure that it is fully accessible for those with disability. Joni and Friends can help.

5. Personally get to know someone with a disability and serve them in any way you can. Listen to their stories and tell those stories to others.

6. Refuse those prenatal tests that lead to the recommendation of abortion and carefully prepare your end-of-life plans to avoid any temptations toward physician-assisted suicide.

12

Giving Marriage to the World, Once Again

This triangle of truisms, of father, mother and child, cannot be destroyed; it can only destroy those civilizations which disregard it.

—G. K. Chesterton

[Jesus] answered, "Have you not read that he who created them from the beginning made them male and female, and said, 'Therefore a man shall leave his father and his mother and hold fast to his wife, and the two shall become one flesh'?"

—Matthew 19:4–5

God did not begin the world with a government or even a church. He started it with a wedding. That's also how it will end. In Genesis we find Adam and Eve, and in Revelation we celebrate the restoration of all things with the wedding feast of the Lamb: the consummation of history in the final and everlasting coming together of Christ and His church.[1]

Marriage was built into the fabric of this world from the very beginning of time. Through marriage, God provided the basic building block of all civilizations, establishing the context within which future generations would be procreated and preserved. In other words, marriage matters.

It was to this design that Jesus pointed the legal experts of His day, who were asking about divorce policy according to the Mosaic Law. It's notable that this Jewish rabbi would refer other Jewish leaders beyond their law to the Garden of Eden, to what was true "from the beginning" (Matt. 19:4–6). Specifically, in His answer to the Pharisees, Jesus identified three aspects of marriage that God wove into the fabric of humanity in creation.

First, Jesus pointed to *sexual diversity* as an essential part of our created design. "Have you not read that he who created them from the beginning made them male and female," Jesus said (19:4). That different but complementary design is not incidental. In fact, it is the grounding for the other aspects Jesus mentions.

Second, because God made them male and female, a *oneness* is achieved in, and only in, marriage. "Therefore, a man shall leave his father and mother and hold fast to his wife, and the two shall become one flesh." This reality that Jesus observes is obvious in our biological makeups. Other than in cases of disability, each of us has the capacity to perform every biological function by ourselves, except one. The procreative process takes two, and requires male and female. The two become one.

The oneness is also very clear in the Genesis account. No living thing, until God made woman, was capable of becoming one flesh with the man. After stating numerous times that His creation was "good," and before the fall, God pronounced the absence of woman as being "not good." Why? Because God gave Adam a job: to fill and form the earth. Without a helper, man was incapable of accomplishing God's purposes for humanity (2:18).

It's curious that Genesis specifically says that the animals were not suitable helpers (2:20). That sounds silly to us today, but think about it. Why aren't animals the sort of help man needs? From the earliest civilizations, animals have been known to be quite useful. They've been used to build up, tear down, carry, till, farm, and perform all kinds of culture-building activities. They aren't bad as far as the "forming" work goes. But what the animals couldn't help with is the "filling." The woman, of course, could (and did).

Together, man and woman could procreate, which would produce others who would also procreate and so on and so on. Because of God's design for His image bearers, they could accomplish their God-given purpose. Of course, marriage is not required for procreation to occur, but in marriage, two become one, united in every possible way: in mind and in body and in purpose. Husbands and wives are more than companions. They are *helpers*. Together, they produce, protect, and preserve future generations of image bearers. We know that when a baby is born, there is a mother nearby. Marriage ensures that the father is also nearby, and together they are committed to the future of their children.

Third, Jesus also points out the *permanence* God intended for marriage. "What therefore God has joined together, let not man separate" (Matt. 19:6). For those who have experienced divorce or abuse, marriage may not seem like the great option it really is. Because failed marriages are the source of so much *insecurity* and *instability*, it is tempting to blame marriage itself. But the fact that failed marriages leave such a negative wake for those involved helps explain why healthy marriages leave such a positive wake. Marriage is a relationship unique from all others. When His questioners respond with the policies of divorce from Mosaic Law, Jesus responds that divorce was an *accommodation* provided only because of the hardness of their hearts. But He quickly adds, "from the beginning *it was not so*" (Matt. 19:8, emphasis added). Jesus understood marriage to be a permanent arrangement.

From Jesus's words, we can conclude that marriage is an institution for all humans and not only for Christians. Christians and non-Christians alike can fulfill the design described in Scripture. The church didn't create marriage, but rather, it recognizes it as a gift of God to His image bearers. Nor is marriage a political institution that belongs to the state. It is a pre-political institution. The state doesn't create marriage, either. Like the church, it can only recognize it. Marriage will always be what marriage was created to be, no matter what activist judges, runaway legislatures, or a majority of voters decide.

Throughout the New Testament, the purpose of marriage as described in Genesis and endorsed by Jesus is never negated. Rather, it is clarified. As created, marriage enabled male and female to reflect God's image together. As redeemed, marriage reflects Christ's love for the church. As created, marriage enabled God's image bearers to spread His rule over all the earth. As redeemed, marriage disciples both current and future generations to spread the gospel over all the earth. As created, marriage is the foundation of social order. As redeemed, marriage commits us to live and restrain our passions for the good of others.

In no way does this mean that only married people can achieve their human purpose and contribute significantly to God's world. The contributions of widows, children, teens, and other singles are just as important as the contributions of married couples, whether those contributions are made in the church or in society. However, marriage plays a central role in teaching future generations and sustaining society. After all, not everyone has children, but everyone does have parents. Strong marriages strengthen the character of future generations, and everyone, whether married or single, benefits.

Marriage unites two individuals in a powerful and public way. People, from old friends to new acquaintances, think of married couples together, and in many social and legal settings, they will be treated as a single unit. There are domestic, financial, conjugal, and familial implications. They have new benefits and responsibilities because of their decision to marry. Together, they are their own entity.

Of course, other types of couples share life together but are not considered a single entity, at least not in the same way. Perhaps two recent college grads, for example, have decided to prolong their roommate arrangement to extend the party or cheapen the rent. They share an Xbox and an apartment, but they are not married just because they share domestic life.

Or imagine two elderly ladies who have lived together for nearly twenty years: a widow whose husband succumbed to cancer and her sister. They care deeply for one another, share everything from their most precious memories to a checking account. They have given each other medical power of attorney and haven't missed an episode of *Jeopardy* since 1995. Theirs is a beautifully committed relationship, but it is not a marriage.

Or what of a romantically involved couple who live together? If you didn't know better, you might even guess they were married, but in fact, they just never got around to tying the knot. They love each other, have children, share a mortgage payment, and dream of retiring together somewhere on a beach. Despite the strong resemblance of their relationship to marriage, neither the culture nor the law considers their relationship to be marriage because there was no public commitment to be faithful to each other for life.

Marriage is a relationship distinct from all others. Neither proximity nor depth of affection nor a sincere commitment to love each other and stay together for life is, on its own, enough to make a relationship marriage. That marriage is unique has been recognized across times and cultures, not least of which by governments who deem it necessary to regulate and, at times, incentivize it. Yet those governments don't deem it necessary to do the same with other real, substantial relationships. Somehow, across time and place, the "oneness" of the marital union is recognizable.

The State of Marriage

As important as it is, marriage in America is not doing well. Data from Pew Research shows that barely half of adults in the United States are married. That's an all-time low. If this trend continues, singles will soon make up the majority of the adult U.S. population.

What's more, the median age of first marriage for both men and women is higher than ever before. In other words, by the time the shrinking cohort that does decide to marry reaches the altar, they're already flirting with thirty.[2]

Sexual behavior before marriage also has a significant impact on marriage success. The National Marriage Project at the University of Virginia found that the way couples "conduct their romantic lives before they tie the knot is linked to their odds of having happy marriages." Though about 90 percent of couples today have sex before marriage, the 23 percent who only sleep with their future spouse have higher marriage stability than the vast majority who sleep around prior to their wedding day.[3] Single life decisions impact future marriages profoundly.

Reversing the Decline

And yet there's also much good news when it comes to marriage. To begin with, researchers both Christian and secular agree that couples in faithful, long-term marriages are happier and healthier, and have happier, healthier, and more successful children. Plus, married couples are, on average, better off financially.

There's more good news about Christian marriages: Despite what you may have read, Christians do not divorce at the same rate as the rest of the world. The idea that the divorce rate of Christians is equal to or perhaps even higher than non-Christians comes from a 2008 Barna Group survey which suggested that 32 percent of "born-again Christians" have divorced at least once. The figure for non–born-again adults was 33 percent.[4]

These statistics seem pretty straightforward and easy to understand. But sociologist Bradley Wright, who has studied both the Barna study and other more exhaustive research, has concluded, "They're just not true." His suspicions of the data first came when he went through a "rough patch" in his own marriage. "We got a lot of help from the church we attended," he said. "To me, it didn't make sense that this sort of support wasn't working for Christians on a large scale. So I did the research and found that it does. Evangelicals have a lower divorce rate."[5]

So what about the other study? The problem, Wright said, is with the methodology that was used: including people in the Christian group because they're not something else, or excluding them from the evangelical group because they don't self-identify as evangelicals.

More exhaustive surveys of Americans and their behaviors and beliefs reveal a very different picture. For example, the General Social Survey, a long-term survey conducted by the University of Chicago, is the best source of data about marriage and religion. According to the GSS, about 50 percent of adults with no religious affiliation are divorced. Those who identify as evangelicals have a 46 percent divorce rate. That's still scandalously high, but it is lower by a statistically significant amount. And according to Wright, even these statistics do not tell the whole story. Among those who attend church weekly, the rate falls to 38 percent, compared to 60 percent for those who never attend church. So practicing one's faith matters more than just claiming it. Also, those couples who did not cohabit and remained faithful in their marriages had an even higher marital success rate.

The bottom line is that Christians who actively practice their faith and behave in ways the Bible says Christians should behave have a likelihood of marital success at 80 percent or more.[6]

If that's true, then why all the bad press? The answer is . . . a bad press! Wright says mainstream media are quick to paint gloomy pictures of Christians because these negative stereotypes reinforce their own ideologies and sell well.[7] But Christian media and Christian celebrity authors also are quick to promote these sorts of stereotypes because, again, they sell well. "They'll find the worst statistics, and tell them in their first chapter, and then spend the next eight chapters telling you how to fix the problem," Wright said.

It's a strategy that sells books and fills seminars, but it also misrepresents Christianity and the many Christians who, by following biblical principles, are seeing good fruit in their married lives. And so, in this chapter we celebrate long-lasting marriages. It's our way of saying that it is possible to remain committed to your spouse over a lifetime, and there are plenty of examples to prove it.

Oh Sweet Lorraine: The Beauty of a Long Marriage

One of the most effective forms of criticism is to present a more beautiful alternative. Michelangelo said, "I criticize by creating something beautiful." The great nineteenth-century preacher Dwight L. Moody reportedly said, "The best way to show that a stick is crooked is not to argue about it or to spend time denouncing it, but to lay a straight stick alongside it."

That's why the best way for Christians to affirm marriage and criticize a culture in which marriage is devalued and debased is to get married and stay married. The second best way is to celebrate godly marriages wherever we find them. That's why, for example, *WORLD* ran a two-year marriage longevity series that celebrated marriages of at least thirty-five years or more. What is striking about these marriages is not that they are filled with heroic deeds or extraordinary circumstances, though some were, but how they exhibited what Kara Tippetts—whom we spoke of in the last chapter—calls "mundane faithfulness." When tempted to become unfaithful, they simply chose to remain faithful. They did the next right thing. Soon, a daily decision became a habit. Before long, their habits had shaped who they had become.

This sort of mundane faithfulness is rare these days, but for one man, it led to him becoming a surprise national phenomenon in 2013.

Fred Stobaugh was ninety-five in 2013, but he still vividly remembered the year 1938. It was the year he met Lorraine at an A&W Root Beer stand in Peoria, Illinois. Soon after that initial meeting, they fell in love and were married.[8]

Almost exactly seventy-five years later, Lorraine died, leaving her husband and their lifetime together behind. About six weeks later, still grieving for her, Fred heard about an on-line singer-songwriter contest sponsored by Green Shoe Studio, a local music business.

Fred, who had never written music before, decided to enter the contest with a tribute to Lorraine, who shared his love of music. "I just sat here kind of hummin' a little bit and it finally came to me," he said.

What came to him was a simple but powerful song, "Oh Sweet Lorraine." It talked about their life together and how Fred still longed for his bride. He wrote the song down, put it in a large envelope, and mailed it in to the contest.

Green Shoe's Jacob Colgan was intrigued by the simple envelope and its contents, even though it was clear Fred couldn't win the contest because he hadn't recorded his song, as the rules stipulated. But Green Shoe Studio has a unique motto: "To change our community, one dream at a time." So rather than throw Fred's entry and lifelong memories away, Colgan decided to learn more about the man who wrote the poignant lyrics.

"I started to read the lyrics," he said, "and was touched by the song. Without even meeting Fred we thought, 'We're going to do something.'" So Green Shoe offered to provide their professional music and recording services to bring "Oh Sweet Lorraine" to life—for free.

That might have been the end of a sweet love story—but then something quite unpredictable happened. Green Shoe posted a video of the song and the story behind it on YouTube.[9] It went viral. Disc jockeys started playing the song on the radio. Green Shoe released it as a single and it entered the Billboard Hot 100, topping out at number 42, making Fred Stobaugh the oldest person ever to have a Billboard Hot 100 hit. As of this writing, the YouTube video has been viewed more than seven million times.

Although we are unsure of Colgan's faith commitments, our hats go off to Green Shoe Studio. They didn't have to care about a bereaved man's love for his departed wife, but they did—and we're all the richer for it. We also can't help but observe that for all the talk today in our culture that traditional one man–one woman marriage is no longer relevant in a culture with all manner of sexual options, something about Fred and Lorraine's marriage still strikes close to the heart of even jaded, postmodern Americans. Fred Stobaugh, we're sure, had no intention of denouncing the current state of marriage. He simply celebrated his own, and millions of people got the message.

From Shattered Dreams to a Life's Work

Stories of long-lasting marriages help us see at least two things. First, we see that real love and successful marriages are not what we see on television or in the movies. They involve commitment. As sociologist Mark Regnerus writes, "Young adults want to know that it's possible for two fellow believers to stay happy together for a lifetime, and they need to hear how the generations preceding them did it."[10] It is also important to see that while no one wants to be in a permanently unhappy state, life and marriage are not and should not be about being happy all the time. The joy that comes from staying committed through the hard times is what really matters. Whatever you think you may or may not have in common with your spouse when you are young and tempted to bail out on a marriage, keep in mind that by the time you've been married for forty years, you will have more in common with your spouse—shared experiences, shared trials and triumphs—than any other person on the planet. And the most important thing you will have in common is a monumental shared achievement: the marriage itself.

A second thing many who have had long marriages can teach us is to look for the new direction in the shattered dream.

That's what happened to Lamar and Twynette Hood when they heard their daughter Jennifer tested positive for Down syndrome: "It was like being hit by a truck," Lamar remembers. "I just didn't believe God would do this to me."[11]

Twynette, Lamar's wife of two years, was waiting at home, praying that their new daughter would be "normal." Her intuition as a mother told her otherwise. Jennifer's disability would ultimately reform their marriage.

Today, after forty-two years together, the Hoods draw attention wherever they go: Lamar, Twynette, and Jennifer—still living at home—with Amy, Amanda, and Jason, three more Hoods, all adopted, all with Down syndrome. The Hoods' dream-shattering crisis has become a mission of mercy.

She was fifteen and he was seventeen when Lamar invited Twynette to a church sweetheart banquet. Three years later, Lamar proposed. "God just put her in my life. He knew exactly who I needed."

After the wedding, Lamar worked as a banker and took night classes to finish college. Twynette clerked at a car dealership. They were busy building the happy life they had planned together, and God was not on their calendar.

Four months after Lamar graduated, Jennifer was born. Her doctors suspected Down syndrome. While waiting for conclusive test results, Lamar assumed the baby was fine. Twynette did not. "We were on opposite ends. He could not tolerate me expressing my feelings."

When the diagnosis finally came, Lamar was crushed. He still tears up when he tells the story. Twynette says, "I never saw Lamar cry before Jennifer was born." In their brokenness, the Hoods drew near to Christ. His comfort in their grief forged a new intimacy of shared suffering and hope. A local church helped the Hoods adjust to Jennifer's disability by embracing her. "Everybody's arms at church opened up," Twynette said. They provided meals, babysitting, and friendship. And the Hoods began to sketch a new plan for a happy life together.

Nine years later, God stirred a desire in Twynette to adopt a child with special needs. Lamar was hesitant. "I didn't think I could love another child that was not my own." Plus adoption was expensive. Lamar prayed, and God gave him the faith he needed. "We can't do it, Lord, but You can."

Within months, God sent Amy into the Hood family. Later, they added Amanda and Jason. Each child's adoption began with a phone call. A voice said, "We have a baby with Down syndrome." And each time, Lamar and Twynette said yes.

When couples in the Hoods' community grieve for their children, Lamar and Twynette pass on the comfort God gave them in their initial sorrow. As Lamar says, "God gave us Jennifer to show us our future and give us our calling—and to bring us to Him."

CONCLUSION AND A TO-DO LIST

Marriage has a bad rap in our society, as does Christian sexual morality. Each is assumed to spoil the sexually free fun a society without religious hang-ups wants to have. The truth is different. God created marriage as a context in which sexuality can be truly free, a context that not only unites the couple that chooses matrimony but also protects and best preserves future generations. Marriage matters to the world. It's one of God's best gifts to us.

How can you become involved in God's redeeming work to restore the family in America?

1. To understand the primary purpose of the institution of marriage, read *What Is Marriage? Man and Woman: A Defense* by Ryan T. Anderson, Sherif Girgis, and Robert P. George. To understand how significantly different it is from marriage's greatest impostor, cohabitation, read *The Ring Makes All the Difference: The Hidden Consequences of Cohabitation and the Strong Benefits of Marriage* by Glenn T. Stanton.

2. Invite friends and family to your house for a viewing of the film *Irreplaceable: The Movie* and afterward discuss the implications of the family for a society.

3. Initiate a small group study at your church using *The Family Project* by Focus on the Family. Be sure to clarify *what marriage is*, not just how to do it.

4. If you are a younger couple headed toward marriage, find an older married couple and ask them questions about their life and experience. If you are an older couple, even if (maybe especially if) your married life has been full of struggles, find a younger couple and invite them into your home. Pastors can be especially effective in connecting couples across generational lines.

5. Evaluate the singles ministry in your church, as well as whether opportunities are granted to singles to lead and serve. Teach clearly about the various types of love found in Scripture (see *The Four Loves* by C. S. Lewis).

6. Always, always, always proclaim the redemptive potential of the gospel of Christ and the forgiveness of sin and restoration of relationships that it promises.

7. Create contexts, personally or through church, for Christ-following singles to meet. Encourage, but don't idolize, marriage.

8. Whenever possible (in sermons, conversations, songs, movies, blog posts, tweets, and wherever), tell the stories of lifelong married love. Include especially the redemptive stories of those who overcame significant struggle and hardship, but don't gloss over the difficulties. There are no fairy tales in real life.

13

Suffer the Little Children

How can you say there are too many children in the world?
That's like saying there are too many flowers.

—Mother Teresa

If anybody understands God's ardor for his children,
it's someone who has rescued an orphan from despair,
for that is what God has done for us. God has adopted
you. God sought you, found you, signed the papers and
took you home.

—Max Lucado[1]

You are the helper of the fatherless. . . . You have heard the
desire of the humble; You will prepare their heart; You
will cause Your ear to hear, to do justice to the fatherless and the oppressed, that the man of the earth may
oppress no more.

—Psalm 10:14, 17–18 (NJKV)

Have you ever said to yourself, "If I just knew what God wanted me
to do, I would do it"? A lot of us, in all kinds of different situations,

174

struggle to know God's will. That may be why we see so many Christian books with words like "God's purpose" and "God's plan" in them.

But consider these words from Scripture: "Religion that is pure and undefiled before God, the Father, is this: to visit orphans and widows in their affliction" (James 1:27).

It is hard to imagine how God could be any more clear or direct. Thus, it's hard to imagine how anyone who claims to be a follower of Christ should not be engaged, in some way, in widow and orphan care. Perhaps you are not called to run an orphanage or look after the widows in your community as a full-time vocation. But if these activities are indeed "pure religion," shouldn't all of us be engaged at some level?

The great news is that many Christians take this charge seriously. Look across America for adoption agencies, foster parents, programs for abandoned and at-risk teens. You will easily find them, and when you do, you will most likely find Christians at work.

Also, by this point in our discussion of God's people at work, this should be increasingly clear: As the old children's song goes, the "head bone connected to the neck bone, the neck bone connected to the back bone." In other words, in the genius of God's economy, all of God's people engaged in God's calling on their lives have a strange and beautiful way of including and complementing all the others.

To help us see that point, let's return to an organization we first met in chapter 2. Detroit's Evangel Ministries, led by Chris Brooks, has realized that declaring the gospel, while vital, is not enough for Christians who want to be heard in a post-Christian world.[2] Our declarations of the gospel seem to be increasingly falling on deaf ears. A skeptical post-Christian world answers back, "Prove it. You say Jesus transforms. Okay, fine. Show me a transformed life, a transformed community, a transformed culture."

In part as a response to that challenge, Evangel Ministries has augmented Brooks's "urban apologetics" approach with just such demonstrations of transformation. One example: "Our church has embraced adoption and foster care in a huge way," Brooks said. "The foster care system is disproportionately populated by minority children. There has been an antagonistic relationship with the state because of the perception that the state somehow profits from pulling our children out of our homes.

"But as we were studying Scripture, talking about the Father God, we encountered the language of adoption in Ephesians 1 and the orphan and the widow in James 1:27. We had to ask, 'What is our obligation to the orphans in our community?'

"We have a goal that there would be no children in our community waiting for a home. There are about 2,000 children waiting, and our goal is to be able to find 2,000 homes for them. We have 3,000 churches in Detroit. So if each church can get just one family to adopt, we can eliminate the need for children to wait. That is a matter of praxis and apologetics: showing how the gospel makes a difference."

Wait No More

Jim Daly, president of Focus on the Family, must be reading from the same playbook as Chris Brooks—the Bible—because they both came up with the same question: Can Christians get kids—and not just a few kids, but a mass number of kids—out of the foster care system and into "forever homes"?

The answer, it turns out, is an emphatic "Yes." The two men also came up with the same idea.

When the Colorado Springs–based ministry Focus on the Family began spearheading the "Wait No More" adoption initiative in November 2008, the state had eight thousand children in foster care.[3] That number included about eight hundred children who were eligible for adoption because their parents had lost parental rights after the state found serious problems in their homes.

By early 2010, five hundred of those eight hundred children had been adopted, according to Sharen Ford, manager of permanency services for the Colorado Department of Human Services. In 2009 alone in Colorado, more than one thousand adoptions became final.

"I'm stunned by the number of kids we've moved off the waiting list," Daly told the *Denver Post*. "I was one of those kids—a kid that doesn't have a mom and dad. I was never adopted, but I was very appreciative of the people who came along to mentor me."[4]

Daly said orphan care is a core mission of Christianity. "If my Bible math is right, God reminds us 47 times to take care of widows and orphans," Daly said. "This country has something like 300,000 churches and 130,000 orphans. The math is pretty simple."

Pastor Rick Warren agrees. In May 2010, he hosted a "civil forum" on the subject of adoption and foster care at the church he pastors, Saddleback Church in Southern California. More than eight hundred people attended, and thousands more watched via webcast from their homes. "Orphans and vulnerable children are not a cause," Warren told the group. "They are a biblical and social mandate we can't ignore. A country half the size of the U.S.—that's how many orphans there are in the world. We're not talking about a small problem."[5]

Both Daly and Ford said the Colorado initiative shows what can happen when churches get involved in a vexing social problem. Ford said, "We don't talk religion. We don't talk politics. We talk kids."[6]

At Focus, the initiative is a national effort, said Kelly Rosati, senior director of the ministry's Sanctity of Life division. In addition to the adoption events in Colorado, Focus has started working in other states, holding meetings of adoption-minded families in St. Louis, Los Angeles, and Fort Lauderdale, Florida. Of those attending, 830 families initiated the adoption process at the events. More than 750 different churches have been involved.

City Kids

On a Saturday afternoon in August, when many families were buying supplies for the coming school year, more than 1,200 children filtered through a large tent at Julliard Park in Santa Rosa, California, about two hours up the coast from San Francisco.

Inside, a young woman in torn jeans was teaching forty school-age kids easy lyrics to a gospel rap song. Other children were in small groups where instructors explained the gospel and handed out free copies of the Bible. Nearby, a Spanish-speaking pastor talked with parents shaded under a tree.

This was all part of an annual event, City Kids, which is now in its tenth year.[7] It is a joint effort of the Redwood Gospel Mission and more than forty local Protestant and Catholic congregations to reach disadvantaged youth with the gospel through family fun and the gift of a free backpack filled with school supplies. Alongside the large tent stood others offering games, haircuts, family portraits, used books, hot dogs, snow cones, and toothbrushes. Large murals with vibrant color created by various churches told of Jesus's life from birth to resurrection.

For years, Redwood Gospel Mission had supplied backpacks to needy families while a handful of local churches had planned a separate back-to-school festival. "We saw we needed each other," said Adam Peacocke, pastor of City Life Fellowship. Redwood executive director Jeff Gillman said church involvement provided a missing link. "The real need for folks is not just to make a decision for Christ, but to connect with others who can help them grow."

Back to the Land

When Travis Crockett stared out of the car at miles of hills, apple trees, and dry grass, and then spotted a deer for the first time in his life, he realized, "This is far, far from home."[8]

"Home" was a gang-dominated set of blocks in Northwest Chicago. The car with Crockett turned from the orchard jungle into an open field with gray-roofed, white-bricked buildings. The air smelled like a farm—fresh-mowed grass, horse manure, and something savory wafting from the cafeteria. "This must be Jubilee," Crockett muttered. The driver turned around and said, "Yeah, this is your new home."

It was April 16, 2013, Crockett's first day at Jubilee Leadership Academy in Prescott, Washington, a Christian residential facility for troubled boys aged thirteen to eighteen. He was a fifteen-year-old city kid who agreed to go to "Washington" because he had assumed it was the capital, not the state. But now Crockett says he's glad Jubilee isn't in DC, because he could have easily run away when things got tough—and lost his last shot at a decent future.

Crockett had been expelled from the eighth grade for fighting rival gang members in school. Every night he cried himself to sleep, stoned from smoking marijuana and guilty and scared over his drug dealing that he knew could cause him to end up dead or in jail. He would ask himself, "Why am I doing this? I want to stop, but I can't stop." But when his troublemaker cousin Keewaun came back from Jubilee transformed, Crockett thought, "I can change."

A year and a half later, Crockett, sixteen, is a model student in Jubilee's leadership program, a mentor to younger students, and an all-star basketball player. He plans for college and hopes for the NBA. Jubilee is a chance—perhaps the last—for students like Crockett to escape a cycle of abuse, crime, addiction, gangs, and despair. Executive director Rick Griffin describes Jubilee as a place where "God wants to level the playing field." In fact, the name Jubilee comes from the biblical idea of erasing debt and allowing the poor and the broken a chance to start over.

Jubilee provides this second chance by interrupting young people's lives in a profound way. The location itself is one very different from the urban settings the boys often come from. Jubilee's 400-acre campus is surrounded by 5,000 more acres owned by Broetje Orchards. Ralph and Cheryl Broetje bought the land and decided to donate it. Before Jubilee opened, in 1995, the Broetjes and Griffin led a group that would gather on the property and pray for "spiritual fruit-bearing" on that land.

Following that season of prayer, Jubilee opened its doors with six students. Today the all-male facility has about fifty students in a fully accredited boarding school. They are led by a staff of forty-five. The facility is also a working farm with cows, pigs, chickens, and twenty-five horses. Jubilee offers therapy sessions, an on-line academic curriculum, vocational programs such as woodshop and welding, and athletic programs with a local high school. The campus also has a football field, basketball court, skateboard rink, outdoor laser-tag park, and zip line, golf, and rope courses.

But Jubilee is no resort. Some boys come under coercion—either court-ordered or "escorted" by a transport service the parents called out of desperation. Once there, they're stuck. The nearest town is about an hour's drive away. Cell phones, laptops, and cash are not allowed.

And by the time they arrive, the boys have accrued emotional scars, anger, and bitterness. It's up to Jubilee to slowly dredge them up.

At first, Jubilee used the traditional punitive method. A misbehaving boy ran laps, dug ditches, or had only a bologna sandwich for dinner. Better behavior yielded more privileges, such as phone calls and video games. But over the years, Griffin realized the penal system was not working. Instead of motivating the kids to change, the disciplinary measures merely solidified mistrust and repressed anger. A kid sullenly following orders to avoid consequences isn't changing, and Jubilee was discharging boys who couldn't seem to change at all.

Griffin left Jubilee from 2004 to 2009 and worked with people with cognitive disabilities, who clearly cannot perform certain normal functions. He started wondering if Jubilee boys, too, aren't subjects of "will not" but "cannot." What if the severe traumas these boys experienced had significantly altered their brain development—and thus their behaviors? After much soul-searching and research, Griffin returned to Jubilee and advocated a total paradigm change.

Today Jubilee follows a three-tiered model of safety, relationships, and skills. Its philosophy: God first wants us to feel safe in Him, then learn from our relationships, and ultimately bless others with gained skills.

For the first thirty days, a staff member accompanies a newcomer everywhere, from breakfast to chapel. Once the student demonstrates a sense of security, the staff teaches him skills to help regulate his emotions and issues through counseling and classes. The vocational programs provide a safe environment for using skills. Horses teach the rider to be more assertive or gentle without being judgmental. Woodworking or welding teaches patience and dexterity.

Since implementing the new model, Jubilee has raised more student mentors and discharged fewer students than ever before—but its Christ-centered mission has been constant, because, Griffin said, "Without Christ, everything else is pretty meaningless." Though spiritual maturity is not a requirement for the boys to graduate, Jubilee is fully intentional about preaching the gospel by word and action.

The independence needed to preach the gospel means Jubilee relies heavily on private donations, not government funds. None of its students can afford to pay the full monthly tuition of $3,500, but Jubilee doesn't turn any student away because of financial status. Had it done so, Travis Crockett and others like him would have continued falling through the cracks in society. One student-turned-intern, Brandon Kohfield, said if it weren't for Jubilee, he would have been "six feet under today—or someplace worse."

Crockett, too, remembers that he expected a future of minimum wage jobs and drugs. But now, whenever he feels discouraged, he recites Jeremiah 29:11 and reaffirms that God has plans to give him hope and a future. He's fallen off the path, but God has put him "back on the straight path through Jubilee, in the middle of nowhere." He confidently says, "I'm a new man now."

CONCLUSION AND A TO-DO LIST

As we said at the beginning of this chapter, the Bible is unambiguous that all Christians are called to play some part in looking after widows and orphans. And many American Christian families have taken this mandate to heart, providing care for orphans in a way far more humane and effective than that offered by government programs. While we need, of course, more families to consider adoption and foster care, particularly for older and disabled children, we also need to keep the quality of care high. Caring for children isn't enough. We must care for them the right way.

Should you and your family consider joining God's redemption of all things by investing your time, love, energy, finances, and family toward caring for a child in need? Here are some ways to get started:

1. Read *Adopted for Life: The Priority of Adoption for Christian Families and Churches* by Russell D. Moore and *Fields of the Fatherless: Discover the Joy of Compassionate Living* by Tom Davis to grasp a theological understanding of the gospel priority of adoption and orphan care.

2. Inspire your family and friends by hosting a screening of the film *The Dropbox* in your home or church.

3. Educate yourself and others on the situation in your community and state. How many are in the foster care system? Are there enough couples willing to care for needy children on short notice? Do local ministries and havens for children have enough resources?

4. Prayerfully consider adoption, foster care, or other ways to be involved. A great place to start is the Christian Alliance for Orphans (www.christianalliancefororphans.org), a clearinghouse for ministries dedicated to caring for needy children around the world. Be sure to read through "Twelve Ways Ordinary People Can Love Orphans."[9]

5. Encourage your pastor to recognize Orphan Sunday (www.orphansunday.org) each November and lead an effort to challenge your congregation with this issue each year.

6. If your church or organization leads short-term mission trips, ensure they are helping and not hurting. See the book *When Helping Hurts* by Steve Corbett and Brian Fikkert.

7. Intentionally make your church a place where children are welcome and safe. Create a network of "safe families" for short-term assistance when children are at risk.

8. Give generously to effective ministries and organizations that care for children locally and abroad.

14

In the Beginning, God Created

I have called by name Bezalel the son of Uri, son of Hur,
of the tribe of Judah, and I have filled him with the Spirit
of God, with ability and intelligence, with knowledge
and all craftsmanship, to devise artistic designs, to work
in gold, silver, and bronze, in cutting stones for setting,
and in carving wood, to work in every craft.

Exodus 31:2–5

Criticize by creating something beautiful.

—Michelangelo

"In the beginning, God created."

The first words of the Bible teach us something about God. God
has an unbelievable imagination, and He is a Creator. So doesn't it
follow that if we are created in His image, we should celebrate the
imagination? Shouldn't we be creators too?

A growing number of Christian artists are not only answering that
question in the affirmative, they are also following Michelangelo's
advice to "criticize by creating something beautiful."

The Artistic Vision of Makoto Fujimura

One of the leaders of this new movement of Christians in the arts is painter Makoto Fujimura. To get an understanding of Fujimura's stature in the art world, let's turn the clock back a bit, to September, 10, 2005.[1] It was the day before the fourth anniversary of the terrorist attacks of 9/11. At the über-hip Sara Tecchia Gallery in New York's Chelsea district, Fujimura stood in a room with twelve of his latest works. They are inspired by Dante's *The Divine Comedy* and depict the fires of hell. *Water Flames*, as Fujimura calls this oversized exhibit, was part of what the city of New York called its "post–9/11 journey." For Fujimura, it was an attempt to make something beautiful and redemptive out of what was a great evil.

The exhibition was much anticipated because in the art world Fujimura is both iconoclast and fixture. His works are on display worldwide (the largest, 17 feet by 23 feet, fills CNN Asia headquarters at the Oxford House in Hong Kong), yet weekends find him at a Presbyterian (PCA) church in Greenwich Village, where he is an elder. Founder and director of the faith-based International Arts Movement, he manages to keep and expand a following among the avant-garde.

The largest canvas in this exhibition is over 10 feet long and nearly 8 feet in height, and carries a list price of $60,000. The paintings—and Fujimura's total body of work—feature hyper-real colors made of imported pigments, chiefly Japanese vermillion and gold, applied using an ancient Japanese technique called *nihonga*.[2]

The flames that surround Fujimura, who paces the middle of the main gallery debating how high to hang each canvas, have a subtext. His work since 9/11—when he spent the morning trapped in a subway beneath the rubble of the World Trade Center—is about "crossing the chasm of history," he says, "back to the fallen Jerusalem that Jeremiah witnessed." The terror attacks and their aftermath prompted questions not only about the meaning of his art but the meaning of his life. "Is New York City like Babylon or Jerusalem? How do I remain faithful here, even among the rubble?"

Water Flames and other works since 9/11 are, Fujimura says, "my personal experience of devastation coming out in art and life with strong faith and resolute hope." While profoundly Christian works are usually shunned in New York art circles, these resonate with outsiders. "He is a profound believer and I am totally secular. But he is like a professor to me," said gallery owner Sara Tecchia. "Fujimura's paintings allow for skeptics as myself to do the one thing that secularism has labeled as a sign of weakness: to hope."[3]

That Fujimura employs abstract forms to telegraph concrete meaning is a revelation in the realm of contemporary artists, where bedrock concepts of truth and beauty—much less biblical concepts of redemption and healing—are usually rejected, and where ironic distance has been stretched to such a limit that most non-artists regard the arts as stubbornly detached from reality and rotating in a narcissistic, varicolored universe.

Among Fujimura's fans are drama critic Terry Teachout,[4] art critic David Gelernter, and Robert Kushner, a 1970s performance artist and acclaimed fabric painter for three decades. "The idea of forging a new kind of art, about hope, healing, redemption, refuge, while maintaining visual sophistication and intellectual integrity is a growing movement, one which finds Fujimura's work at the vanguard," wrote Kushner in a review of *Water Flames*.

Greg Wolfe, editor of the arts magazine *Image Journal*, summed up the importance of Fujimura's art: "It's been a catastrophe for the church that we have abandoned high culture. One generation's high culture has a way of becoming the next generation's pop culture. And Mako is one of America's leading visual artists."[5]

Infusing Christianity into LA's Giant Murals

As Makoto Fujimura was making a name for himself in New York, Kent Twitchell was already a household name in the art world on the other coast.

Twitchell made a splash on the American art scene in 1971 when he painted a mural of actor Steve McQueen that covered the entire side of a house in Los Angeles. He's gone on to paint even more impressive murals, some of them eight stories tall, and all of them distinctive. Perhaps the most striking are his paintings of Jesus, which he's put on walls, overpasses, and other public spaces.

Far from being the temperamental, eccentric artist that we've come to expect because of the popular biographies of men like Andy Warhol, Jackson Pollock, and Pablo Picasso, Twitchell has a gentle, understated manner. In fact, he clearly doesn't love being called the "grandfather" or the "godfather" of mural painting in a city known for its mural paintings. "I blush a little bit when I hear that," he said. "There were others. The LA Fine Arts Squad was before me and painted some beautiful pieces a couple of years before I did back in the late '60s. Art Mortimer, another artist, started about the same time I did on the west side. I guess I just kept doing it, and I've done them in a dramatic enough way that it's been in the news longer."[6]

Twitchell has certainly been in the news, in part because—as he said—his paintings are dramatic and they are unavoidable. His painting of the LA Chamber Orchestra is eight stories tall on the side of a building that overlooks the Harbor Freeway, one of LA's busiest thoroughfares.

Twitchell's paintings are both lifelike and a bit ghostly. His figures, especially the paintings of Jesus, for which he is best known, sometimes look as if the figures are emerging from clouds or fog. Twitchell said this appearance is no accident.

"I went to a Bible church when I was a teenager in Lansing, Michigan," he said. "Behind the sanctuary was a giant painting of Jesus all in white coming again in the clouds. I remember every Sunday just sitting in there sketching that." Twitchell would sketch in the blank pages of his Bible. "I always had this fascination with painting Christ, the Messiah, coming again in the clouds."

Twitchell hopes all of his paintings, even those that do not include depictions of Jesus, will point people toward God. The painting of Steve McQueen, for example, has bright eyes, not unlike the fiery eyes of Moses when he came down from Mount Sinai. "I painted McQueen as if he were Moses and he had just seen God," Twitchell said. He said he often paints heroic figures, such as the Lone Ranger, as "metaphors for Christ saving people."

For this reason, Twitchell sometimes calls himself an "underground religious painter." He said, "I couldn't get up in the morning and have the inspiration to do them if it wasn't something that was very personal to me. There are people who paint from [the perspective of] eastern mysticism, from Marxism, from atheism, from you-name-it, or nihilism. None of those ring a bell with me, but I'm Christian, and I'd be untrue to who I am inside if I didn't paint something that was informed by my Christianity."

And it seems that people "get it," even in the city that some conservative Christians think of as America's Babylon. You can be stuck in traffic on the Harbor Freeway, or another of the clogged Los Angeles freeways, and if a Kent Twitchell painting comes into view, it's like taking a quick exit to a museum. Twitchell says he wants his paintings to provide a moment of peace in an otherwise chaotic world, and perhaps even to get people to see Jesus in a new way. "The context is unexpected," he said. "And it's that unexpected, face-to-face confrontation with Jesus that I'm looking for. I always wanted my pieces to be oases for the poor person who has to drive in the rush-hour traffic; just something that's beautiful, handmade. Something that will uplift a little teeny section of time."

It does "uplift a little teeny section of time," as Twitchell said, but one of the great things about art is that it also creates the opportunity to last—and contribute to people's thinking—for a very long time, in ways that entertainment culture in most cases will not. Makoto Fujimura said, "The arts are a 500-year conversation. Art is about looking at works by the Angelicos, Michelangelos, and Da Vincis. It's about finding yourself on this path and looking 500 years ahead. If the Lord returns before then, that'll be great, but we have an opportunity to leave something for the next generation and the generation after that: a conversation that is rehumanized and can speak of philosophies and theologies of the past, bringing art as well as science into envisioning the future. Great art will always do that."[7]

Art for the Rest of Us

Kent Twitchell and Makoto Fujimura have gained widespread acceptance in the elite art world on the coasts, but what about "flyover country," that vast land between the galleries and museums of New York and Los Angeles? Are Christians having an impact there?

The short answer to that question is "Yes." A complete answer would fill another book, but to give you just a sample of what's going on, we are going to take a quick tour of the art world in America, pausing only briefly in places where Christians are having an impact.

Our first stop is Grand Rapids, Michigan, where ArtPrize attracted 1,536 artists hoping to win more than $500,000 in prize money. What is different about ArtPrize is that ordinary people can vote for the submissions, and their votes help determine who wins the prize money.[8]

Carol Roeda's *Color Out the Darkness* was one of twenty works that made it into the finals of the public vote grand prize competition in 2014. Twenty-five tubes, each 10 feet tall, formed a semicircle. Written in white on black panels on the exterior of the semicircle were quotes on suffering, hope, dark, and light—by St. Augustine, Solzhenitsyn, C. S. Lewis, and others. Inside the semicircle, the tubes burst with bright colors and stylized flowers. Roeda explained the theme on an accompanying brochure. "The light shines in the darkness, and the darkness has not overcome it. John 1:5"[9]

Nicholas Kroeze's three-dimensional display of a pond during a rainfall was also one of the twenty finalists for the public vote grand prize. Created with the help of his two sons and son-in-law, *The Pond* consists of wooden raindrops hung by clear filament from a 10-foot-tall hexagonal gazebo. Carved wooden ripples and splashes adorn the surface of a pond below. Kroeze is a former missionary to Mexico and is now president of Kuyper College in Grand Rapids. Theological ideas permeate his work. He said the carved "snapshot" of a pond during rainfall represents God's common grace. "He sends His rain on all alike."

South by southwest from Grand Rapids is Austin, Texas, where every year the South by Southwest festival draws more than two hundred thousand people to participate in one of the world's largest music, film, and interactive media festivals.

In 2013, a group of Austin churches and artists thought it would be interesting to have a redemptive presence at "South by," as it is often called. So they asked the questions: What if Jesus came to the South by Southwest festival? What would He do? What would He say? Where would He spend His time?

The answer to these questions became the subject of a large mural conceived by artist Jim Janknegt. He and a team of artists painted the mural at SXSW 2013 on Sixth Street, "Main Street" for Austin's music scene and near the heart of the festival.

The mural, called *Touch the Word*, shows Jesus in modern clothing—including a hoodie and sneakers—touching people on Austin's Sixth Street, with the bright lights of Austin's music venues all around. Ten scenes from the Bible, including Jesus's interaction with the Roman centurion and His healing of the woman with the issue of blood, are depicted.

"This is a riff on medieval paintings that showed Jesus in contemporary settings," said Janknegt, who has been an Austin artist for more than thirty years.

Every place in the mural where Jesus has touched someone is noted by a flash, or a spark.

"One of my challenges was to make visual things that are not visible," Janknegt said. "The spark is my attempt to do that. Not only do you see sparks when Jesus touches someone, or when they touch Him, but also when people who have been touched by Jesus touch others. That's the power Jesus gives to His disciples."

The mural was part of The Wall Project at SXSW, a joint ministry of Austin's nondenominational Hope Chapel and the Anglican Christ Church. Terri Fisher, who leads the arts ministry at Christ Church and coordinates the project, said, "We love Austin and we want this project to be a presence of Christ in the city of Austin, and we want to bless the city with the gift of art."

Janknegt and his assistants paint the overwhelming majority of the mural's large panels (which are 8 by 12 feet each). However, they leave a 6-inch border around the entire image so passersby can make their own contributions. In addition, two on-site handmade journals—one for words and the other for images—allow others, including artists and writers from the participating churches, to take part.[10]

Entertainment That Inspires

During one of his *BreakPoint* commentaries, our friend Eric Metaxas asked an interesting question: "Should Christian believers enter into the highly secular world of comedy—say, in Las Vegas? Or should they stick safely to 'Christian' comedy in Christian settings before Christian audiences?"[11]

It's an interesting and difficult question. An implicit message of this book is that there is no arena of life over which Christ does not have a legitimate claim of sovereignty. But what about such areas as comedy? Hip-hop music? Pop music generally? Can Christians have a redemptive, restorative influence there too?

Metaxas answers that question by telling the story of his friend Brad Stine. After listening to Chuck Colson discuss the importance of "letting the Christian worldview penetrate all aspects of our individual and cultural lives," Stine wondered: Would it be possible to bring the Christian worldview to professional comedy at the highest levels?

Stine thought the answer to that question was "Yes," but he acknowledged, "Any believer who finds himself drawn to the arts usually discovers he's in a never-ending dilemma: Battling with secular mentality that doesn't necessarily want what he's selling, and a religious mentality that doesn't want him selling it there."[12]

Stine said people who go to secular clubs are comfortable with dark comedy that has coarse language and gratuitous sexual references. When that's what people want, he said, "it's difficult to pull people back into the light." But rather than flee that environment, Stine took it as a challenge. He said the people who "got it" first were often the other comics, who knew how hard it was to be funny without being crude. One of those comics became a Christian. Stine said he had shared his faith with that comic, but he thinks the man was more impressed by his commitment to God than his talk about God.

"Did this guy become saved strictly because of me?" Stine asked. "Of course not! But for one moment in time, I was where I was supposed to be. A field of ripe harvest that had no farmers because for years Christians would rather let this particular crop rot than bring it in the barn!" Stine continued, "I was a piece of the machine God had constructed to bring another of His children home. But it only occurred because I was on the mission field of a nightclub."

Lecrae and KB: Redeeming Hip-Hop

If the story of Brad Stine doesn't convince you that God is a lover of diverse gifts and that He wants us to "go into all the world and make disciples," consider the story of hip-hop artist Lecrae and one of his disciples, KB.

Before we dive into their story, it's important that we understand a bit of the environment from which their art springs. Indeed, if you doubt that art imitates life, and vice versa, look no further than hip-hop or "rap" music. Columbia University professor John McWhorter thinks it's one of the clearest (and saddest) examples of how art—for better or worse—shapes imaginations, which in turn shape behavior.

"The rise of nihilistic rap," he wrote over a decade ago, "has mirrored the breakdown of community norms among inner-city youth."

Rap stars produce music videos "flashing jewelry, driving souped-up cars, sporting weapons, angrily gesticulating at the camera, and cavorting with interchangeable, mindlessly gyrating, scantily clad women."[13]

McWhorter believes rap music portrayed what was going on in inner-city neighborhoods in America and provided models for perpetuating that behavior. The lyrics and videos are crammed full of four-letter words, celebration of crime and drugs, the objectification of women, and the rejection of authority.

"It was just as gangsta rap hit its stride," he writes, "that neighborhood elders began . . . to notice that they'd lost control of young black men, who were frequently drifting into lives of gang violence and drug dealing . . . hip-hop, with its fantasies of revolution [in] community and politics, is more than entertainment. It forms a bedrock of young black identity."[14]

But Christian hip-hop artist Lecrae Moore, who goes simply by Lecrae, hopes to turn the philosophical "nothingness" of the genre into something redemptive. In fact, his first number one single, "Nuthin'," addressed that nihilism head-on: "Here we go again in circles / I think I heard it all / We been here before / But we need something more."

"I wanted to say something meaningful [with "Nuthin'"]," he explained after his recent appearance on Jimmy Fallon's *Tonight Show*. "And I just wanted to articulate that I love music, I love hip-hop . . . and I wanted hip-hop to have some substance."[15]

Prior to becoming a Christian, Lecrae says, he lived to imitate his favorite rappers' lyrics and values. "My whole world," he confesses, "was surrounded by guns and drugs and gangs. By 16 I was getting high on a daily basis. I got involved with woman after woman. When you mix drugs, you mix alcohol, you mix youth, it's a cause for an explosion."

That explosion came in the form of a car accident that should have killed him. Despite flipping his truck while wearing no seat belt, Lecrae emerged with barely a scratch. And that was when he surrendered his life to the Savior he knew had spared it.

Shortly afterward he began rapping for inmates at a juvenile detention center. Their positive reaction to the "hope and encouragement" of his story and performance convinced Lecrae that his passion for hip-hop didn't have to die with his old life.

Fast-forward fifteen years, and he's become the most successful Christian hip-hop artist. He's earned a reputation for theological depth, catchy music, and a message of restoration for his genre. Lecrae uses his art as a vehicle for smashing idols and offering an alternative to the "nothing" of hip-hop culture. And he's not afraid to use the J-word, reminding fans regularly that Jesus is the reason behind his rhymes.

Lecrae is also taking seriously his responsibility to bring other hip-hop artists along with him. One of them is KB, the stage name for Kevin Burgess, whom Lecrae signed to his label, Reach Records, after seeing a YouTube video of KB performing and doing street evangelism in Tampa, Florida.

KB's early life was safe and stable. He was raised by two married parents on a military base. Until he was about eleven or twelve years old, he said the worst thing he had ever seen "was a high-schooler smoking a cigarette."[16]

But his parents divorced and his mother moved to Florida, "smack-dab in the middle of the 'hood," KB said. "There were soldiers in the 'hood, but they didn't work for the government, so I saw a lot of things I had seen before, except they were being done by people who were committing crimes. My environment had completely shifted. I felt unsafe all the time. Gunshots every night—and then I'm here, [without a] father, trying to figure out who I am and what I want to do and how do I fit in with this new environment. I found myself spiraling into this darkness of more questions than answers, and, in the midst of that, Jesus stepped in."

He came in the form of rap music. A man ministering in KB's neighborhood gave him a CD that had seven Christian hip-hop songs on it. "The eighth song was a gospel presentation, and I've been walking with the Lord ever since," KB said. Did that experience heighten his belief that what he's doing can make a difference in people's lives? "Absolutely," KB answers. "You couldn't tell me otherwise."

Since that day, KB graduated from Bible college in Florida, signed with Lecrae's Reach Records, and the two of them often tour together. Though KB hasn't yet seen the success Lecrae has experienced, he saw his first album make the Billboard charts, and he continues to create and tour.

And, by the way, he also continues to study the Bible and theology. "My number one guy is Charles Haddon Spurgeon," KB said. "I have never read or encountered anybody better with words than Charles Spurgeon—nobody. No rapper—Eminem, Kanye, Jay-Z—nobody. He owns the wordsmith manual. The man spoke in parables, in allegories. Hip-hop has a lot of that kind of storytelling. It's bringing home a moment, leading people up to a point, and then driving home your point. That's Charles Spurgeon. He was a rapper, man."

Redemptive Stories in Film

One final story before we close, and we've been saving this story till last because not only does it help us make some of the key points in this chapter, but it also helps us make one of the key points of this book: storytelling matters.

Twenty-five years ago, Jason Jones was a wild seventeen-year-old in the U.S. Army, stationed in Fort Benning, Georgia. He openly disdained Christianity, but when his girlfriend told him she was pregnant, something happened in his mind and heart. He now says it was God who opened up his heart to love that unborn child.[17] So Jason decided to fly home on the first available leave the army would give him to marry his girlfriend. But before he could get home, the girl's father forced her to have an abortion.

Jason's heart was broken, but what Satan intended for evil, God turned into good. Jason resolved then that he would dedicate his life to ending abortion. Even before he became a Christian he became a pro-life activist. His activism put him in close touch with many Christians in the pro-life movement, and eventually Jones professed Christ himself, and he continued his pro-life activism. His activism put him in touch with Christians involved in the filmmaking business. He started promoting pro-life projects, and ultimately became a producer himself, raising money for such projects as the pro-life films *Bella* and *October Baby*. He put up a website encouraging abortion-minded women who had seen *Bella* to tell their stories. Jason said he had documentation of more than a thousand women who had been planning on having an abortion but had changed their minds after seeing that movie.[18]

His most recent project is a short film called *Crescendo*, about the early life of Ludwig van Beethoven. Many people don't know that Beethoven was conceived in an abusive relationship and his mother attempted to abort him. This film makes plain what a tragedy it would have been for the world had Beethoven never existed. Indeed, over the closing credits of the movie plays the famous theme from Beethoven's Ninth Symphony, the famous "Ode to Joy." This unabashedly pro-life film has received standing ovations at industry screenings and recently won top prize at the Hollywood Film Festival.

But Jones is most proud of the fact that the film has been used by pregnancy care centers around the country to raise money for their local operations. The pregnancy care centers will rent a movie theatre and show *Crescendo* and another short film in which Jason and Justin Bieber's mother, Pattie Mallette, describe their experiences with abortion. They then ask the audience to support the center hosting this screening. Thousands of people have responded, and this 17-minute film about the life of Beethoven has raised more than $5 million for centers across the country. "I have seen this little film create a greater pro-life impact than my 20 years of relentless pro-life activism," Jones said. That's now why he says he is committed to "storytelling in film as a powerful way to reach a culture with the message of the gospel and the message of life." His organization, Movie to Movement, is committed to "fulfilling the Great Commission through film and sharing the gospel of Jesus Christ through art."

On the power of storytelling and art generally to carry God's truth, Jones is fond of quoting Damon of Athens, a musician who lived in the fifth century BC. He said, "Give me the songs of a nation, and I care not who writes its laws."

CONCLUSIONS AND A TO-DO LIST

Just as God is a Creator, we who are in His image were created to be creators. Throughout history Christians have given the world some of its most precious paintings, stories, songs, and sculptures. From the most inspiring cathedrals of Europe, to the great music of Bach and Handel, to the religious art of the Renaissance, the church and Christian artists have pointed our imaginations to God.

Today we are seeing a renaissance of Christians in the arts. Artists like Makoto Fujimura and his International Arts Mission are being intentional about making art that pierces the veil of postmodern secularism to give us a glimpse of the transcendent. Charlie Peacock, Michael Card, and Andrew Peterson—to name but a few of many—are doing the same thing in music. Greg Wolfe and *Image* are helping Christians to recover their artistic vision and voice. If you have artistic inclinations, God has claimed them for His purposes. Those not particularly gifted ought to recognize the hand of God and redemptive potential of artistic gifts to the world. Here's how:

1. Read *Art for God's Sake* by Philip Ryken and the Francis Schaeffer classic *Art and the Bible* to learn more about a biblical worldview of artistic endeavors. To learn how Christian faith inspired some of our world's most significant musicians, read *Spiritual Lives of the Great Composers* by Patrick Kavanaugh. To learn about how art influences culture, read *Saving Leonardo: A Call to Resist the Secular Assault on Mind, Morals, and Meaning* by Nancy Pearcey.

2. Evaluate whether your church intentionally includes artists in its life and ministry. For ideas on how to get started, consider the Arts Ministry of the Center for Faith and Work (http://www.faithandwork.com/arts/).

3. Create a list of great works of art and literature and develop a plan for working your way through that list with friends or family members.

4. Learn about the local artists and musicians in your town, where and how they live and work, and find ways to support them.

5. Invite nonbelieving friends to attend exhibitions, concerts, movies, and readings with you. Use the content of the presentations to discuss matters of eternal significance.

6. Consider establishing an "artist in residence" position at your church or organization with the purpose of challenging the larger congregation or community with things of truth, meaning, and beauty.

15

Aim Small, Miss Small

One person committed to a cause is far more effective
than a thousand who are merely interested.

—William E. Brown

Whatever your hand finds to do, do it with all your might.

—Ecclesiastes 9:10 (NIV)

A mentor of ours once said, "If you want to change the world, start
by cleaning your room."

Well-meaning people and self-help gurus tell us to "reach for the
stars" and "change the world." We ought to dream big dreams and
try hard things, but in our attempts to "live large," it is tempting to
neglect needs closer at hand and within our actual reach. Without
exception, the stories of this book tell of people who refused to overlook a need they had the capacity, vision, and ability to address. Our
prayer is that these stories will be both examples and inspiration for
God's people, you and me, to live redemptively here and now, wherever
God has placed us.

Without question, much about our current cultural situation seems dire. The needs can be overwhelming. The real question we all must face is not whether we can in fact change the world but how we will respond to the next opportunity to do something. Will we act? Will we do whatever we do well?

The title to this chapter comes from one of our favorite movies. *The Patriot* tells the story of a father facing tough choices during the Revolutionary War. Mel Gibson plays a hero of the French and Indian Wars who, because he knows the horrors of war, wants to avoid this new war, if at all possible. His hopes to avoid conflict are dashed when his oldest son, eager to enter the conflict with the British, joins the South Carolina militia. In front of his father and siblings, the son is taken captive by a ruthless British general and is marched away from the house, facing execution.

The father gathers his two younger sons and goes to ambush the British patrol and rescue his captured son, played by Heath Ledger. Hiding in the woods and waiting for an opportunity to attack, the father steadies his sons by reminding them of what they know. "What did I tell you about shooting?" They reply, "Aim small, miss small."

The lesson for them and for us is clear: Aim for a specific spot. Even if you miss the spot, you are still likely to hit the target.

In the introduction of this book, we challenged readers to wrestle with four questions. First, w*hat is good in our culture that we can promote, protect, and celebrate?* Second, *what is missing in our culture that we can creatively contribute?* Third, *what is evil in our culture that we can stop?* And finally, *what is broken in our culture that we can restore?*

Then, in the first chapter, we challenged readers with the strategic significance of "mediating institutions." The strength of any society, we argued, is its middle. When there is a robust civil society, bolstered by everyday citizens coming together to confront local needs with local solutions, people can flourish and real change can happen.

This is our version of "Aim small, miss small."

When Chuck Colson was challenged about what his legacy would be, he was committed that it not be merely buildings, books, or even the organizations he founded. As important as his writings and institutions continue to be, even after his death, he saw his legacy to be "little platoons" of Christians trained to understand the gospel's implications for all of life and sent out to be restorers in all areas of culture. This vision was the genesis of the Centurions Program, a yearlong training course that initiated a community of Christian worldview champions all across America. Over the last years of his life, Chuck devoted much of his time and energy into this program. To date, over nine hundred Centurions have been trained and commissioned in areas as diverse as politics, education, business, and family.

Chuck called on T. M. Moore to architect this program. Moore understood that for a program to be successful, the training must be more than informational. It must be formational, and Centurions needed to have a blueprint for kingdom engagement. T. M. developed a process, based out of the Great Commission of our Lord, to lead Centurions toward a customized blueprint for living out their faith in their spheres of influence. He calls it "the personal mission field."[1]

Jesus commissioned His followers in Matthew 28:18–20: "All authority in heaven and on earth has been given to me. Go therefore and make disciples of all nations, baptizing them in the name of the Father and of the Son and of the Holy Spirit, teaching them to observe all that I have commanded you. And behold, I am with you always, to the end of the age."

Many believers, though familiar with Jesus's words in this passage, mistakenly believe the command in this passage to be "Go!" In the original Greek, however, that is not a command. The only command in the passage is "Make disciples of all nations." Moore rightly notes that the preface to that command is "as you go" or "wherever you go."

Moore suggests to the Centurions that they should first identify where they go. Over the course of a week, we find ourselves in all kinds of personal and social settings: at work, at home, at church, in our communities, at the voting booth, at the store, and around our neighborhoods. Once we identify the places we spend our time, we can identify the relationships we have in those spaces. Then we can begin to think through the needs of these places and what we might do to join God's work there.

Underneath this exercise is the classic Christian understanding of vocation. Vocation comes from the Latin word *vocare*, which means "to call." Today, vocation is often confused with occupation, or what we do to make a living. The Protestant Reformers understood vocation differently. They understood anywhere and everywhere we go as our "stations," situations and relationships ordained by God for us.

This idea of "station" is key. If we see the various situations and relationships in our lives as accidental, we will never have a proper understanding of vocation. Instead, we should see our various stations as places and people to which God has called us. A calling, after all, requires a "caller." As Paul told the Epicurean and Stoic philosophers during his famous "Mars Hill" sermon, "[God] made from one man every nation of mankind to live on all the face of the earth, having determined allotted periods and the boundaries of their dwelling place" (Acts 17:26).

So God determines when and where we live. It is no accident where we find ourselves, whether in Budapest or Boston, in Singapore or Soddy Daisy, Tennessee. And it is no accident if we are brothers, daughters, employees, neighbors, and citizens. God is writing our stories into His Grand Narrative of the Story of All Things.

We cannot and should not do everything. How ridiculous would *Romeo and Juliet* be if one actor played both parts? So how do we discern our part, our vocation, in God's Grand Narrative?

First, we should take seriously the particular gifts, abilities, and passions we all have. Just as it is no accident where we find ourselves, it is no accident that each of us has been created in unique ways. How we engage the world will largely depend on the unique ways God has made us. As we grow and mature, many of us will find new things that interest us and engage our passions. So we should ask ourselves, "What do I love doing?" Or better yet, "What makes me come alive?" Early in this book we quoted from the movie *Chariots of Fire*, in which Eric Liddell said, "When I run I feel God's pleasure." What causes you to feel God's pleasure?

It may be that we thrive on creativity, or analytics. It may be that we love to see systems built that benefit others, or we are bent toward giving, or cooking, or painting. Our passions are windows into our design.

Second, we have to understand the specific brokenness of our culture. There are particular evils in any time and place, including ours. Os Guinness explains, "Many followers of Jesus today have not begun to wrestle with the full dimensions of the truth of calling because they have not been stretched by the real challenges of today's world and by the momentousness of the present hour."[2]

Along these lines, we should ask ourselves, "What breaks my heart?" Or, "What are the cultural trends leading people away from truth?" Historically, we can see how Christians identified evils like racism, slavery, poverty, greed, sloth, or other specific forms of injustice that were prevalent in their time and place. We should too.

199

If God created us in particular ways and put us in particular places, it only follows that we should look for those places where our gifts and our culture's brokenness intersect. Frederick Buechner suggests that at these intersections we will find the clearest sense of our vocations:

> There are all different kinds of voices calling you to all different kinds of work, and the problem is to find out which is the voice of God. . . . By and large a good rule for finding out is this: the kind of work God usually calls you to is the kind of work (a) *that you need most to do* and (b) *that the world most needs to have done.*
>
> If you really get a kick out of your work, you've presumably met requirement (a), but if your work is writing cigarette ads, the chances are you've missed requirement (b). On the other hand, if your work is being a doctor in a leper colony, you have probably met requirement (b), but if most of the time you're bored or depressed by it, the chances are you have not only bypassed (a), but probably aren't helping your patients much either. . . .
>
> *The place God calls you to is the place where your deep gladness and the world's deep hunger meet.*[3]

Finally, we must embrace that all Christians, not just professional ministers and nonprofit leaders, have sacred vocations. The idea that some are called "into the ministry," usually meaning pastors and missionaries, while the rest of us are not is just not true. All Christians have been reconciled and are given "the ministry of reconciliation" (2 Cor. 5:14–21).

Our friend Scott Rae often tells of a church service in which volunteers for Vacation Bible School were called forward. "We are going to pray for these folks who will be doing ministry this week," the pastor said. That was, of course, an appropriate thing to do. However, as one teacher quipped, "I've been a public school teacher for twenty years, and no one has ever prayed for me."

Let this observation from John Stott sink in:

> We often give the impression that if a young man is really keen for Christ he will undoubtedly become a foreign missionary, that if he is not quite as keen as that he will stay at home and become a pastor, that if he lacks the dedication to be a pastor, he will no doubt be a doctor or teacher, while those who end up in social work or the media or (worst of all) politics are not far removed from serious backsliding.[4]

It simply is not true that a person's calling is more sacred on the basis of *where they work*.[5] To be Christian is to be called to God's redeeming work in the world. And anyone who is in Christ can and should seek to glorify God wherever they are.

We close this book with two final challenges to all who will take their redemptive calling seriously. First, wherever we go and in whatever ways we seek to make a difference in the world, we must also proclaim the gospel we are seeking to model. It's tempting to be silent, particularly in times like ours, when speaking Christian truth can lead to disdain or ridicule. "Preach the gospel at all times," we've heard. "When necessary, use words." Often attributed to Saint Francis of Assisi, that compelling line can mislead us.

Even if Saint Francis said those words, which he most likely did not, Christianity is a proclaimed religion.[6] Its truth is a truth that is to be seen and heard, just as Jesus was one who lived and taught, pointing us to the truth about God, our sinful condition, and the possibility of forgiveness and redemption. In other words, we cannot think that our actions remove our responsibility to personally share Christ with others.

Second, we can be encouraged to know that success is faithfulness, nothing more and nothing less. Will we see the restoration of our particular culture because of our efforts? We cannot guarantee that Western civilization will be "saved" in the sense that many speak. But this we know, Christ has risen from the dead. He will restore all things.

We cannot say it any better than Richard John Neuhaus, and so we end our reflections with his words:

> And will we overcome? Will we prevail? We have overcome and have prevailed ultimately because He has overcome and He has prevailed. There are days in which you and I get discouraged. On those days I tell myself—I suppose almost every day I tell myself, sometimes several times a day—those marvelous lines from T. S. Eliot's "East Coker," where Eliot says, "For us there is only the trying. The rest is not our business."
>
> For us there is only the trying. The rest is not our business. Some people read those lines as lines of resignation, kind of shrugging your shoulders and saying, "What can you do?" But I read them as lines of vibrant hope. The rest is not our business. The rest is God's business. Thank God, we are not God. Thank God, God is God.[7]

And all God's people say, "Amen."

Conclusion

Two Personal Stories

> Small is beautiful.
> —E. F. Schumacher

One reason we are so convinced of the power of redemptive stories to change lives is that we are both witnesses of and participants in stories that demonstrate that power. Christians who took everyday redemption seriously, who were not celebrities or seeking glory, intentionally entered our lives and altered our trajectories toward the good, the true, and the beautiful.

And so, as we wind down this book, we each offer a story of our own.

John's Story

In ninth grade, I was a knucklehead. Even worse, I was a *Christian school* knucklehead. Those are the worst kind. Six days a week, between that Christian school and the church that operated it, I was in the same building hearing the same Bible lessons, often from the same people.

This was my tenth year at this school (including kindergarten), so I knew the Christian answers to the Christian questions but didn't really have much faith that I could call my own. It wasn't a very big place, either. That year, the principal (who was also the assistant pastor of the church) taught the Bible class for all the boys from ninth through twelfth grades.

It was sometimes difficult to know where the church ended and the school began. Church projects often became school projects, and school students often became volunteers, though not always voluntarily. And that's the reason I met Ms. Buckner on the last day of classes before Christmas break in December 1990.

We all know what is supposed to happen on the last day of classes before Christmas break: *not much*. Certainly not anything resembling academia. Perhaps a party is called for, and that's what I was expecting that day.

Instead, our Bible teacher/pastor/principal announced that our boys Bible class was being sent out two by two to visit the elderly "shut-ins" of our church. I suppose the intention was to bring Christmas cheer, but as you might imagine, that's not what happened. The only thing we wanted to do less than academic work on the last day of classes before Christmas break was visit old people we had never met.

My only respite was that I was paired with my friend I'll call Nathan. Two years older and a recent transfer to our school, Nathan shared my disdain for the assignment we had been given.

"What are we going to do?" I asked. "I don't want to go see any *old* people."

"I've got an idea," Nathan replied. "We'll go visit one person but say that we couldn't find the other person's house. That way, we'll be done fast and can go to the mall and meet some girls."

I liked Nathan. He knew how to formulate a plan. And he shared my inflated view of our prowess with women.

So one of the papers we had been given with a name and address was thrown in the garbage. The name on the other paper: Omega Buckner. She lived down a windy, rural Virginia road in a small apartment her grandson had built for her on the end of his farmhouse.

She invited us inside, and there we were: an eleventh grader, a ninth grader, and an eighty-nine-year-old widow. We didn't have a lot in common. The small talk, you might say, dragged.

Just when we thought it couldn't possibly get any more awkward, Ms. Buckner said, "I've got an idea. Let's sing Christmas carols together." We stumbled our way through "Silent Night," and she decided one carol was enough.

"Well, Ms. Buckner," Nathan said, "we'd best be on our way."

"Yes," I lied, "we still have one more person to visit before heading back to school."

"Can we pray together before you go?" she asked.

So I prayed, and then Nathan prayed. It took about forty-five seconds. Then Ms. Buckner prayed.

At that point, I had been in the church my whole life. I had heard thousands of prayers, including the verbose, flowery kinds of prayers from evangelists, pastors, and other deep-voiced, God-invoking folks. But I had *never* heard anything like this. In the middle of the prayer, I remember, I looked up just to make sure Jesus wasn't sitting next to her, because it sounded like He was. She spoke to God as if she *knew* Him, with a simultaneous confidence and humility that only comes when you know you are being heard.

We left her house and headed to the mall, soon distracted by proclaiming our overeager expectations to meet girls. I do remember, however, Nathan saying to me, "She's a cool old woman." I agreed.

Two years later, I woke up with the strangest feeling. It was late November, I think, and I was now in eleventh grade at the same Christian school, still with no real faith to speak of. Typically, I would wake up thinking about basketball and my girlfriend, but I woke up this particular morning thinking of Ms. Buckner. To this day, I have no idea why.

"I need to go visit this lady," I told my girlfriend.

"Why?" she asked.

"I can't explain it. I met her a couple of years ago, and I need to go see her."

She still didn't understand, but since I didn't have a driver's license, she finally agreed to drive me back down that windy road to Ms. Buckner's apartment. Still, just so I would know how stupid she found my idea, she refused to get out of the car.

"Ms. Buckner," I said when she opened her door, "you probably don't remember me, but two years ago I came here with my friend Nathan. My name is John."

"John." She smiled. "I remember you. I prayed for you this morning."

I wish I could say that her statement had the immediate impact on me it should have. Instead, this began an unlikely, and yet very important, friendship. Within a year or so, my posture toward Christ had dramatically changed and was only strengthened by my frequent visits with Ms. Buckner.

She prayed for me every day for the remainder of her life. To this day, I cannot imagine what she has prayed me out of and into. And if I ever asked her to pray for something specific, she would remember and ask me about it the next time we'd visit. On more than one occasion, she asked me about something I had forgotten.

During my summers at college, I served as a youth ministry intern at my church, and I purposed to take as many students to see her as would go. After one such visit, I remember one ninth grader I was mentoring saying to another, "When I grow up, I want to marry someone like her." She was then ninety-three. Everyone I ever took to see her walked out of her door solemn, with head shaking, muttering something like, "Wow . . . she's incredible."

After graduating from college, I asked her to pray about a decision I faced, whether to begin seminary or to spend a year on a short-term mission project to Jamaica. When I told her I had chosen to go to Jamaica, her eyes lit up, and through a big smile she said, "Oh, I just knew that's where God was going to take you." I took that as confirmation.

That day was the last I was to see her. At age ninety-seven, she was still very sharp mentally but not so much physically. She had faced an especially tough series of health challenges, and we both knew that she would likely not live until I returned from Jamaica. That day, we did not say good-bye. Instead, we said, "I'll see you in heaven."

I had only been in Jamaica about a month when a message came through from my mother. Ms. Buckner had passed peacefully into the presence of Jesus. Though I could not attend her funeral, I was named as an honorary pallbearer.

A few years ago, my high school alma mater asked me to be their graduation speaker. I had told the story of Ms. Buckner many times, but on this night in that place, the mere mention of her name brought tears to literally dozens of eyes across that auditorium and smiles to even more faces. I wasn't the only one in that community with a Ms. Buckner story.

At age fourteen, I found myself—seemingly by chance—in the home of an eighty-nine-year-old woman I didn't know and didn't particularly like. I didn't want to be there. I lied to her. And yet God used her to alter the trajectory of my life and to influence an entire community.

Warren's Story

My story involves not the faithfulness of someone who invested in my life but the faithfulness of someone I never met, will never meet, and who never knew me. Yet because of his faithfulness, my life and the lives of my children were eternally altered.

In 1951, my father—Carlos Smith—was a twenty-one-year-old infantry rifleman a long way from home. He was, in fact, sitting on a mountaintop about forty miles north of Seoul. This particular mountaintop was one of those hills that formed the infamous Punchbowl region near what would become the border between North and South Korea.

As my father put it, "To the north were a half million enemy soldiers. To the south was the way home. I was scared, cold, hungry, and very lonely."

You could see for miles in most any direction. Fierce fighting on these mountainsides, fighting that included regular mortar barrages, had more or less stripped the mountains of any vegetation. It was a cold, barren, exposed wasteland.

That's why my father couldn't help but notice a vehicle moving up the ridge toward him, just behind the MLR—the Main Line of Resistance, which is what they called the "front line." Eventually he could make out that the vehicle was a jeep driven by one man. My father assumed he was a soldier. From my father's high and forward vantage point, he could follow the jeep's progress over the next couple of hours. My father observed that several times the driver came to forks in the road—no more than a dirt trail, really—that would have allowed him to turn back to safer and less-exposed territory. But he did not turn back. He kept coming.

The road terminated at my father's position. He and several other soldiers—the men in his platoon—had dug in on that hill surrounding an almost level spot that was no larger than three or four parking spaces. A man my father estimated to be in his forties remained sitting in the jeep but nodded a friendly greeting to several of the soldiers.

207

They were members, like my father, of the famed 2nd Infantry Division, sometimes called the 2ID, or the "Indianhead Division," after the division's shoulder insignia, which featured the profile of a Native American in battle headdress.

This older man was not, however, a soldier himself. He was dressed in army fatigues, but they had no rank or any insignia to reveal who or what he was.

"He stepped from the jeep," my father said, "and he faced the small circle of us that had formed around him." He introduced himself by saying his name, but more than fifty years later, when my father first told me this story, he said he couldn't remember it. What my father did remember is this: This man was a member of the Salvation Army.

This minister of the gospel, whose name is now lost to history, then asked these soldiers, some of whom had been on the front lines for weeks without a break, how he could serve them. He had writing paper and envelopes. Did anyone need them? He asked if anyone needed a letter written for him. He would be glad to do that too. He also said he had a limited supply of razor blades, toothpaste, and toothbrushes. "All was free for the asking," my father said.

The man's visit was brief, but it made a huge difference to those soldiers keeping watch on what that year would become the bloodiest battlefields of the Korean War. The Battle of Heartbreak Ridge, in which my father and others gathered around that jeep would fight months later, took the lives of 3,700 American and Allied soldiers. The North Koreans and Chinese lost 25,000 men.

As the Salvation Army minister prepared to leave, he asked if anyone would mind if he said a prayer. No one did, so they bowed their heads as he prayed. He then shook hands with each of the soldiers. Years later, my father could not remember what he had prayed, but he did remember that as he shook hands with the men gathered on that ridge, he said the same words to each: "God bless you."

When I was about ten years old and my father was in his thirties, he made a public profession of faith in Christ. He will tell you today that this unknown but quietly faithful Salvation Army chaplain is part of the reason why. "He served us without a desire for recognition, glory, or prestige," my father said. "There was something different about him." That difference helped my father to understand the gospel, and because of that, the history of my family changed.

And that story, in a nutshell, is what this book is all about.

Notes

Introduction

1. Abraham Kuyper, "Sphere Sovereignty," in *Abraham Kuyper: A Centennial Reader*, ed. James D. Bratt (Grand Rapids: Eerdmans, 1998), 488.

2. We don't use these words indifferently. Careful readers know they come from sociologist Christian Smith's important 2005 work describing the worldview of modern evangelical teenagers as "moralistic, therapeutic deism." For more on this topic, see *Soul Searching: The Religious and Spiritual Lives of American Teenagers* by Christian Smith and Melinda Lundquist Denton (Oxford: Oxford University Press, 2005).

3. Lesslie Newbigin, *A Walk Through the Bible*, 2nd ed. (Kansas City, MO: Barefoot Ministries, 2011; Triangle, 1999), 12–13.

4. A phrase used by Francis Schaeffer in *Christian Manifesto* (Good News, 2005).

5. See for example two helpful books on the idea of "worldview": William E. Brown, W. Gary Phillips, and John Stonestreet, *Making Sense of Your World: A Biblical Worldview*, 2nd ed. (Sheffield, IA: Sheffield Press, 2007) and Charles W. Colson and Nancy Pearcey, *How Now Shall We Live?* (Wheaton: Tyndale House, 2004).

6. C. S. Lewis, *Miracles* (New York: HarperOne, 2001, reprint ed.), 51.

7. Thomas Howard, *Evangelical Is Not Enough: Worship of God in Liturgy and Sacraments* (San Francisco: Ignatius Press, 1984), 36–37.

8. Richard John Neuhaus, "Telling the World Its Own Story" (The Colson Center Library). Available on-line at http://www.colsoncenter.org/search-library/search?view= searchdetail&id=21199.

9. Gabe Lyons also articulated these questions in the opening address of the 2014 Q Conference in Nashville, TN. See http://qnashville.qideas.org/.

Chapter 1 Great News!

1. "Poverty: Not Always with Us," *The Economist*, June 1, 2013.

2. Alexis de Tocqueville, *Democracy in America* (New York: Penguin, 2003).

3. Thomas Kidd, "Tocqueville's Uncanny Vision," *Patheos*, March 4, 2014.

4. In 2012, the total size of the nonprofit sector in this country was 5.5 percent of the gross domestic product, or about $886 million of the $16 billion GDP. Source: The National Center of Charitable Statistics. http://nccs.urban.org/statistics/quickfacts.cfm

5. Cited in Everett Carll Ladd, "A Nation of Joiners: That Peculiarly American Form of Behavior," *Philanthropy*, Nov/Dec 1999.

6. Charles Murray, *Coming Apart: The State of White America 1960–2010* (Washington, DC: Crown Forum, 2013).

7. Jill Lacy, "The Other Washington," *WORLD*, April 10, 2010, 51–52.

8. David Eldridge, "Biden Comfortable with Gay Marriage, Cites 'Will & Grace,'" *Washington Times*, May 6, 2012.

9. For a fuller account of how the cultural imagination was swayed toward embracing same-sex marriage, see Sean McDowell and John Stonestreet, *Same-Sex Marriage: A Thoughtful Approach to God's Design for Marriage* (Grand Rapids: Baker, 2014), 17–23.

10. Rodney Stark, *The Rise of Christianity: How the Obscure, Marginal Jesus Movement Became the Dominant Religious Force in the Western World in a Few Centuries* (San Francisco: HarperSanFrancisco, 1997).

11. Ibid., 82.

12. Ibid.

13. To hear the report: http://www.npr.org/2014/10/09/354890862/in-collecting-and-cremating-ebola-victims-a-grim-public-service.

14. Eric Metaxas, "Running toward the Plague: Christians and Ebola," *BreakPoint* commentary, Oct. 15, 2014. Available on-line at http://www.breakpoint.org/bpcommentaries/entry/13/26237.

Chapter 2 Helping That Helps

1. Quoted in *PovertyCure: From Aid to Enterprise*. DVD series by The Acton Institute, 2013.

2. "The Westminster Shorter Catechism," available on-line from the Center for Reformed Theology and Apologetics at http://www.reformed.org/documents/wsc/index.html?_top=http://www.reformed.org/documents/WSC.html.

3. Marvin Olasky, *The Tragedy of American Compassion* (Washington, DC: Regnery Publishing, 1994).

4. Steve Corbett and Brian Fikkert, *When Helping Hurts: How to Alleviate Poverty without Hurting the Poor and Yourself* (Chicago: Moody, 2009).

5. Jim Towey, author's interview with Mother Teresa's attorney, published as "Jesus in His 'Distressing Disguise,'" *Charlotte World*, May 6, 2005.

6. Steven W. Mosher. *Population Control: Real Costs, Illusory Benefits* (Edison, NJ: Transaction Publishers, 2008), 4.

7. See "Not Always with Us" from *The Economist* (June 1, 2013). Available on-line at http://www.economist.com/news/briefing/21578643-world-has-astonishing-chance-take-billion-people-out-extreme-poverty-2030-not.

8. *PovertyCure: From Aid to Enterprise.* DVD series by The Acton Institute, 2013.

9. Kathleen Thorne, "Ruths and Naomis," *WORLD*, Sept. 2, 2006.

10. Allie Cook, "On the March Again," *WORLD*, Sept. 1, 2007.

11. Mary Hopkins, "Cooking for Christ," *WORLD*, July 16, 2011.

12. A version of the story of Friends Ministry was published in *WORLD* as "Cultivating Change" by Daniel James Devine, July 24, 2014. Used with permission.

13. Ibid.

14. Bob Lupton, *Toxic Charity: How Churches and Charities Hurt Those They Help and How to Reverse It* (New York: HarperOne, 2012); Bob Lupton, *Theirs Is The Kingdom: Celebrating the Gospel in Urban America* (New York: HarperOne, 2011).

15. This section is based on personal conversations with Renny Scott and information found in Carol Knight, "The Book," Making Housing Happen, February 13, 2014, http://makinghousinghappen.net/the-book/get-inspired-featured-organizations/#stockade.

16. Mark Binelli, "City of Stray Dogs: Detroit's Epidemic of 50,000 Stray Dogs," *Rolling Stone*, March 20, 2012.

17. For more about Evangel's history, see the church's website: http://www.evangelministries.org.

18. Christopher Brooks, *Urban Apologetics: Why the Gospel Is Good News for the City* (Grand Rapids: Kregel, 2014).

19. Andy Crouch, "Why Apologetics Is Different—and Working—in the Hood," *Christianity Today*, Oct. 22, 2013.

20. Ibid.

21. Ibid.

22. This idea originally belongs to William B. Wichterman, from his article "The Culture: 'Upstream' from Politics," in a *A Healthy Culture: Strategies for an American Renaissance*, ed. Don Eberly (Grand Rapids: Eerdmans, 2001), 76–101.

23. Ibid.

24. Ibid.

25. Peter Marshall, *The Light and the Glory* (Grand Rapids: Revell, 1977), 242.

Chapter 3 Capitalism for the Common Good

1. Henry Hazlitt, *Economics in One Lesson* (New York: Three Rivers Press, 1979), 17.

2. Michael Sieply, "Film's Wall Street Predator to Make a Comeback," *New York Times*, May 7, 2007.

3. Ayn Rand, *Capitalism: The Unknown Ideal* (New York: Signet, 1967), 195.

4. Jay Richards, *Money, Greed, and God: Why Capitalism Is the Solution and Not the Problem* (New York: HarperOne, 2009), 111–112.

5. Much of this section appeared in a somewhat different form as "More Than an Entrepreneur: Farewell Truett Cathy," *BreakPoint* commentary, Sept. 10, 2014.

6. This mission statement is on the wall of all Chick-fil-A restaurants.

7. Shane Windmeyer, "Dan and Me: My Coming Out as a Friend of Dan Cathy and Chick-fil-A," *Huffington Post*, Jan. 28, 2013.

8. Ibid.

9. Quintin Ellison, "From Bankruptcy to Riches: Phil Drake Builds a Business Empire," *Smoky Mountain News*, Sept. 14, 2011.

10. Ibid.

11. Ibid.

12. Ibid.

13. Ibid.

14. Marvin Olasky, "Timely Teaching: Texas Business School Teaches That Leading a Meaningful Life Is More Important Than Dollar Signs," WORLD, Aug. 25, 2012.

15. Ibid.

16. Ibid.

17. Ibid.

Chapter 4 This Will Stop in Our Lifetime

1. We'll have more to say about China's one-child policy in chapter 5, "Women at the Well," when we share the story of Reggie Littlejohn, the founder of Women's Rights Without Borders.

2. WORLD has an annual pro-life issue devoted almost exclusively to the pro-life movement. It is published on the anniversary of the *Roe v. Wade* decision, which is also the date of the annual March for Life in Washington.

3. From "A Passion to Serve: How Pregnancy Resource Centers Empower Women, Help Families, and Strengthen Communities," 2009, www.APassion ToServe.org.

4. Heartbeat International is another major player in this movement. Though CareNet is significantly larger in the United States, Heartbeat International has 1,800 affiliates on six continents and describes itself as the largest organization of its kind in the world.

5. Recent surveys by Gallup and several other polling organizations document this shift. For a summary of these surveys: http://en.wikipedia.org/wiki/Societal _attitudes_towards_abortion#mediaviewer/File:USA_Gallup_abortion_opinion _poll_stacked_area.svg.

6. A pregnancy care center is just one of the many ministries of this entre-preneurial and innovative church. For more: Marvin Olasky, "Doing Well, Doing Good," WORLD, Aug. 20, 2005.

7. Christian Care Center, http://www.christiancarecenter.org/ministries/ pregnancy-and-family-care-center/.

8. Much of the material in this section was originally published as Courtney Crandell, "Art in the Center of Life with Down Syndrome: People with Different Ability Levels Need the Arts, and the Arts Need Them Too," WORLD, Oct. 21, 2014. Used with permission.

9. C. Mansfield, S. Hopfer, and T. M. Marteau, "Termination Rates after Prenatal Diagnosis of Down Syndrome, Spina Bifida, Anencephaly, and Turner

and Klinefelter Syndromes: A Systematic Literature Review," *Prenatal Diagnosis* 19:9 (Sept. 1999): 808–12.

10. Kimberly Winston, "Richard Dawkins Stands by Remarks on Sexism, Pedophilia, Down Syndrome," Religion News Service, Nov. 18, 2014.

11. Jamie Edgin and Fabian Fernandez, "The Truth about Down Syndrome," *New York Times*, Aug. 28, 2014.

12. Ibid.

13. Crandell, "Art in the Center of Life with Down Syndrome."

14. Ibid.

Chapter 5 Women at the Well

1. From Harriet Beecher Stowe, "The Chimney-Corner" from *Household Papers and Stories* in *The Writings of Harriet Beecher Stowe: With Biographical Introduction, Portraits, and Other Illustrations,* vol. VIII (Cambridge: Riverside Press, 1896), 252.

2. Nicholas Kristof and Sheryl Wudunn, *Half the Sky: Turning Oppression into Opportunity for Women Worldwide* (London: Vintage, 2010). There is also an accompanying film series.

3. See *It's a Girl*. Film. Shadowline Films, 2012.

4. *The Epistle of Mathetes to Diognetus* (c. AD 130). Available on-line at http://www.earlychristianwritings.com/text/diognetus-roberts.html.

5. See a detailed explanation in Rodney Stark, *The Rise of Christianity: How the Obscure, Marginal Jesus Movement Became the Dominant Religious Force in the Western World in a Few Centuries* (San Francisco: HarperSanFrancisco, 1997), 95–128.

6. Jonathon Seidl, "A Way Out: Rescuing Women from Prostitution, Strip Clubs, and Drugs," WORLD, Aug. 23, 2008. Available on-line at: http://www.worldmag.com/2008/08/a_way_out.

7. Ibid.

8. Through 2008, A Way Out claimed that of 248 women helped since the program's inception, only 7 have ever returned to the industry after completing the program. Since then, the program has grown. Currently, A Way Out provides services to between 40 and 50 women a year.

9. Kathy K. Martin, "Spiritual Rescue: A Way Out Helps Women Escape Sex Trade through Healing Power of Jesus," *The (Memphis) Commercial Appeal*, July 9, 2011.

10. This idea of "arrested adolescence" is one that is beyond the scope of this book, but it seems to play a key role in the problems we are discussing throughout the book. See, for example, the stories we tell of Jubilee Leadership Academy in chapter 13, "Suffer the Little Children." Mentoring boys and helping them to "grow up" and take on increasingly adult responsibilities is a key part of their recovery process.

11. This section depends heavily on Marvin Olasky's interview with Reggie Littlejohn, published as "Complete Dependence: God Used Reggie Littlejohn's Suffering to Shape Her into an Advocate for China's Voiceless," WORLD, July 12, 2014.

12. "Skip" Vaccarello, "A Woman on a Mission," www.FindingGodInSilicon Valley.com, Dec. 3, 2013.

13. Ibid.

14. Available on-line at http://www.thea21campaign.org/content/21-ways -to-help/gjdpl5?linkid=2675.

Chapter 6 Coloring Outside the Lines

1. T. S. Eliot, "The Aims of Education: Can Education Be Defined?" *To Criticize the Critic and Other Writings* (Lincoln, NE: University of Nebraska Press, 1992), 75–76.

2. Quoted in Steven Garber, *The Fabric of Faithfulness: Weaving Together Belief and Behavior* (Downers Grove, IL: InterVarsity, 2007), 93.

3. Neil Postman, *Technopoly: The Surrender of Culture to Technology* (London: Vintage, 1993), 186.

4. Jill Lacey, "Cornerstone School," *WORLD*, April 10, 2010, 52–53. Clay Hanna is no longer the director of Cornerstone Schools. He is currently an officer in the Tennessee National Guard and writes for such publications as *Politico* about his experiences in Iraq.

5. Ibid.

6. Jamie Dean, "West Side Story," *WORLD*, March 24, 2007.

7. Disclosure: John Stonestreet is a regular speaker at Impact 360.

8. For more on these various offerings from Summit Ministries, visit www. summit.org.

9. See http://www.johnjayinstitute.org/.

10. Charles Howard, "The John Jay Institute: Cultivating Leadership through Dialogue," *Huffington Post*, Nov. 1, 2011.

11. Jennifer Anderson, "Film Spotlights Roosevelt-SouthLake Bond," *Portland Tribune*, Jan. 24, 2013.

12. Ibid.

13. Ibid.

Chapter 7 Justice That Restores

1. Charles W. Colson, *Loving God* (Grand Rapids: Zondervan, 1987), 25.

2. Heather Rice-Minus, personal interview.

3. Interview with Warren Cole Smith, Feb. 8, 2014. Aired as an episode of the WORLD News Group radio program *Listening In*, Feb. 15, 2014. Available on-line: www.wng.org/ListeningIn.

4. Ibid.

5. Eric Metaxas, "Prisoners' Children Need You," *BreakPoint* commentary, Oct. 24, 2014.

6. Daniel James Devine, "Free Retainer: Administer Justice Helps the Poor Get Their Day in Court," *WORLD*, Aug. 10, 2013.

7. Ibid.

8. Ibid.

9. Ibid.

10. He also wrote a book that more fully tells his story: Bruce Strom, *Gospel Justice: Joining Together to Provide Health and Hope for Those Oppressed by Legal Injustice* (Chicago: Moody, 2013).

11. Daniel Olasky, "Surrogate Parents: New Horizons Builds Relationship Triangles with Prisoners and Their Newborn Children," *WORLD*, April 24, 2010.

Chapter 8 Forgiveness Heals, Time Doesn't

1. From Andrew White, *Father, Forgive: Reflections on Peacemaking* (Oxford, England: Monarch Books, 2013), 30.

2. Michael O. Emerson and Christian Smith, *Divided by Faith: Evangelical Religion and the Problem of Race in America* (London: Oxford University Press, 2001). The Society for the Scientific Study of Religion named it "Outstanding Book of the Year" for 2001.

3. Anthony Bradley is a professor at The King's College, a research fellow at The Acton Institute, an evangelical college in New York City, and the author of several books on race and culture.

4. Thomas Sowell, *Affirmative Action around the World* (New Haven, CT: Yale University Press, 2004).

5. A personal conversation between the Reverend Carl Ellis and John Stonestreet (February 2002). Used by permission.

6. Quoted in Eric Metaxas, *Bonhoeffer: Pastor, Martyr, Prophet, Spy—A Righteous Gentile vs. the Third Reich* (Nashville: Thomas Nelson, 2010), back cover flap.

7. Angela Lu, "Churches Step into Ferguson's Pain: The Anger and Hurt Coursing through the St. Louis Suburb Gives Christians the Opportunity to Speak Grace and Show Love," *WORLD*, Nov. 25, 2014.

8. Ibid.

9. Marilyn Stewart, "Former KKK Terrorist Cites C. S. Lewis' Faithful Obedience," *Baptist Press*, Aug. 9, 2006.

10. Kristie Jackson, "Tuesday Testimony: Tom Tarrants," www.kristieejackson.com, Jan. 25, 2011.

11. Thomas Tarrants, *The Conversion of a Klansman* (New York: Doubleday, 1979).

12. John Perkins and Thomas Tarrants, *He's My Brother: Former Racial Foes Offer Strategy for Reconciliation* (Grand Rapids: Baker, 1994).

13. Steve Almasy, "NFL Player's Thoughtful Ferguson Response Draws Applause," *CNN*, Nov. 28, 2014.

Chapter 9 Loving God with All Your Mind

1. G. K. Chesterton, *Heretics* (1905; repr. Rockville, MD: Serenity, 2009), 146.

2. Vinoth Ramachandra, *Subverting Global Myths* (Downer's Grove, IL: InterVarsity, 2008), 154–5.

3. Quoted in "Johannes Kepler," *Hellenica*. Available on-line at http://www.mlahanas.de/Physics/Bios/JohannesKepler.html.

4. See Gary A. Tobin and Aryeh K. Weinberg, "Religious Beliefs and Behavior of College Faculty," *Profiles of the American University*, vol. 2. Available on-line at http://www.jewishresearch.org/PDFs2/FacultyReligion07.pdf.

5. Howard Kurtz, "College Faculties a Most Liberal Lot, Study Finds," *Washington Post* (March 29, 2005), C01. Available on-line at http://www.washington post.com/wp-dyn/articles/A8427-2005Mar28.html.

6. A phrase coined by Arthur Holmes. See his helpful book *All Truth Is God's Truth* (Grand Rapids: Eerdmans, 1977).

7. J. Gresham Machen, "Christianity and Culture," *The Princeton Theological Review*, vols. 11–12 (Princeton University Press, 1913), 7.

8. See for example, Kelly James Clark and Michael Rea, *Reason, Metaphysics, and Mind: New Essays on the Philosophy of Alvin Plantinga* (Oxford University Press, 2012).

9. Even a top atheist philosopher like Thomas Nagel admits this. See "A Philosopher Defends Religion," *New York Review of Books* (September 27, 2012). Available on-line at http://www.nybooks.com/articles/archives/2012/sep/27/philosopher -defends-religion/.

10. More than 300 colleagues and former students gathered at the University of Notre Dame to celebrate the work of Alvin Plantinga in May 2010. See "Alvin Plantinga Retirement Celebration," *Center for Philosophy of Religion*. Videos and other resources available at http://philreligion.nd.edu/videos/conference-videos/ alvin-plantinga-retirement-celebration/.

11. Jamie Dean, "Less Than Ideal: Study Challenges Rosy Assumptions about Homosexual Parenting," *WORLD*, June 30, 2012.

12. Ibid.

13. Tara Merrigan, "UT Investigates Professor's Study on Children with Gay Parents," *The Statesman* (Austin, Texas), July 11, 2012.

14. Warren Cole Smith, "Good Deeds Punished: Texas Sociologist Gets Caught in an Academic Witch Hunt," *WORLD*, Aug. 25, 2012.

15. David Barash, "God, Darwin and My College Biology Class," *New York Times*, Sept. 27, 2014.

16. Dick Peterson, "Evicting God from the College Classroom," *WORLD*, Oct. 15, 2014.

17. Interview with Stephen Meyer by Warren Cole Smith, Nov. 21, 2014. Meyer's book on this topic is *Darwin's Doubt: The Explosive Origin of Animal Life and the Case for Intelligent Design* (New York: HarperOne, 2014).

18. Much of this section comes from various interviews with Mike Adams conducted by Warren Cole Smith in the summer of 2014 and aired as part of WORLD's radio program *Listening In* on July 5, 2014. Some quotes also came from a speech by Adams to the Alliance Defending Freedom's Legal Academy in Naples, Florida, on July 11, 2014.

19. Mike S. Adams, *Welcome to the Ivory Tower of Babel: Confessions of a Conservative College Professor* (Boyne City, MI: Harbor House, 2004).

Chapter 10 It Doesn't Define You

1. See Stephen Jimenez, *The Book of Matt: Hidden Truths about the Murder of Matthew Shepard* (Hanover, NH: Steerforth, 2013).

2. For more on these thinkers, see Benjamin Wiker's helpful summary of each author in *10 Books That Screwed Up the World: And 5 Others That Didn't Help* (Washington, DC: Regnery, 2008).

3. See Pitirim Sorokin, *The Crisis of Our Age: A Prophetic View of the Future by One of the Masterminds of the Generation* (New York: Dutton, 1941).

4. Rosaria Butterfield, *The Secret Thoughts of an Unlikely Convert* (Pittsburgh: Crown & Covenant, 2013).

5. Marvin Olasky, "From Lesbianism to the Parking Lot to Church: An Interview with Author Rosaria Butterfield," *WORLD*, March 23, 2013.

6. Ibid.

7. Ibid.

8. Ibid.

9. Ibid.

10. Ibid.

11. Ibid.

12. Ibid.

13. Marvin Olasky, "From Gay to Joyous: Author Christopher Yuan Journeyed out of a Pit into the Arms of God," *WORLD*, Feb. 8, 2014.

14. Ibid.

15. Christopher and Angela Yuan's story is told in full in Christopher Yuan and Angela Yuan, *Out of a Far Country: A Gay Son's Journey to God, A Broken Mother's Search for Hope* (Colorado Springs: WaterBrook, 2011).

16. This section comes from the written testimony of Ricky Chelette shared with the authors in November 2014.

Chapter 11 Not the Least of These

1. "Euthanasia: The Right to Die Can So Easily Become the Duty to Die," *The Mirror*, Aug. 19, 2013. Available on-line at http://www.mirror.co.uk/news/uk-news/euthanasia-right-die-can-easily-2182129.

2. Quoted in Beth Greenfield, "Mom's Fight to Let 12-Year-Old Daughter Die in Peace," *Yahoo! Parenting*, Oct. 28, 2014, https://www.yahoo.com/parenting/moms-fight-to-let-12-year-old-daughter-die-in-peace-101190836767.html.

3. Mansfield, Hopfer, and Marteau, "Termination Rates after Prenatal Diagnosis."

4. Joni Eareckson Tada, "The Disability Double Standard: Instead of Helping the Disabled Live Full Lives, New Laws Seek to Help Them Die," *Wall Street Journal*, Jan. 9, 2014. Available on-line at http://online.wsj.com/articles/SB10001424052702303933104579302893600224348.

5. The thoughts in the next several paragraphs were first articulated in a *BreakPoint* commentary. See John Stonestreet, "One Life Lost, All Lives Diminished: Brittany Maynard and Assisted Suicide," *BreakPoint* commentary, Nov. 10, 2014. Available on-line at http://www.breakpoint.org/bpcommentaries/breakpoint-commentaries-archive/entry/13/26371.

6. John Donne, "Meditation XVII," *The Works of John Donne*, vol. III, ed. Henry Alford (London: John W. Parker, 1839), 574–75.

7. This profile with Tada is from an interview with her by Warren Cole Smith at the National Religious Broadcasters' 2014 convention, Feb. 24, 2014. Also

published in a somewhat different form as "Suffering Is Sacred" by Warren Cole Smith, *WORLD*, Oct. 22, 2014.

8. Jill Lacy, "The Other Washington," *WORLD*, April 10, 2010.

9. This section based on an interview with Kara Tippetts by Warren Cole Smith and originally published as "Trusting God with Terminal Cancer" by Warren Cole Smith, *WORLD*, Sept. 29, 2014.

10. *The Hardest Peace: Expecting Grace in the Midst of Life's Hard* (Colorado Springs: David C Cook, 2014).

11. John Stonestreet, "Inheriting Pro-Life: How a Son Learned from His Father to Defend the Weak," *BreakPoint* commentary, July 23, 2013.

12. Jonathan Mummolo, "Father Who Died Saving Son Known for Sacrifice," *Washington Post*, Sept. 10, 2008.

13. Ashlee Vance, "Crowded Searches for Medical Miracles," *Bloomberg BusinessWeek*, Aug. 2, 2012.

14. Ibid.

15. Maya's mother, Dana, blogs about their experiences at http://niederfamily.blogspot.com/.

16. Interview with C. Jimmy Lin by John Stonestreet, May 24, 2013.

Chapter 12 Giving Marriage to the World, Once Again

1. Much of the material in this section is adapted from a chapter entitled "What Is Marriage?: Part 1: What God Thinks" in Sean McDowell and John Stonestreet, *Same-Sex Marriage: A Thoughtful Approach to God's Design for Marriage* (Grand Rapids: Baker, 2014), 35–42.

2. John Stonestreet, "Intentionally Married, Happily Married: Reversing an Unhappy Trend," *BreakPoint* commentary, Oct. 20, 2014.

3. Ibid.

4. See Audrey Barrick, "Study: Christian Divorce Rate Identical to National Average," *Christian Post*, April 4, 2008, http://www.christianpost.com/news/study-christian-divorce-rate-identical-to-national-average-31815/.

5. Warren Cole Smith, "Not Dead Yet: Students Taught about the Death of Culture and Christianity Should Hear the Other Side from Sociologist Bradley Wright," *WORLD*, Aug. 27, 2011.

6. For much more on this topic, see Bradley Wright, *Upside: Surprising Good News About the State of Our World* (Minneapolis: Bethany House, 2011). See also David G. Myers, *The American Paradox: Spiritual Hunger in an Age of Plenty* (New Haven: Yale University Press, 2000), 48.

7. For more on the bias of the press, see Marvin Olasky and Warren Cole Smith, *Prodigal Press: The Anti-Christian Bias of the American News Media* (Phillipsburg, NJ: P&R Publishing, 2013).

8. He was 95 when John Stonestreet told this story on a *BreakPoint* commentary on Oct. 10, 2013.

9. See https://www.youtube.com/watch?v=KDi4hBWsvkY.

10. Mark Regnerus, "The Case for Early Marriage," *Christianity Today*, July 31, 2009.

11. A version of this story appeared in Gary Spooner, "From Shattered Dreams to a Mission of Mercy," *WORLD*, June 22, 2013. Used with permission.

Chapter 13 Suffer the Little Children

1. Max Lucado, *The Great House of God* (Nashville: Thomas Nelson, 2001), 15.

2. Quotations from Brooks in this section are from personal interviews with the author as well as Andy Crouch, "Why Apologetics Is Different—and Working—in the Hood," *Christianity Today*, Oct. 22, 2013.

3. Electa Draper, "Adoption Initiative Halves Numbers of Kids Needing Families," *Denver Post*, March 5, 2010.

4. Ibid.

5. Naomi S. Riley, "Adoption Season for Evangelicals," *Wall Street Journal*, Sept. 24, 2010.

6. Draper, "Adoption Initiative."

7. Mary Jackson, "City Kids," *WORLD*, Sept. 20, 2014.

8. This section based on reporting by Sophia Lee originally published as "Growing on the Farm," *WORLD*, Oct. 4, 2014.

9. Available on-line at http://www.christianalliancefororphans.org/wp-content/uploads/Twelve-Ways-to-Love-the-Orphan.pdf.

Chapter 14 In the Beginning, God Created

1. Mindy Belz, "Art Aflame: WORLD's Daniel of the Year Makoto Fujimura Restores Art's Good Name among Christians and Gives Christians a Good Name in the Arts," *WORLD*, Dec. 17, 2005.

2. Ibid.

3. Ibid.

4. Terry Teachout, "About Last Night," *WORLD*, July 2, 2008.

5. Belz, "Art Aflame."

6. Warren Cole Smith, "Infusing Christianity into LA's Giant Murals," *WORLD*, Nov. 14, 2014.

7. Marvin Olasky, "Envisioning the Future: Makoto Fujimura Says the Arts Are a 500-Year Conversation on Philosophy and Theology," *WORLD*, April 24, 2010.

8. Emily Scheie, "Art for the Common Man: Grand Rapids Competition Brings Judges and the Rest of Us Together," *WORLD*, Dec. 13, 2014.

9. Ibid.

10. Warren Cole Smith, "Innocents in Austin: A Spark of Christ in the City" *WORLD*, March 14, 2013. This on-line story also has photos of the mural, and a video of the artist explaining his technique: www.worldmag.com/2013/03/innocents_in_austin_a_spark_of_christ_in_the_city.

11. Eric Metaxas, "God's Comic," *BreakPoint* commentary, Oct. 2, 2012.

12. Brad Stine, *Being a Christian without Being an Idiot* (Nashville: Word Distribution, 2004).

13. John H. McWhorter, "How Hip-Hop Holds Blacks Back," *City Journal*, Summer 2003, on-line at http://www.city-journal.org/html/13_3_how_hip_hop.html.

14. Ibid.

15. John Stonestreet, "Lecrae Calls Hip-Hop Higher," *BreakPoint* commentary, Sept. 29, 2014.

16. Warren Cole Smith, "Real Music about Real Change," *WORLD*, Nov. 6, 2014.

17. Interview with Warren Cole Smith, July 19, 2014.

18. Ibid.

Chapter 15 Aim Small, Miss Small

1. See T. M. Moore, "Personal Mission Field." Available on-line at http://www.colsoncenter.org/get-involved-in-the-center/personal-mission-field.

2. Os Guinness, *The Call: Finding and Fulfilling the Central Purpose of Your Life* (Nashville: Thomas Nelson, 2003), 58.

3. Frederick Buechner, "Vocation," from *Wishful Thinking: A Theological ABC* (New York: Harper and Row, 1973), 95. Emphasis added.

4. John R. W. Stott, *Christian Mission in the Modern World* (Downers Grove, IL: InterVarsity, 1975), 31.

5. See David Naugle, "Redeeming Vocation" from *The Christian Worldview Journal* (May 24, 2010). Available on-line at http://www.colsoncenter.org/the-center/columns/indepth/15248-redeeming-vocation.

6. See Ed Stetzer, "Preach the Gospel, and Since It's Necessary, Use Words," *Christian Post,* June 26, 2012, http://www.christianpost.com/news/preach-the-gospel-and-since-its-necessary-use-words-77231/ (accessed Nov. 2014).

7. Richard John Neuhaus, "Telling the World Its Own Story." Available on-line at http://www.colsoncenter.org/search-library/search?view=searchdetail&id=21199.

Bibliography

We are both "book guys." That's why you find a lot of our favorite books cited in our book. But loving books is, we believe, more than just a quirk or a matter of personal taste. We both believe it was no coincidence that when God wanted to reveal Himself to us, He gave us a book: the Bible. We both strongly subscribe to the notion that "readers are leaders, and leaders are readers." Books shape us. Books, unlike movies or television or almost any other medium, both force us and allow us to slow down and really think things through.

That's why we've compiled this bibliography of books cited in this book, plus a few more for those who want to read more deeply about the subjects we have introduced in *Restoring All Things*.

Adams, Mike S. *Welcome to the Ivory Tower of Babel: Confessions of a Conservative College Professor*. Boyne City, MI: Harbor House, 2004.

Bales, Kevin, and Ron Soodalter. *The Slave Next Door: Human Trafficking and Slavery in America Today*. Oakland: University of California Press, 2010.

Belles, Nita. *In Our Backyard: A Christian Perspective on Human Trafficking in the United States*. Decorah, IA: Free River, 2011.

Brooks, Christopher. *Urban Apologetics: Why the Gospel Is Good News for the City*. Grand Rapids: Kregel, 2014.

Butterfield, Rosaria. *The Secret Thoughts of an Unlikely Convert*. Pittsburgh: Crown & Covenant Publications, 2013.

Colson, Charles W. *Justice That Restores*. Wheaton: Tyndale, 2001.

———. *Loving God*. Grand Rapids: Zondervan, 1997.

Colson, Emily. *Dancing with Max: A Mother and Son Who Broke Free*. Grand Rapids: Zondervan, 2012.

Corbett, Steve, and Brian Fikkert. *When Helping Hurts*. Chicago: Moody Publishers, 2009.

David, Tom. *Fields of the Fatherless: Discover the Joy of Compassionate Living*. Colorado Springs: David C Cook, 2008.

De Tocqueville, Alexis. *Democracy in America*. New York: Penguin Classics, 2003.

Drop Box, The. Film. Kindred Image, 2015.

Emerson, Michael O., and Christian Smith. *Divided by Faith: Evangelical Religion and the Problem of Race in America*. London: Oxford University Press, 2001.

Ensor, John, and Scott Klusendorf. *Stand for Life: Answering the Call, Making the Case, Saving Lives*. Peabody, MA: Hendrickson, 2012.

Family Project, The. Colorado Springs: Focus on the Family, 2014.

Fujimura, Makoto. *Refractions: A Journey of Faith, Art, and Culture*. Colorado Springs: NavPress, 2009.

Garber, Steven. *The Fabric of Faithfulness: Weaving Together Belief and Behavior*. Downers Grove, IL: InterVarsity, 2007.

George, Robert P., Sherif Girgis, and Ryan T. Anderson. *What Is Marriage? Man and Woman: A Defense*. New York: Encounter, 2012.

Guinness, Os. *The Call: Finding and Fulfilling the Central Purpose of Your Life*. Nashville: Thomas Nelson, 2003.

Hazlitt, Henry. *Economics in One Lesson*. New York: Three Rivers Press, 1979.

Hill, Wesley. *Washed and Waiting: Reflections on Christian Faithfulness and Homosexuality*. Grand Rapids: Zondervan, 2010.

Holmes, Arthur. *All Truth Is God's Truth*. Grand Rapids: Eerdmans, 1977.

Irreplaceable the Movie. Pine Creek Entertainment, 2014.

Ivie, Brian, with Ted Kluck. *The Drop Box*. Colorado Springs: David C Cook, 2015.

Kavanaugh, Patrick. *Spiritual Lives of the Great Composers*. Grand Rapids: Zondervan, 1996.

Larson, Catherine Claire. *As We Forgive: Stories of Reconciliation from Rwanda*. Grand Rapids: Zondervan, 2009.

Lewis, C. S. *The Abolition of Man*. Collected Letters of C. S. Lewis Series. New York: HarperOne, 2009.

———. *The Four Loves: The Much Beloved Exploration of the Nature of Love*. New York: Mariner Books, 1971.

Lupton, Bob. *Theirs Is the Kingdom: Celebrating the Gospel in Urban America*. New York: HarperOne 2011.

———. *Toxic Charity: How Churches and Charities Hurt Those They Help, and How to Reverse It*. New York: HarperOne, 2012.

Machen, J. Gresham. *Education, Christianity and the State*. 2nd ed. Unicoi, TN: Trinity Foundation, 2004.

McDowell, Sean, and John Stonestreet. *Same-Sex Marriage: A Thoughtful Approach to God's Design for Marriage*. Grand Rapids: Baker, 2014.

Metaxas, Eric. *Bonhoeffer: Pastor, Martyr, Prophet, Spy*. Nashville: Thomas Nelson, 2010.

Meyer, Stephen C. *Darwin's Doubt: The Explosive Origin of Animal Life and the Case for Intelligent Design*. New York: HarperOne, 2014.

Miller, Darrow. *Discipling Nations: The Power of Truth to Transform Nations*. YWAM, 2001.

Mitchell, C. Ben, and Joy Riley. *Christian Bioethics: A Guide for Pastors, Health Care Professionals, and Families*. Nashville: B&H, 2014.

Moore, Russell D. *Adopted for Life: The Priority of Adoption for Christian Families and Churches*. Memphis: Crossway, 2009.

Moore, T. M. "Personal Mission Field." Colson Center Library. Available online at http://www.colsoncenter.org/get-involved-in-the-center/personal-mission-field.

Moreland, J. P. *Love Your God with All Your Mind: The Role of Reason in the Life of the Soul*. Rev. ed. Colorado Springs: NavPress, 2012.

Morrow, Jonathan. *Welcome to College: A Christ Follower's Guide to the Journey*. Grand Rapids: Kregel, 2008.

Murray, Charles. *Coming Apart: The State of White America 1960–2010*. New York: Crown Forum, 2013.

Myers, David G. *The American Paradox: Spiritual Hunger in an Age of Plenty*. New Haven, CT: Yale University Press, 2000.

Neuhaus, Richard John. "Telling the World Its Own Story." Colson Center Library. Available online at http://www.colsoncenter.org/search-library/search?view=searchdetail&id=21199.

Noll, Mark A. *Jesus Christ and the Life of the Mind*. Grand Rapids: Eerdmans, 2013.

Olasky, Marvin. *The Tragedy of American Compassion*. Washington, DC: Regnery Publishing, 1994.

Olasky, Marvin and Warren Cole Smith. *Prodigal Press: Confronting the Anti-Christian Bias of the American News Media*. Phillipsburg, NJ: P&R Publishing, 2013.

Pearcey, Nancy. *Saving Leonardo: A Call to Resist the Secular Assault on Mind, Morals, and Meaning.* Nashville: B & H, 2010.

Perkins, John and Thomas Tarrants. *He's My Brother: Former Racial Foes Offer Strategy for Reconciliation.* Grand Rapids: Baker, 1994.

Postman, Neil. *Amusing Ourselves to Death: Public Discourse in the Age of Show Business.* New York: Penguin, 1985.

PovertyCure: From Aid to Enterprise. DVD. The Acton Institute, 2013.

Ramachandra, Vinoth. *Subverting Global Myths: Theology and the Public Issues Shaping Our World.* Downers Grove, IL: InterVarsity, 2008.

Reynolds, Matt. *The White Umbrella: Walking with Survivors of Sex Trafficking.* Chicago: Moody, 2012.

Richards, Jay. *Money, Greed, and God: Why Capitalism Is the Solution and Not the Problem.* New York: HarperOne, 2009.

Ryken, Philip. *Art for God's Sake: A Call to Recover the Arts.* P&R Publishing, 2006.

Schaeffer, Francis A. *Art and the Bible.* 2nd ed. Downers Grove, IL: InterVarsity, 2006.

Smith, Warren Cole. *A Lover's Quarrel with the Evangelical Church.* Downers Grove, IL: InterVarsity, 2009.

Sorokin, Pitirim. *The Crisis of Our Age: A Prophetic View of the Future by One of the Masterminds of the Generation.* New York: Dutton, 1941.

Stanton, Glenn T. *Loving My (LGBT) Neighbor: Being Friends in Grace and Truth.* Chicago: Moody, 2014.

———. *The Ring Makes All the Difference: The Hidden Consequences of Cohabitation and the Strong Benefits of Marriage.* Chicago: Moody, 2011.

Stark, Rodney. *The Victory of Reason: How Christianity Led to Freedom, Capitalism, and Western Success.* New York: Random House, 2006.

Stine, Brad. *Being a Christian without Being an Idiot.* Nashville: Word Distribution, 2004.

Strom, Bruce. *Gospel Justice: Joining Together to Provide Health and Hope for Those Oppressed by Legal Injustice.* Chicago: Moody, 2013.

Stott, John R. W. *Christian Mission in the Modern World.* Downers Grove, IL: InterVarsity, 1975.

Tarrants, Thomas. *The Conversion of a Klansman.* New York: Doubleday, 1979.

Tippetts, Kara. *The Hardest Peace: Expecting Grace in the Midst of Life's Hard.* Colorado Springs: David C Cook, 2014.

UnDivided The Movie: The Unbelievable Love Story of a Church and a Public School. Film. Lightning Strikes Entertainment, 2013.

Waiting for Superman. Film. Walden Media, 2010.

Webber, Robert E. *Who Gets to Narrate the World? Contending for the Christian Story in an Age of Rivals*. Downers Grove, IL: InterVarsity, 2008.

White, Andrew. *Father, Forgive: Reflections on Peacemaking*. Oxford, England: Monarch Books, 2013.

Wiker, Benjamin. *10 Books that Screwed Up the World: And 5 Others That Didn't Help*. Washington, DC: Regnery, 2008.

Wright, Bradley. *Christians Are Hate-Filled Hypocrites . . . and Other Lies You've Been Told*. Minneapolis: Bethany, 2010.

————. *Upside: Surprising Good News about the State of Our World*. Minneapolis: Bethany House, 2011.

Yuan, Christopher, and Angela Yuan. *Out of a Far Country: A Gay Son's Journey to God, A Broken Mother's Search for Hope*. Colorado Springs: WaterBrook, 2011.

Index

Warren Cole Smith is the vice president of WORLD News Group, publisher of *WORLD* magazine, and producer of the nationally syndicated radio program *The World and Everything in It*. He has written, co-written, or edited more than ten books, including *A Lover's Quarrel with the Evangelical Church* and *Confronting the Anti-Christian Bias of the American News Media*. He lives in Charlotte, North Carolina.

John Stonestreet is a speaker and author for the Chuck Colson Center for Christian Worldview. He is a gifted communicator on areas of faith and culture, theology, worldview, education, and apologetics, and he is a sought-after speaker at conferences, colleges, churches, schools, and other various gatherings each year. Co-host with Eric Metaxas of *BreakPoint* and the voice of *The Point*, a daily national radio feature, he is the coauthor of *Making Sense of Your World*. He and his wife, Sarah, have three daughters and a dog and live in Colorado Springs, Colorado.

PROVIDING CLARITY TO THE NEWS THAT MATTERS MOST

YOUR SOURCE FOR RELIABLE CHRISTIAN WORLDVIEW NEWS

YOUR WORLD MEMBERSHIP INCLUDES:

WORLD
MAGAZINE

BIWEEKLY ISSUES OF AWARD-WINNING
WORLD MAGAZINE

WORLD
RADIO

THE DYNAMIC DAILY AND WEEKEND
PROGRAMMING OF WORLD RADIO

WORLD
DIGITAL

THE EXPANDED AND FULLY SHAREABLE CONTENT OF
WORLD DIGITAL, PROVIDING ANYTIME ACCESS TO
WORLD'S COVERAGE OF IMPORTANT EVENTS

WORLD will arm you with honest reporting and wise insights you can rely on, through fully considered Christian worldview journalism that brings true clarity to the news that matters most.

Become a WORLD member today for only $4.98 per month or $59.76 per year. Simply go to wng.org/becomeamember or call 800-951-6397, Monday-Friday between 9:00 AM and 7:00 PM ET.

Go to wng.org/becomeamember to get started today!

BREAK◖◗POINT™

For the best in Christian commentary on today's news and trends, listen to *BreakPoint*® with John Stonestreet and Eric Metaxas.

Visit www.BreakPoint.org for radio listings or to listen online. Or get John and Eric's *BreakPoint* commentaries each weekday in your inbox.

And don't miss John's hard-hitting one-minute commentary, *The Point*®.

www.BreakPoint.org

Also from
JOHN STONESTREET

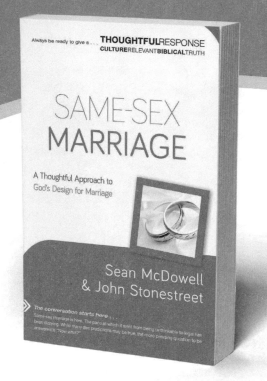

Always be ready to give a . . . **THOUGHTFUL**RESPONSE
CULTURERELEVANT**BIBLICAL**TRUTH

SAME-SEX MARRIAGE

A Thoughtful Approach to
God's Design for Marriage

Sean McDowell
& John Stonestreet

ISBN 978-0-8010-1834-3

Sean McDowell and John Stonestreet

Same-sex marriage is here, presenting unique challenges and opportunities. How do those who follow Christ faithfully articulate the case for one-man, one-woman marriage in everyday conversation?

Sean McDowell and John Stonestreet believe a thoughtful approach to God's design for marriage is the answer. The key is not a contentious attitude toward those who believe in same-sex marriage but a winsome perspective that is faithful to Christ, committed to truth, and shaped by a love for God and others.

BakerBooks
a division of Baker Publishing Group
www.BakerBooks.com

Available wherever books and ebooks are sold.